TEAM SPIRIT

The Elusive Experience

John Syer

The Kingswood Press

The Kingswood Press
an imprint of William Heinemann Ltd
10 Upper Grosvenor Street, London W1X 9PA

LONDON   MELBOURNE
JOHANNESBURG   AUCKLAND

First published 1986

ISBN 0 434 98096 X

Photoset and printed in Great Britain by
Redwood Burn Limited
Trowbridge, Wiltshire

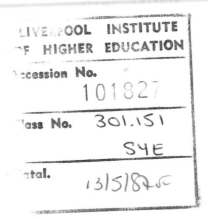

This book is dedicated to
Alan and Mary Syer
co-leaders of my very first team

My heart-felt acknowledgements to

Carol A O'Connor for pointing the way and
for being the best
Christopher Connolly for giving me time off
and for patient support
My clients for allowing me to tell bits of their
stories
Derek Wyatt for good humour, good ideas
and faith that it would happen
Richard Heller for stirring things up
and Mary-Lou Grimberg, who worked a two-
week miracle right at the end.

CONTENTS

Introduction   1

1 So what is team spirit?   13
  Morale   14
  Cohesion-   15
  Confluence   20
  Synergy   22
  Low cohesion   24
  Negative confluence   25
  Low synergy   26
  Positive and negative team spirit   27
  Glossary   29

2 Conflict   30
  Encountering a challenge   31
  Challenging opponents   39
  When the individual experiences
      conflict within himself   46
  Conflict within the team   47

3 Conformity   54
  Symbols of conformity   54
  Norms   56
  The non-conformist   57
  Cultural conformity   59
  The importance of the individual
      within the team   60

4 Relationships   71
  The relationship between
    coach and individual   72
  The relationship between
    coach and team   83
  The relationship between players   86
  The relationship between players
    and their opponents   94

5 Communication   98
  Communication between coach
    and athlete   99
  Communication between coach
    and team   103
  Communication between players   110
  Criticism   115
  Questions   115
  Instructions   116
  Encouragement   118

6 Motivation   121
  What is motivation?   121
  How can I motivate an athlete?   123
  How can I motivate my team?   127
  How can an athlete motivate himself?   132
  How may an athlete be helped
    towards self motivation?   134
  How can I as coach help my
    team towards self-motivation?   138

7 Confidence   144
  How to gain confidence   150
   (i) Helping the individual   150
  (ii) Helping the team   165

8 Stress   174
  Stress defined   174
  The signs of stress   175
  The causes of stress   176
  Results of stress   182
  How to reduce stress   184
   (i) What the coach can do   184
  (ii) What the individual can do   189

Epilogue   198
Appendix A: Situational Leadership: A Behaviourist Model   208
Appendix B: Leadership at Findhorn: A Humanist Model   215
Appendix C: The Sporting Bodymind   222

Bibliography   224
Index   227

INTRODUCTION

It was the 1982 Milk Cup Soccer Final. Large lights had blazed Steve Archibald's name high above the packed Wembley stands for at least half an hour. Tottenham 1, Liverpool 0. The blue and white Tottenham crowd were going wild, whistles shrilling from thousands of lips to tell the referee to blow full time. My own palms were damp with excitement. I wanted Tottenham to win and, because he had been the first player to tune in to mental training and had worked at it hard and consistently, I wanted Steve to score the winning goal. Then, suddenly, Liverpool equalised.

The shock was numbing. Throughout the break before extra time, the Tottenham team stayed scattered over a wide area, some lying on their backs gazing dully at the sky. I'm convinced we lost the match in those moments. Spread out, disconsolate and alone, each player was more aware of his disappointment and physical tiredness than he would have been together with other members of the team. Liverpool won 3–1 in extra time.

Two years later, we had learned our lesson. We were playing Anderlecht in the final of the UEFA Cup. At the end of full time, the teams were equal and we were still equal at the end of extra time. At that point the issue had to be settled by penalty kicks and, watching from the stand, I saw Tottenham players grouped together around goal-keeper Tony Parks who was suddenly thrown into a highly stressful situation. This time it was the Anderlecht players who were dispersed, standing exhausted or collapsed on the grass. Ray Clemence, Tottenham's injured first choice goalie, came out on to the pitch, put his arm around Tony's shoulders and walked with him to the goal-mouth, osten-

1

sibly just giving advice and verbal encouragement but in fact transmitting total confidence. The Anderlecht goal-keeper had no such loving support and looked a forlorn figure compared with Tony. In the end, Tottenham's almost tangible team spirit won the day. Tony saved penalties, Anderlecht did not and Tottenham were presented with the Cup.

I stood and applauded, my face split wide with a smile, and remembered a time years earlier when, as Scottish national men's volleyball team coach, I'd fully experienced what the Tottenham players were experiencing now . . .

At about 9.40 pm on 6 April 1971, our 'universal' Charlie Ferguson read the Norwegian's set perfectly and closed with Ronnie Hamilton. As one formidable unit they jumped, reached far across the eight-foot-high net and deflected the considerable force of Ivar Hellesnes' spike back into the attacking court. Two men dived in vain: in a split second the ball had hammered into the floor and Scotland had won by three sets to nil, our first international victory abroad.

That moment I experienced an intense team spirit. There had been five years of preparation, five years of wrestling with the conflicting needs and emotions of a squad of very different, very young and gifted individuals. I'd not been *trained* as a coach. I'd made many mistakes, giving in when I should have stood firm, standing firm when I should have given in. There were players I liked immensely and I'd sometimes been blinded by my liking. From some players I'd sometimes felt distant and from that distance I'd failed to distinguish and develop qualities of which the team was badly in need. Yet at this moment, in which all our disparate efforts were rewarded, we formed a single living unit.

There are many ways to experience happiness. As a player I'd felt it as a limitless power and ability, when all six of us under pressure had thought of the same tactic at once and had moved as a unit, each executing his own part, surprising into error our over confident opponents.

As a coach, I'd experienced it as surprise when players improved and produced together something that only could have come from them, yet of which I had never thought. Sometimes, it was the discovery of trust and security. One morning at the European Championships in Italy, long after it was our turn to train, I still couldn't persuade the Israeli team to move from the practice court. I stepped back discouraged, only to see my players casually take a volleyball and begin to play football behind, then around and then amongst the Israelis. Distracted, the Israelis stopped and angrily tried to take possession of the 'football', yet for all their superior skill as volleyball players they found themselves outclassed. 'Hey!' I thought with astonishment, 'I don't *have* to know all the answers. Our strength, even our imagination as a unit *really* doesn't all depend on me.'

I want this book to be a map on which I can place my various perceptions of team spirit, both positive and negative, sporting and otherwise, direct and vicarious. At seven years old, I went to boarding school and the first memory of my sporting career is as a small boy clutching a rugby ball, running for dear life amid what I took to be shouts of encouragement, touching the ball down, turning in shy triumph and discovering that I'd run in the wrong direction. Despite this early trauma, I soon found that sport, in all its startling unpredictability, could be an endless source of excitement and delight. I also found that I was much better at hockey than at rugby. When I left school to begin two years of national service, my selection for the Scottish Command hockey team gave balance to claustrophobic life as a colonel's office clerk at Scottish Command HQ.

Between national service and a volleyball career that began at Edinburgh University, I had three years in French territory – as a student in Grenoble where I lived in the community of a French boarding house; as an English 'assistant' at the French lycée in Oran, where I struggled uneasily between the teaching staff group (who were understandable but distant) and the student body (who were incomprehensible but friendly); and once again as a member of an office community, this time in a Parisian insurance company where I earned money to attend classes at the Sorbonne.

Apart from the army hockey team, none of these group experiences had been entirely positive and so it was with the Edinburgh University and Scottish volleyball teams that I first had a sustained encounter with genuine team spirit. I also played for Great Britain for two years of this time, under coach Dave James, a valuable if less integrated experience. Eventually, I became National Director as well as National Coach of the Scottish Volleyball Association and learnt a great deal about teamwork at the executive level of the business world.

In 1976, I joined the Findhorn Foundation, the spiritual community and educational Trust on the Moray Firth, one of the first centres of alternative or 'New Age' culture in Britain. Between resigning my post with the Scottish Volleyball Association and leaving for Findhorn, I had a recurrent nightmare of finding myself back in my boarding school classroom. As it turned out, this new experience was indeed very much a return to the group living of school and army. However, it was as if I had travelled a full circle and discovered that the circle was the first turn of a spiral. Not only did I come back to my starting point with a wealth of understanding I had gained in the interim but Findhorn itself, though superficially similar, turned out to be a 'higher' and vastly more meaningful dimension of community life than anything I had experienced the first time round. It was here that I also began to find an alternative way of viewing sport.

Although the break from Edinburgh to Findhorn was sudden in the eyes of my friends, there had been connecting experiences. Whilst still Director of the Scottish Volleyball Association, I'd become a yoga student, a member of a Jungian dream-analysis group and had attended some Gestalt and Encounter workshops. Findhorn helped me synthesise so many disparate experiences. I thought I'd give up competitive sport for good but immediately met Christopher Connolly, with whom I later developed the Sporting Bodymind consultancy, and within two months found myself coaching a Findhorn Foundation volleyball team. Above all, in the context of this book, it was my experience as a member of the Foundation's guest department and the responsibility of leading groups of people visiting the community for the first time, people from all over the world, all professions, all ages, that gave me a new and deeper perception of team spirit. From Findhorn I went on a staff exchange programme to the Esalen Institute in California, where I renewed my acquaintance with Gestalt Therapy and met early 'bodymind' exponents Ken Dychtwald, Bob Kriegel and Mike Murphy. When The Sporting Bodymind was launched early in 1979 by Christopher and golfer Sandy Dunlop in London, I came straight back to join them, though I continued to maintain a connection with California through my Gestalt training with George and Judith Brown of the University of California at Santa Barbara.

Developing the consultancy has in itself been one prolonged experience of teamwork. Sandy and I sparked spectacular electrical storms from each other with Christopher holding the focus as the foundation was laid. However Sandy moved to a business management consultancy in December of that first year. Since then Christopher and I have created, developed, adapted, agreed, disagreed, argued, brainstormed, co-operated and, if there is such a word, 'synergised' (see chapter one, page 22). We are very different from each other and, as a team, we are different again. Neither of us could have thought out Sporting Bodymind as it now, alone. It was a time of particular satisfaction when our book *Sporting Body, Sporting Mind: An Athlete's Guide to Mental Training*, was published (May 1984) because it seemed to put all that we had achieved together over the previous five years into perspective.

One key element of that time was our work with Tottenham Hotspur Football Club. This began in October 1980 when the club's physiotherapist Mike Varney introduced us to manager Keith Burkinshaw. Keith invited us to sit in on a few team meetings and to discuss their dynamic with him afterwards. I then remained at Tottenham on a part-time basis until March 1983 (we decided I would continue alone after May 82) and returned after more time in America, to work with the next manager, Peter Shreeve, for the whole of the 1984/85 season. Sometime during our first season at 'Spurs' we told the players about individual mental training and Steve Archibald decided to give it a try. One by one, other players followed suit until all but a couple of first team players had had at least one or two meetings.

Nineteen-eighty/eighty-one and 1981/82 were great seasons, culminating in FA Cup Final victories at Wembley but, although I enjoyed all the work that I did then, particularly the development of communication skills through small and large group meetings, I probably worked best in my final season, 1984/85. Peter Shreeve employed me primarily to work with players on an individual basis but such work had its place in the context of the team as a whole. Working effectively with individual players automatically reinforced positive connections between players, between each player and the captain and between each player and the coaching staff. During this final year I developed a new method of working with two players at once, which would help to reinforce some specific link between them. In the end we won no trophies but finished a satisfying third in the league.

I write 'we' as I have occasionally done further on in this book when referring to my work with Spurs. That was the way I felt and talked about my working relationship with the players. To say 'you' to them would have implied a distance that was neither correct nor helpful. However, in the wider context of the club, it was more complicated. Two years after our debut, the popular press were still shrieking 'Mindbenders!' (*Morning Star*) and 'Brainwashing!' (*Daily Mirror*), whilst Danny Blanchflower, perhaps Tottenham's all-time favourite son, titled one of his *Sunday Express* articles 'The Spectres of White Hart Lane'. Keith and

Peter brushed such comments aside but they did reflect the layman's view. The problem was that the role of a sports psychologist within the manager's team wasn't clear. Indeed, my territory seemed to overlap the territory traditionally occupied by the manager himself. What was it I could do that he wasn't doing anyway? This vagueness affected the day-to-day logistics of my attendance. For all the goodwill I was shown by Keith and Peter, I was sometimes left wondering when I should attend, where I should work and who I should work with. It was in such moments of doubt, moments *between* my sessions with the players, that I was occasionally prone to questioning my use of the pronoun 'we'.

It was only after I left the club in May 1985, after Peter's first season as manager, that I had the opportunity to clear the confusion in my own mind. In November 1985, Christopher and I were asked to build a course based on *Sporting Body, Sporting Mind* for the in-flight and ground managers of Scandinavian Airlines (SAS). We began by writing the script for a video which would show a coach making all kinds of horrendous mistakes in dealing with his players. The SAS managers would then discuss how far they could identify with the situations they saw on the screen. Whilst considering the role of a manager in this new light, I realised he *should* be part teacher, part counsellor and part facilitator – or at least that these are generally the roles he is left to play. He's expected to *teach* physical, technical and mental skills for individual athletes (or business subordinates) to use on their own; *counsel* in the sense of helping an athlete (or subordinate) to identify his goals and take decisions as to how he might reach them; and *facilitate* or lead team (or departmental) discussions and develop team spirit. The trouble is that few sports coaches are taught to do any of this bar the teaching of physical and technical skills. The rest, which constitutes the whole area of mental training, is either ignored or partially acquired through trial and error.

In point of fact, I doubt if either Keith or Peter would agree that the manager's role is so wide. Basically their interest was in results and the players were a means to an end. If they'd been totally confident that results could have been achieved without teaching mental exercises, without talking to players individually and without team discussions, I suspect they wouldn't have been interested. I feel that it was partly the fact that they weren't sure, which accounted for their somewhat ambivalent relationship with me. Looking back, I'm grateful that they were prepared to stay with the concept as long as they did. I too learnt a great deal at Spurs and, over the four-year period, saw my skills develop and change. I enjoyed my work enormously and a few of the people I encountered then have become my friends.

If you leaf through the pages ahead, you'll find that every chapter begins with a consideration of the individual athlete, perhaps to the point where you wonder why the book is called *Team Spirit*. However, I don't think you can develop team spirit without caring for the individual within the team, in addition to caring for the team as a whole. Each individual team member needs to learn how and when to merge with the team and how and when to withdraw. If you are his coach, you may need to help him to do that, teaching him or ensuring that he is taught the required mental skills. In fact, the whole area of individual mental training as well as training for the group is important to you, if you want your team to be inspired with a sense of their own team spirit. I think it is worth going over this before we go any further.

If physical skills may be listed as stamina, strength, balance, timing, speed, agility and flexibility, and technical skills (in volleyball for instance) as serving, receiving, setting, spiking, diving and rolling, *mental skills* include the individual ones of concentration, confidence, relaxation, the ability to deal with stress, quality of performance (such as perseverence, patience, aggression), correct attitude (towards oneself, one's team-mates, one's opponents and one's environment) and motivation, *plus*

Skills required for Volleyball

Physical	Technical	Mental		
stamina	serving	1. *Individual*		2. *Team*
strength	receiving	concentration		communication
balance	setting	confidence		relationships
timing	spiking	relaxation		team spirit
speed	diving	coping with stress		
agility	rolling	qualities		
flexibility		(eg perseverence, patience, aggression)		
		correct attitude (towards oneself, others and environment)		
		motivation		

the team ones of communication, relationships and team spirit.

Mental training consists of a body of exercises to improve not just mental skills but physical skills and technical skills as well. These mental exercises are in part 'right-brain' (eg visualisation, and the use of music, pictures and symbols) and in part 'left-brain' (eg goal-setting, preparation, analysis, affirmations and slogans).

The Sporting Bodymind Mental Training Exercises

(These exercises are outlined in more detail in *Sporting Body, Sporting Mind*.)

Left-brain exercises	Right-brain exercises
goal-setting	
planning (tactics)	visualisation (all types)
analysis	symbols
completing questionnaires	acting
affirmations	music
slogans	pictures
evocative words	drawing
keeping performance log for	relaxation methods
physical and mental training	body awareness exercises.
speed writing	
journal writing	

Types of visualisation

1. Mental rehearsal:
   (i) Performance practice
      – basic performance practice
      – ideal model
      – top performance practice
      – right place/right time
      – substitution rehearsal
   (ii) instant replay
   (iii) during performance or 'as if . . .' visualisation
   (iv) instant replay
   (v) performance review

2. Problem solving:
   (i) the black box
   (ii) the quiet place
   (iii) visual re-editing
   (iv) the Wise Old Man

Sporting Body, Sporting Mind: An Athlete's Guide to Mental Training is a compendium of mental training exercises and I refer to it frequently in this book, to which it is a companion volume.

You may know little of these exercises and therefore of mental training. Instead, if you are a coach, you probably devise physical and technical training exercises which coincidentally improve mental skills and indeed, consciously or unconsciously, this is how most coaches *do* develop their athletes' mental skills. When you increase load or repetitions in weightlifting, you are not only increasing the athlete's strength but also his confidence as he experiences the heightening of his physical ability. When you devise any technical pressure drill, you are not only improving the technique or techniques concerned but *also* improving the athlete's ability to deal with stress. The concept that *any* physical, technical or mental exercise may, with some ingenuity, be used to develop any physical, technical or mental skill may be expressed diagrammatically for any sport. Using tennis as an example, the following table shows how just one physical exercise (weights) or one technical exercise (feeding balls) or one mental exercise (visualisation) may be used to develop each of the three different types of skill (one example only being given of each).

	Physical skills	Technical skills	Mental skills
Physical training	weights improve *strength*	weights around wrist when volleying at the net improves *volley*	a gradual increase of load in weight training increases *confidence*
Technical training	feeding balls non-stop to alternate sides of player improves *stamina*	feeding balls to forehand improves *forehand*	feeding balls to the forehand for ten minutes non-stop improves *concentration*
Mental training	visualising oneself doing a perfect half-volley improves *timing*	visualising oneself doing a perfect service improves *service*	're-editing' a memory of a bad accident and visualising the new version will improve *ability to deal with stress*

Having looked at what the individual needs if he is to become a valuable member of the team, let's return to the team as a whole. Team spirit is itself a mental skill and if your target is that it be developed in your team, you may achieve this by physical training exercises (stretching in pairs, for instance), by technical training exercises (eg a drill where one player's achievement is made to depend on another's), or by mental training exercises (eg team meetings). However, in my view, if you don't introduce mental training exercises, it is going to take you much longer than it would do otherwise. Mental training is a distinct third way to help an athlete or a team to improve their performance and, as such, is an invaluable adjunct to the training you already conduct. When the individual adopts a suitable programme of mental training exercises, he will progress faster. When you hold a team meeting, with a little skill, you can remove long-standing, half-recognised blocks quite quickly.

This book is a record of my own development and experience as a sports psychologist and coach. It describes how I now teach and counsel individual team members and how I lead group meetings, adding to the information already given in *Sporting Body, Sporting Mind*. If you would ike to develop these skills, this book suggests the first step – a possibly new way of viewing your role. Some of the suggestions and exercises can be adopted quite easily, especially those concerned with 'facilitating' skills – ways of leading team meetings. Many of the individual counselling or mental exercises need expertise and you may want to engage a 'mental trainer' to lead them, just as you may already engage a physical trainer to conduct physical training.

How far you will want to go in this direction will partly depend on your attitude to coaching. As you go through this book, you'll see that I refer to two extreme types of coach, the authoritarian 'behaviourist' who tells his players what to do and motivates them through some system of reward and punishment and the democratic 'humanist', who asks players for their opinions and helps them to discover their own motivation. Most coaches fall somewhere between the two or vary their approach according to the situation but, in professional sport at least, the accepted way of coaching is very much towards the behaviourist end of the scale. Since my own training and approach is humanistic, my first objective is to provoke thought and reflection. What are you aiming to achieve? How do you normally ensure that you achieve it? What sort of obstacles do you habitually encounter? Then comes the question What is new in the humanistic approach which you would feel comfortable with and would like to try? So long as you don't expect to become a sports psychologist overnight, this book can help you to better understand present behaviourist attitudes you might hold, know when you might best call in outside assistance, and develop your personal style of coaching so that it embodies any part of the humanistic approach that appeals to you. Above all, the book is intended to show you how you may use mental training to promote the experience of team spirit.

Communication, leadership, harmony and relationship are issues for all of us in one context or another. Team spirit is usually a potent unacknowledged factor in even the individual sportsperson's experience as well as in the experiences of those engaged in team events. Both positive and negative team spirit is experienced as commonly in business, in politics, in the theatre, in the classroom, or in any other group situation as it is in the sports team. Sometimes I use the word 'manager' rather than 'coach' because, in addition to being the term used to designate the 'head coach' in soccer, American football and baseball, it is also used in business, to which much of this book is applicable.

Indeed, although this book is about sport and is addressed primarily to the coach, I trust that it will be of interest not just to other leaders – be they called captains, managers, directors, officers or teachers – but also to those who are 'led'. When appropriate, I have used the words 'athlete', 'sportsperson', 'performance' or 'competition', rather than 'player' or 'match' which have a more restricted application. For the sake of simplicity, I have used the pronouns 'he' and 'him' throughout – I'm not entirely happy with this decision but tried writing 'or she' and 'or her' and found the result disjointed. The book is obviously intended for coaches and athletes, leaders and followers, of either sex.

The first chapter explains my view of team spirit and how it differs from some popular (often negative) assumptions. I then look at various factors that affect team spirit, starting with conflict because it is out of conflict that come new ideas. New ideas can be stifled by imposed conformity and we'll look at this before moving on to relationships and communication – two issues so bound up with team spirit that they surface in other chapters as well. The sixth chapter is on motivation, whilst the last two – confidence and stress – give some further indication on the way I work with team-members individually. However, I consider the manager's relationship to individual members of his 'team' as well as to the team as a whole, in the context of *each* chapter's theme. This on the principle that a team only reaches *its* potential if each of its individual members are helped to reach *their* potential. The epilogue and first two appendices explore the differences between behaviourist and humanistic leadership in more detail.

Sometimes I refer to my background in Gestalt, psychosynthesis, yoga and group dynamics. Sometimes I relate stories I have read or been told and sometimes I draw on my own experience of teams. I quote a lot from Fritz Perls, 'father' of Gestalt, whose writings have always excited me, from my favourite brand of journalism – the sports profile – and from certain books, none more so than John Madden's *Hey Wait a Minute!* which, despite my scant knowledge of American football, had me laughing out loud.

This book seems to have taken three years to write, the last-minute additions driving my publisher to distraction. I trust it won't take you as long to read and that it makes some connection with your own experience. So often the teams of which we are part will crash through one discord after another, yet occasionally the perfect combination of notes will surprise us. I believe that if we are prepared to see and respond to each other more clearly, we may eventually learn to sound the elusive harmony of team spirit at will. If my book can encourage you to experiment anew with the means at your disposal, it will have fulfilled its purpose.

1

SO WHAT IS TEAM SPIRIT?

'You'd better phone her,' said my editor, speaking of a new copy-editor he'd brought in at the eleventh hour. 'Sure . . . Why?' I asked. 'She's scared to phone you.' Intrigued, I dialled the number he gave me. Within seconds I knew it would be fine: instant rapport. Then: 'What's he going on about?' I asked politely. 'I can't stand the title,' blurted Mary Lou. 'I like the book but I'd *never* pick it up in a bookshop, with a title like *Team Spirit*. It's so boring. I mean Rah! Rah! Rah! Come on chaps! All together now! I had enough of that at school.'

An old friend called by that evening. I tried him. '*Team Spirit*, Hugo. What do you think?' 'Let's all pull together, you mean?' asked Hugo, giving me a sidelong look through the flash of his glasses. '"Play up, play up and play the game . . ." Now where's that from, I wonder? Was it *Tell England* by Ernest Raymond?' 'Hugo,' I sighed, 'you *know* that's not what I mean. What shall I call the bloody thing?' He phoned the next morning. 'How about *All Together Now*?' he suggested. 'You know. Music hall style.'

Although I had long before identified some *negative* aspects of team spirit, I was surprised. For me, the rah-rah-rah rantings of coaches, teachers, managers or officers are the *empty shell* of team spirit, what remains when the experience has been lost. Even the experience itself goes by different names. One evening deep into the 1985/86 season, I bumped into Tottenham mid-field player Chris Hughton, in Hampstead. 'How's it going?' I asked, very glad to see him. 'Well, morale is so-so,' he said, spreading his hands, and I knew what he meant, despite morale having other connotations for me. I feel that 'morale', 'cohesion', 'confluence'

13

and 'synergy' are all words that refer to team spirit but reflect different points of view. It is worth looking at each of these in turn.

Morale

'Morale' like 'team spirit' is an emotive non-technical term. *For me* it has the negative connotation of large impersonal institutions. In particular I associate it with the army, where the majority have little say in their fate and the 'level of morale' is not only judged by the officer in charge but thought to be his responsibility. 'Morale' is something that can 'fail' through extreme pressure or inadequate leadership and may be 'raised' by good management. The group's leader, ever aware of the possibility of his followers becoming depressed and losing confidence, tries hard to stay one step ahead. On the whole, he's concerned that his followers help each other to achieve an end that is dear to his heart or to the heart of those to whom he is himself subordinate.

In this kind of situation, the group is often together through force of circumstances rather than through eager choice but 'morale' is also used of nurses who work in understaffed and insanitary conditions and of school-teachers after prolonged industrial action. In this case, the term relates to groups whose members may well *choose* to belong, consciously and conscientiously, but whose membership is large, imprecise or politically organised. For me, there is still some sense of members being caught up in something too big to be wholly in their control.

The structure of a professional football club is in many ways similar to that of the military services. For this reason, both managers and players occasionally refer to the team's 'morale'. In fact, when I first attended a day's training at Tottenham, I was reminded of my national service days. The players ('men') sat in line on a couple of benches, at the start of the day, and the manager ('commanding officer') stood in front of them and gave a morale-boosting talk. At lunchtime, the coaching staff ('officers') sat at a separate table from the players, . . . and before leaving the training ground the manager called two players into his office on matters of discipline.

The shape and the format of team meetings changed over the following two years and the team won two trophies but, midway through my third season, there was a period when confidence fell and the manager once again felt responsible for raising 'morale'. This meant another rousing talk, although by then there had been changes and he asked the players to speak as well.

Cohesion

'Cohesion' is an academic word which reflects a relatively dry view of team spirit. It is mainly used by behaviourists, people who believe that (in the field of sport) an athlete acts only according to the promise of reward or the threat of punishment. Reward may be selection, promotion or an increase in salary; punishment may be being dropped, being fined or not being praised for things done well. Since many coaches and even some athletes do see motivation in this way, it's worth looking at the academic behaviourists' view of team spirit in some detail.

An early definition of cohesion (sometimes called 'cohesiveness') was 'the sum of all forces that make members remain in a group. (Festinger *et al.*, see bibliography.) These forces were identified as: (i) a commitment to success or 'task motivation', with each individual concerned to achieve the same team objective; (ii) (as a negative factor) the difficulty of withdrawing from the team, whether because of a contract, fear of letting teammates down or inertia; and/or (iii) social needs or the attraction to other team members, stemming from admiration or empathy. Of these, 'attraction to other team members' seemed the most powerful, not just to coaches who demanded that their players play for each other but to many academics as well. The accompanying assumption was that cohesion (largely the attraction of other team members) improved the team's communication and co-ordination and therefore of course its performance.

Not all academics agreed with these theories. Some felt that cohesion was the *result* rather than the cause of improved performance and there are athletes who hold a similar view. Steve Archibald, the most forthright, imaginative non-conformist I have ever met in a team sport, felt during his Tottenham days that team spirit 'is an illusion that you only see after you've won'. (When he joined Barcelona FC, he soon came to feel differently.) This view is supported by the experience of the East German rowing eight who won the 1968 Olympic Gold Medal in Mexico, despite the fact they couldn't stand each other. (Hans Lenk, see bibliography.) In the 1984 Superbowl, the Los Angeles Raiders – once based in Oakland and called 'the Oakland A's' – thrashed the Washington Redskins, who prided themselves on being a 'family'. Raider's tight end, Todd Christensen commented:

'Camaraderie is over-rated. We're close but I don't invite Howie Long and Lyle Alzado over to dinner every night. The Oakland A's fought all the time and won three straight World Series.' (*Los Angeles Times*, 25 January 1984.)

The East German experience suggested that the business of sharing a *task objective* meant more to cohesion than player's mutual attraction or, at least, that task sharing contributed more to successful performance. After all, a team is a 'unit with a task that no individual members can do alone'. (Lenk.) Teams may achieve success even when their members have no liking for each other or even dislike each other. Fulfilling the task set for the team is more satisfying to the members than the business of getting along with each other or making friends. The formation of friendships within a team will even hinder its performance if cliques and jealousies are created and energy is diverted away from the team's task.

I don't believe this is the whole story but, when I was a member of the unsuccessful British volleyball team in Holland in 1968, the team fell into two distinct cliques and this can only have restricted our ability to succeed. Although one clique was the first six, the other contained most of the substitutes, so that when a substitution was made the players on court no longer constituted a cohesive team.

At Spurs, feelings were rarely expressed in public. Perhaps ties of friendship are less strong in professional than in amateur teams and no doubt affiliative needs are rarely a reason for joining a professional club. Friendships and antagonisms existed but there was no glaring divide. The only times I suspected that team performance suffered from cliquishness were when reserve team players were suddenly promoted to a first team role. Despite the fact that first team squad players play for the reserves when they lose form or return from injury, the regular reserve team players had their own dressing room, own coach and own customs. When, as sometimes happened, two or three reserves were selected to make up the substitutes bench on away European Cup matches (when five subs are allowed rather than the customary two), they invariably shared rooms with each other, ate together and played cards together in the evening. Though there was a real chance that they be called upon to integrate with the first team in the middle of the match, little effort was made by either side to achieve integration prior to the match.

Yet in general my own experience has been that strong social bonds between players complement and reinforce rather than exclude their motivation to perform a common task. This seems to have been the case with John Biglow, the US rower who failed to gain a medal in the single sculls at the 1984 Olympics but, five years earlier in only his junior year, had stroked the Yale boat to their first victory over Harvard for sixteen years. Biglow, reports David Halberstam in his compelling mystery-style book *The Amateurs*, 'was unsure of himself academically and socially and he knew he wanted to be part of something that gave him a sense of self and a sense of belonging'. Eventually he chose rowing over a singing group he was drawn to 'because oarsmen all had to sacrifice so much for their sport' which meant 'their relationships with each other were far more intense'. Personally, the joy of working towards a shared objective with a group of which I am glad to be part is an even greater pleasure than just hanging out together, though that too is an important part of the relationship's rhythm. For me, therefore, the affiliation needs of team members do not necessarily result in the formation of cliques which work against each other. It should also be said that a skilful leader can teach cliques that are in discord to appreciate each other and achieve more together in terms of enjoyment, satisfaction and task performance than any sub-group can alone.

In the school classroom, high cohesion based on strong affiliation needs are as likely to improve performance as not. It all depends on the norms of the group or class. In fact, it has been found that the highest level of cohesion (defined as 'interpersonal attraction') is to be found in the worst and the best groups of performers: in the first case where the group norm is *against* doing school work and in the second case where it supports school work. In both cases cohesion helps them in their resolve. The teacher can promote both learning and cohesion by replacing the traditional straight-line rows of desks, which all face the front, by small groups of desks, at which the students sit and help rather than compete against each other.

As regards the story of the successful, bickering East German rowing team, it has been suggested – this section on cohesion is largely inspired by A Carron and P Chelladurai (see bibliography) – that cohesion, whether task or socially motivated, can affect performance only through interaction. Two-way communication is essential. Yet the only inter-personal communication required in a rowing eight is between the cox and the unit as a whole, and even that is a one-way process. The East German rowers had no avenue of communication with each other during a race, each member of the eight having his own task and being directly responsible to the cox. The dislike they felt for each other was therefore inevitably contained and cohesion or the lack of it could have no effect on their performance.

This conjures up a picture of a boatful of robots and evokes Max Beerbohm's definition of a crew – 'Eight minds with but a single thought . . . if that.' The trouble is that it leaves out the crucial subliminal element of team spirit, a level which has nothing to do with words, which we shall examine in a moment. It certainly does not mesh with Andrew Ellison's comment about his crew, after winning the 1984 Olympic four-oar event: 'The important thing is not what style you've got but that you're compatible. We're very compatible and very motivated.' (*Sunday Times*, 12 August 1984.)

Strong social and task achievement needs *can* co-exist, team spirit does make a difference and if the East German team had had a more harmonious relationship they would probably have done even better. However, it is true that however angry they were with each other, they could hardly have formed into warring cliques and pursued that war in competition. Some sports are markedly more interactive than others and some teams do not need interdependence for success. Other teams do but achieve success by means other than communication. Even those needing good communication do not necessarily need mutual attraction between team members.

Important distinctions can be drawn between, (i) *co-active* sports such as rowing eights and tug of war, where individual team members are all dependent on the same outside source to initiate and control their efforts; (ii) *reactive/proactive* sports, such as cricket or American football, where interaction between teammates is only one way, with one (always the same) athlete being dependent on another (always the same) to initiate action; and (iii) *interactive* sports, such as soccer, basketball, volleyball and hockey, where players are all dependent on each other with the role of initiator changing constantly.

A team has to co-ordinate its efforts if it is to be successful. In the case of co-active sports the coach *rules* in advance how individual athletes will co-ordinate, since no adjustment or communication is necessary during competition. In reactive/proactive sports the coach co-ordinates his team by *planning and practicing* set moves in advance, which need only minor adjustments and little communication during the competition. In interactive sports, the coach cannot rule or plan to any significant extent, the athletes must co-ordinate through *mutual adjustment* during the competition and communication is essential. From this it is argued that only interactive sports teams need to cultivate cohesion because only they need to communicate during performance in order to achieve co-ordination.

It is interesting that 'cohesion' is defined scientifically as the 'molecular force of attraction between similar kinds of molecules'. This does reflect the formation of cliques, where people with similar feelings, views and norms turn inwards towards each other, shutting out the rest of the team or new members who seem strange. However, for me, true team spirit corresponds much better to the definition of *adhesion* – 'the molecular force of attraction between *different* kinds of molecules'. In fact, I believe that team spirit has much more to do with respect, appreciation and delight in the *different* characteristics of individual team members than it has to do with liking and conformity, and these were qualities I looked for as coach to the Scottish men's volleyball team.

Before Clive Lloyd became captain of the West Indies cricket team in 1974, the West Indians, according to a profile of Lloyd in the *Observer*, 'were renowned as flamboyant, happy-go-lucky, "calypso" cricketers, lacking in that great Victorian virtue of temperament. Lloyd, by bridling that unbridled enthusiasm, has made them flamboyant yet utterly professional'. (19 August 1984.) He united 'various religious, political and socio-economic backgrounds, compounded by the insular tendencies of island people'. In the end, something quite new and overwhelmingly successful emerged: the first ever national team with four out-and-out fast bowlers.

Somerset cricket team captain Peter Roebuck said at the end of the 1985 season: 'Team spirit and friendliness aren't the same thing. Team spirit is going through something together.' When the great Japanese baseball player, Sadaharu Oh described his relationship with his illustrious team-mate Nagashima, he wrote: 'A team of course is composed of different individuals. There is no need for team-mates to be friends; in fact, there is something about being team-mates that can make friendship not especially desirable. It is hard for example to be perfectly objective with a friend. But the fact that Nagashima-san and I were so different and yet so prominent on the same team gave rise to speculation that we did not get along. This was not the case.' (Sadaharu Oh and David Faulkner, *Sadaharu Oh: A Zen Way of Baseball*.) To find a more holistic inspirational view of team spirit we need to move on from cohesion to the concept of confluence.

Confluence

Confluence is a state experienced by most individuals as well as team athletes, peak experiences of intense concentration and awareness when it seems impossible to do wrong. Tony Jacklin the British golfer used to call this a 'cocoon' of concentration. Racing drivers have described moments when they are suddenly at one with the car, the track and the smell of the newly-mown grass beside the track. Billie-Jean King has described the perfect shot as one she could almost 'feel' coming. Tennis players describe such feelings of confluence as being 'in the zone' (see also pages 135–7).

Confluence, then, is a Gestalt concept which in its positive form denotes the individual's feeling of oneness with his or her environment. 'Parts and the whole are indistinguishable from one another. Newborn infants live in confluence, they have no sense of any distinction between inside and outside, between self and other. In moments of ecstasy or extreme concentration, grown people too feel confluent with their environment. Ritual demands this sense of confluence, in which boundaries disappear and the individual feels most himself because he is so closely identified with the group. Part of the reason ritual produces a sense of exaltation and heightened experience is that normally we feel the self-other boundary quite sharply and its temporary dissolution is consequently felt as a tremendously impactful thing.' (Fritz Perls, *The Gestalt Approach*.)

Gestalt is an educational ('humanistic') psychology in which the 'teacher' helps the 'student' to recognise and fulfil his potential ability. Gestalt was developed by Fritz Perls, a contemporary of Sigmund Freud, who nevertheless felt that more is to be learnt from our experience of the present than from an understanding of our past.

Gestalt exercises are therefore designed to increase awareness of the interplay of our physical, emotional and mental reactions to our environment. These exercises include acting out our perceptions of others; alternating full awareness of the environment with complete withdrawal from it; noticing that what we imagine about what we see affects how we feel; and recognising the resentments, demands and appreciations we experience in relation to other people. A Gestalt 'teacher' tends to ask questions beginning with 'How?' and 'What?' rather than questions beginning with 'Why?'.

In team sports, confluence is a sense of oneness with performers in one's own team, as well as with the total environment. After a match in which Glenn Hoddle kept finding Tony Galvin with long passes of pin-point accuracy, one of which led to a spectacular goal, Tony said 'We didn't speak but I was on his wavelength'. It also happens in rowing. 'When most oarsmen talked about their perfect moments in a boat, they referred not so much to winning a race but to the feel of the boat, all eight oars in the water together, the synchronization almost perfect. In moments like that, the boat seemed to lift right out of the water. Oarsmen called that the moment of *swing*. John Biglow loved that moment too but he spoke of it in an interesting manner. What he liked about it, he said, was that it allowed you to *trust* the other men in the boat. A boat did not have swing unless everyone was putting out in exact measure and because of that, and only because of that, there was the possibility of true trust among oarsmen.' (Halberstam.)

The sense of 'oneness' (see also pages 000–000), the team athlete's peak experience, would seem to occur at a point beyond the top of the team spirit scale, higher even than the 'All for one and one for all' affirmation of the Three Musketeers, fiercely delivered before each match by Ray Clemence, on leaving the dressing room. Many teams attempt to reach this state consciously or unconsciously through some form of ritual, over and above a rousing pep-talk from the coach. 'Ritual,' observed Perls, 'joins people together'. (*The Gestalt Approach*.) At Tottenham, each player touched the head, back or hand of each other player, saying that player's name and wishing him 'All the best!', in the final moments of the dressing room warm-up.

Superstition can serve a similar purpose for most individual as well as team athletes. Diver Greg Lougarnis, winning two gold medals in Los Angeles, played with his teddy 'Garvey the Bear' between dives, rolled around with him on a nearby trampoline and even took him to the bathroom. When Jack Nicklaus lost his favourite ball-mark repairer on the eve of the 1984 US PGA Championships, John Hopkins wrote in the *Sunday Times*: 'Nicklaus is very superstitious. For 20 years he has always worn white gloves and shoes and carried in his pocket the same three pennies and this little metal gadget. Without it he was a shorn Samson'. (26 August 1984.) And Bjorn Borg, before each match of his five year reign as Wimbledon champion, 'packed and repacked his tennis bag to exact specifications. To Wimbledon he would only ride in a car with a stereo radio. The driver would always have to take the same route over Hammersmith Bridge, never Putney Bridge. Exactly four days before the Championship, he would start his beard.' (Frank Keating, The *Guardian*, 26 January 1983.) The form of the superstition or ritual is unimportant. What matters is its ability to intensify awareness and concentration, to lead the athlete into his 'zone'.

Sacred ritual, as in the oldest forms of circle dance as well as more current religious services, has always aimed to create the high feeling of oneness that is confluence. Often such unity has been fostered to better fight in battle. John Bertrand, skipper of *Australia II*, saw the Carlton Football Club win the VFL Grand Final in September 1982 and described their mental preparation: 'Just before the Carlton players ran out, some of them were seen embracing each other. In other words, they were going to *war* together . . . a matter of life and death.' (John Bertrand, *Born to Win*.) Inspired, Bertrand engaged Laurie Hayden, the Club's sports psychologist, to help prepare his crew and build similar powerful rituals. Ritual demands total participation: 'Only a full participation of the entire personality will result in that religious feeling of intensified existence, of exaltation of integration, without diminishing the full awareness of both the individual and the group, both the self and the other, and the full awareness of the individual that he is part of the group.' (Perls, *The Gestalt Approach*.)

Synergy

The difference between synergy and confluence, both aspects of team spirit, is one of emphasis. Whilst confluence denotes the sense of being 'one' with other members of the team, synergy (in its positive form) denotes the sense of additional energy being available when a team of individuals work together harmoniously. It is the energy, strength or creative ability of a team when it is greater than the energy, strength or creative ability possessed by the totality of that team's members. It is a concept that can explain why a team of moderately gifted individuals may sometimes beat a team of supremely gifted individuals who lack team spirit. A synergetic whole is greater than the sum of its parts.

'If the combination of separate elements between orchestra and conductor fits together, then you can achieve something beyond the actual notes,' Esa-Pekker Salonen, the Finnish principle guest conductor of the Philharmonia Orchestra told Edward Greenfield of the *Guardian*. (7 February 1986.) The synergetic whole is far more than a group of individuals 'bound together'. *Yes*, the individual member retains awareness of his individuality but he *also* experiences a sense of being completely merged in some entity greater than himself.

'Whatever advantage we had in talent,' wrote Sadaharu Oh of the 1965/66 Giants team, 'we also possessed the kind of confidence as a collective unit that separated us from everyone else.' It is an exciting process. 'Synergy means the working together of unlike elements to create desirable results, unobtainable from any combination of independent efforts... The search for new solutions becomes an adventure in openness and creativity that is far more satisfying than attacking or resisting each other's initial proposals.' (James and Marguerite Craig, *Synergic Power*.) Differences are indeed not just respected but are appreciated with surprise and delight as the sparks which light up a whole new way of understanding. Virgin Atlantic Airways came about through a meeting of Randolph Fields of Fields Investments and Richard Branson of Virgin Records. 'Something "very magical happened" when Fields met Branson, says Fields. "The Americans call it synergy. The combination of us and our businesses just seemed to be so much greater than the individual parts."' (Mick Brown, *Sunday Times*, 17 June 1984.) Synergy occurs most dramatically when the differences of the component parts are greatest. Within a team setting, it is then that controversy can generate the most original of ideas. Hence perhaps the disgust of Miss Daphne Park, Principal of Somerville College, on hearing of Margaret Thatcher's failure to gain an honorary Fellowship: 'You don't stop someone becoming a fellow of an academic body because you dislike them!'

The synergistic effect of two opposed cliques breaking through to mutual respect was well described by Jimmy Boyle, as he discussed *The Nutcracker Suite*, a play he wrote about his experiences as a man imprisoned for murder in the special unit at Barlinnie prison: 'What I hope this play will show very clearly is that what happened in the special unit wasn't simply a matter of them converting us to their values. It was a two-way process, to do with two groups of people who had been trained to regard each other as almost sub-human, beyond the pale, suddenly beginning to perceive each other as human beings and as equals. In a sense, the impact of the unit on the prisoners is the predictable bit; what I find exciting in the play, as we've adapted it, is the way it shows the impact on the prison officers, so that in the end the special unit became just that, a unit, representing a united opposition to the values of the conventional prison system.' (Joyce McMillan, *Guardian*, 10 October 1985.)

A study that compared the individual ability of baseball and basketball team players (M Jones, see bibliography) discovered that measurements of physical ability allowed a ninety per cent correct prediction of the baseball players' performance but only a thirty-five per cent correct prediction of the basketball players' performance. This not only reflects the relatively high demand on basketball players for improvisation but suggests that the main variable in their performance is the degree of team spirit or synergy that exists in the team. In fact, it is likely that the thirty-five per cent predictability refers to a base-level where no synergy exists at all, each individual member on the team operating with minimum support from the rest. Beyond this point, the chemistry of synergy comes into play.

Everton ran away with the English Football League title in 1984/85, yet it was only at the end of the season (in which they also won the European Cup Winner's Cup and were beaten finalists in the FA Cup), that individual players were identified and extensively profiled in the press. Such is the mark of a synergetic team. The ability of interacting teams has always the potential of being greater than the sum of the abilities of their individual players. This gives hope to the accomplished coach with limited resources. *Sunday Times* football correspondent, Brian Glanville, once noted that Billy Bingham's Northern Ireland team 'assess their own strengths and play to them. [They] continue to make a virtue out of necessity, to make the most out of a limited range of players.' (16 September 1984.)

Anthropologist Ruth Benedict was puzzled as to why some primitive cultures are friendly, open and generous, whilst others are suspicious, stingy and hostile. She found the explanation in synergy. In the friendly cultures people had developed relationships based on working together, with much energy and creativity. By doing so, they developed high positive synergy – producing more together than the sum of each individual's contributions. The hostile cultures were so inept at working together, or so hostile to each other, that they developed negative synergy – producing less together than if each individual had acted separately. (Craig and Craig.)

Low cohesion

Team spirit is not always a positive factor. *Low cohesion* has been identified with disconsolate cliques working against each other, but a negative *bonding* can exist when cohesion occurs through fear of an outside force or when leadership or coaching of the group is authoritarian and wholly task-oriented. A group that has been intimidated has its potential for creativity driven beneath the surface, from whence it may erupt in bursts of resentment and destruction. If the eruption is against inappropriate leadership, performance as defined by the leader's objectives will suffer.

In January 1986, when Defence Secretary Michael Heseltine stormed out of a cabinet meeting, protesting that Margaret Thatcher demanded conformity to her views, the *Observer* commented: 'Even before she reached no. 10, she was brazenly warning her prospective colleagues: "As Prime Minister, I couldn't waste time having internal arguments". It can at least be said on her behalf that she has been as good as her word. The roll-call of those, now 10 in all, who have been dismissed from her Cabinet, is one demonstration of this. The cowed demeanour of her present colleagues is an even more vivid one. Mr Heseltine's act of defiance may have been hurtful to the Prime Minister and generally unhelpful to the Government: it has also even more certainly been good for the future democratic health of the Conservative party.'

We'll consider the role of positive leadership in creating team spirit in a later chapter but, as Stilgar says in Frank Herbert's science fiction novel *Dune*: '"A leader, you see, is one of the things that distinguishes a mob from a people. He maintains the level of individuals. Too few individuals and a people reverts to a mob."' The negative side of team spirit is typified by a mob. In the climate of low cohesion, individual members drag each other down to their lowest common denominator, fear of or infatuation with the mob's instigators being the most likely cause.

Negative confluence

Those who are in most danger, whether physical or simply of performing poorly, are those who can no longer distinguish between self and other and who either deny their own needs in order 'to meet the expectations of others' or can't tell which need is dominant. A common example is the golfing partner who has agreed to your suggestion to play a match on a mid-week afternoon and then spends his whole time on the golf course worrying about the work he has to do at his office. The result is that he is neither fully present nor has he fully withdrawn: he is caught in a 'middle zone'. So is the team athlete who doesn't pace himself properly, driving himself mercilessly in support of team effort and then letting the team down by collapsing twenty minutes before the match ends.

This is one reason why any team athlete should develop his kinaesthetic sense or 'body awareness'. With practice, he needs just a moment to take a deep breath, let it out slowly and withdraw. He needs to take his attention from events, other people or his emotional feelings and put it instead on his physical sensation, asking 'Okay, so what do you need, body?' This done, he can return his attention to the competitive situation with renewed attention and excitement.

I had a theory that those players at Tottenham who were injured least were those who best understood the need to withdraw at the right time. By the same token these were often the players who were most committed during a match. Steve Perryman, who was perhaps the most committed player of all, once told me about his 'sixth sense' for impending injury: 'Normally on a challenge, you stay solid and carry right through. You're the governor of the situation. But sometimes, perhaps when you've had to come in from a distance, something tells you, after you've committed yourself, that you have to get out. That's when you see me sailing through the air, you almost get a ride from the other fellow – not because of the strength of the challenge but because of me having to get out. Ironically, it then *looks* as if my opponent has fouled but in fact it is my body adjusting.' Michael Clark, 'Britain's undisputed star of non-establishment dance' is able to recognise this need for withdrawal in members of his group. When he was asked by John Percival of *The Times* why he arranged an intensive course in classical ballet technique in preparation for his latest production, he replied, 'We had an exhausting tour and we were starting to get injuries. Concentration on technique [which involves increased body awareness] helps to save us from injury. Ballet is the basis of all my work.' (26 August 1985.) The inability to withdraw and vulnerability to the herd or mass instinct are signs of negative confluence.

Low synergy

Low synergy was defined by Ruth Benedict as occurring in suspicious hostile groups where joint output can fall far below what it would be if the individuals acted separately. 'War is the example par excellence of low synergy: nations interact but output in terms of human satisfaction, is much less than if there was no interaction.' Often people try to resolve conflict by low synergetic means – 'by force, cunning or compromise'. Members of the group feel powerless and ill-informed so that 'they are unable to make conscious informed choices about matters that affect them'. 'A low synergy climate diminishes trust, arouses resentments, mystifies, belittles many of the persons interacting and stifles their creativity.' (Craig and Craig.)

The rowing camp, directed by National Coach, Harry Parker, at which the athletes who would fill the USA pair and quad boats were to be chosen, had such a climate. 'If rowing was an estimable sport filled with virtue and honor and strength, then there was something about the team camp that was the reverse of that. They became its Darwinian lowest common denominator. This camp was, if anything, worse; it was filled with anxiety and tension that turned inevitably into paranoia... Every sculler in those tense moments was watching Harry Parker, wondering if he was on Parker's good or bad side and wondering what Parker, so quiet and enigmatic, really thought. In this hothouse atmosphere, old friends first became rivals and then enemies, while old rivals, in the new juxtaposition of loyalties, became allies.' (Halberstam.)

Positive and negative team spirit

So what other signs are there of positive and negative team spirit in a sports team? It seems that members of a team with high cohesion will not take 'high personal credit for success' nor 'low blame for failure' (Patricia and Richard Schmuck, *Group Processes in the Classroom*), whereas the reverse is true where cohesion is low. Positive team spirit may not be aligned to mutual attraction but more surely with appreciation, the creative use of differences and commitment to a common goal.

Negative team spirit can be perceived in the formation of cliques and in individual members who neither fully take part nor fully withdraw, who attend but do not commit themselves to an opinion, who are neither relaxed nor fully mobilised and effective.

All team members need to be capable of total withdrawal and this is often concommittant with total contact with another group in their lives. However, matters relating to the team need to be shared and discussed with the team as a whole and not, as is sometimes the case, only with friends, acquaintances and relations outside. When this happens energy that belongs to the team leaks away and the outside group is itself a kind of clique. At Tottenham there was at least one player who told me he preferred to discuss his football with his family than to talk about it with other team members, especially rather than talk about it in a team meeting. I felt the fact that, on a bad day, this player was often described as 'isolated' on the field was a reflection of the fact that he didn't discuss the games with his fellow players and thereby tie the invisible knots of intuitive relationship with them and become totally part of the team performance.

Almost all athletes perform better for being part of some sort of team. Prior to the Olympics in Los Angeles, Ed Moses trained with Daley Thompson at USC Irvine. Like Daley Thompson he is independent, not easily part of a squad. *Sports Illustrated* reported: 'On more than one occasion Moses has said "I don't need anybody". But he probably *did* need his wife Myrella, Gordon Baskin his business manager and Ken Yoshimo his physiotherapist.' (30 July 1984.) Tessa Sanderson, after gaining her javelin gold medal, recounted how Daley Thompson himself helped her, was part of *her* team, in that he kept telling her to think 'I can do it. I can do it'. When Fuzzy Zoeller won the 1984 Masters Championship, *Sports Illustrated* wrote: 'Even a big wheel needs spokes and Zoeller gets a lot of support from his family and friends ... and that covers just about everybody in New Albany, Indiana.' (6 August 1984.)

After helping Europe to win the 1985 Ryder Cup, golfer Manuel Pinero told John Hopkins of the *Sunday Times* that he believes he plays better when part of a team. 'When I play for myself I'm thinking of the other players, officials, the spectators, the courses we are competing on. But when I play for my country I can see in my mind a picture of the whole Iberian peninsula as clearly as if I'm reading a book. I think of the people there and I think I mustn't let them down. I must try my best.' (22 September 1985.)

This is commitment. Few people can say they have no opportunity to be part of a team but not everyone makes the choice. Commitment to a group is a gift we may be reluctant to make. We may rightly fear the authoritarian leader or distrust potential 'saboteurs' amongst the team, those who drain the team's energy with destructive remarks.

Yet even as ordinary team members there will be opportunities to contribute and lead. More often than not commitment brings new insight and unexpected rewards and, like Manuel Pinero, we may find that our performance improves. The strength of the group becomes our own and we discover the surprising sense of being part of something greater than ourselves. This is the spiritual element of team spirit. As Nikki Lauder said on winning the 1984 World Motor Racing Championship: 'We human folk have many more resources of spirit which we do not use at all.' (*Guardian*, 22 October 1984.)

Glossary

Team spirit is sometimes called 'morale', 'cohesion', 'confluence' or 'synergy', each term reflecting a different viewpoint.

Morale: a term with military connotations, usually used where a leader is made responsible for maintaining team spirit and where followers are part of the group through force of circumstances rather than active choice.

Cohesion: an academic term, meaning the sticking together of like elements. It also implies a passivity on the part of the followers and manipulation by the leader towards his own ends.

Confluence: a positive merging of different elements, so that the contact boundary between them disappears. It is the Gestalt term for the experience of the individual who momentarily feels one with the group and the environment of which he is part.

Synergy: the additional quota of energy and creative ability available to a group of dissimilar individuals who discover the pattern that maximises their individual abilities when they work together.

When team spirit is weak or lacking, morale cohesion and synergy are said to be low and confluence may be negative.

Low morale: primarily a problem for the leader and usually denoting depression, lack of confidence or sullen silence.

Low cohesion: either implying subgroups or cliques working against each other or otherwise the negative bonding of the whole group through fear – a fear that results in subservience or in the unity of a mob.

Negative confluence: the experience of the individual who loses all sense of individuality and unthinkingly identifies himself with the group of which he is a part.

Low synergy: experienced by a group whose members work against each other and where the joint output is less than what it would be if the individuals acted separately.

2

CONFLICT

In the narrow context of a stressful present situation, conflict can seem entirely negative but, in this chapter, I want to suggest that it can *always* be viewed as an opportunity for improvement and the discovery of new horizons. The most obvious ingredient of conflict is intense energy. Some normal gentle flow of intent has been blocked or opposed and it builds up like water behind a dam. The moment of release into a clear channel has great creative power. As a Gestalt psychologist, I also view aggression positively and experience it as a life-affirming force, a positive statement to the world. I reserve the term 'violence' for its usual negative connotations.

The creative team athlete meets opposition and conflict in four different situations:

1. He encounters it as a challenge made by his opponents.
2. He experiences it as his own aggression, the frank challenge he makes *to* his opponents and the clash that results from his attack.
3. He experiences it as moments of indecision within himself.
4. He is involved in disagreement on tactics or in personality clashes between members of his team.

As coach, you will teach him to attack and defend positively, to welcome conflict as an opportunity to discover more of his ability. You will also see that he learns how to solve inner conflict and you'll guide any conflict that arises within the team towards a fruitful conclusion.

This chapter considers each type of conflict in turn and some ways in which the athlete may be helped to deal with them. Since

30

altering his focus of attention is one way for an athlete to change a negative response to challenge, I have included a passage on concentration in section 1, *Encountering a challenge*. I should also point out that my fourth section, *conflict within the team*, does *not* include conflict between yourself and one of your athletes, since I've included this in the wider context of chapter four, *Relationships*.

1. *Encountering a challenge*

Fritz Perls says: 'Without frustration there is no reason to mobilise your resources.' (*Gestalt Therapy Verbatim*.) We *need* conflict in order to discover our worth. No work of art, no scientific discovery, no perfect sports performance is achieved without overcoming innumerable barriers. In fact, it is barriers that oblige us to develop new muscles, increase our skill and discover unsuspected horizons. Even Ed Moses, so long undefeated in the 110 metre high hurdles, regards the tough competition of his early days as responsible for his development. Questioned about his attitude to losing, he replied 'I lost a lot in high school and college. Maybe as often as I won. I just didn't think about it in terms of losing. I was *preparing*.' (*Sports Illustrated*, 30 July 1984.)

When Chris Lloyd beat Martina Navratilova to win the 1985 French Tennis Championships, she was thirty years old and had beaten her opponent only once in the previous sixteen meetings. However, this victory almost levelled the tally of matches between the two players at thirty-two to thirty-three. Speaking of the change of fortune over the years, Chris Lloyd said afterwards: 'Of course things would sometimes have been easier if Martina hadn't been there but her presence gave me new goals to reach. I once dominated women's tennis, as Martina does today. I wonder how long that can go on without becoming overwhelmed by boredom. So, of course, the fact that she's there has encouraged me to work harder. If I had stayed No.1 I would probably have given up already. Now I always have goals to reach. To concentrate on the Grand Slam tournaments and try to beat her.'

By the same token, John McEnroe felt abandoned when Bjorn Borg retired. In the poetic words of Jacques Carducci (*L'Equipe*, 10 June 85): '... et puisqu'on parle de Borg, McEnroe ne lui a jamais pardonné d'avoir dit goodbye, alors qu'ils étaient partis pour naviguer sur les sommets. Il ne lui a jamais pardonné de l'avoir laisse en plan, sans être allés ensemble plus loin dans leur exploration mutuelle du jeu.'

The same principle applies to a team. If a team is to develop its ability, it must test itself against worthy opponents. Failure to do so, not only means no improvement, but the level of performance will deteriorate. Without competition, the team will fall apart. Members will join other clubs, give up the sport or drift into opposing camps within the team. Fritz Perls says 'The avoidance of external conflicts results in the creation of internal ones.' (*Ego, Hunger and Aggression.*) The team splits into cliques and, if there is no common outside boundary, the cliques will fight each other.

Any outside opposition is better than none. When all English soccer teams were banned from playing abroad, following the Huysell stadium disaster of May 1985, Tottenham's pre-season tour to the West Indies was cancelled. On hearing this, Peter Shreeve immediately organised a tour to the south-west of England. The need for match practice is in part to provide individual players a realistic setting in which to test their skills but also to heighten their perception of themselves as part of the team, to experience fully the contrast between 'us' and 'not us'. Even a match between the first team (or first six in volleyball) and reserves (or second six) does not fully awaken the sense of this contrast. Teams in the West Country may have been weaker than Tottenham's own reserves but they provided a true if not worthy opposition and the fact of being in alien surroundings heightened Tottenham's sense of identity and team spirit.

Although any opposition is better than none, teams do need worthy opponents if they are to maintain form as well as unity. John Madden's Los Angeles Raiders were so good that they needed not just the pressure of high class opponents but the additional pressure of prime-time exposure on television. 'Those guys wanted the pressure,' says Madden. 'That's what made them so great. Especially on Monday night. "The whole world's watching," I always reminded them. That's all they wanted to hear. They loved it. In nine seasons of Monday night games the Raiders had an 11–1–1 record, the best of any team in that span. It wasn't an accident. I had great players on that great stage.' (John Madden with Dave Anderson, *Hey Wait a Minute (I wrote a book!).*)

Peter Roebuck of Somerset Cricket Club speculated that it may have been the additional stimulus of being derided as a 'backwoods team' as they moved into the eighties, that pushed the team to winning the John Player League in 1983 for the first time. Once they had achieved recognition and respect, the challenge was diminished and their response was proportionately less. In 1985, despite still having Viv Richards, Ian Botham and Joel Garner in the team, they were bottom of the league again.

Fritz Perls said that 'the more hostility threatens from without, the greater will be the integrative function of individuals and groups.' (*Ego, Hunger Aggression.*) This is true up to a point. The 'tightening' process is observable prior to any big match. The loose circle of players will close. Differences still to be resolved are put to one side until after the competition. Mutual support and encouragement is the norm. However, the experience of meeting overwhelming hostility can end in humiliation and be as detrimental to team spirit as having no challenge at all. Such an eventuality should be foreseen, long before the match begins. If it is and you guide your team to choosing a realistic goal, one much less than winning but that demands improvement in *some* facet of performance, you may *increase* team spirit even in defeat.

Helping the athlete to meet a challenge
I've already suggested that the team must seek worthy opposition and deal with potentially overwhelming hostility by choosing an appropriate realistic goal that will be less than winning. However, within the team, individual athletes will sometimes have difficulty in making an appropriate response to an opponent's challenge. When Glenn Hoddle was returning to the side after a long bout of injury, he used mental rehearsal to practice dealing with aggressive, potentially dangerous challenges and his ability to avoid or ride the hard tackle (see page 162).

Mental rehearsal is a right-brain technique, thoughts originating in the right hemisphere of the brain being visual rather than verbal, intuitive rather than logical and associative rather than analytical. (See the table in Introduction page 8. A more detailed account of this mode of classification is given in *Sporting Body, Sporting Mind*.) However, a player can also solve problems arising out of an opponent's challenge through the use of analytical left-brain thinking. Graham Roberts was, for a long time, liable to respond physically to violent tackles or other real or imagined provocation and to be penalised by the referee. Despite feeling justified and ill-treated at the time, he would readily recognise a few moments later that he'd been outwitted by his opponent and had let down his own team. Tony Galvin had a similar conflict, in that he would become enraged by any referee's decision which he considered to be unjust. He too would let the side down by being penalised for arguing too strongly. In both cases, the answer was to work with their own rational assessment of the situation in the quiet of a one-to-one session and ask them how else they might respond to such incidents. I suggested to each of them that they consider their problem as one of concentration and that if, by acting as they usually did, they could be said to be losing their concentration, that in turn meant that their attention became fixed on a factor within the total situation which was unhelpful to their performance. Their task was to decide where they might more usefully direct their attention and then practice making this switch.

Since any source of conflict may potentially cause a loss of concentration, it's worth staying with this concept a little longer. In any sport, an athlete is required to shift his attention continually from one point to another. If he focuses too long on a single factor, he's said to 'lose concentration' because the situation and its demands are continually changing and his attention hasn't stayed with it.

Robert Nideffer points out that attention may move along two different scales: from *broad* to *narrow* from *external* to *internal* (see bibliography). If we apply this to team ball games, it means that *broad* attention is required by the athlete with the ball, as he scans his options in terms of team-mates to whom he may pass; *narrow* attention is required by the defender who sees his opponent approaching with the ball and shuts out all other information in a bid to dispossess him. Each of these two examples are also examples of *external* attention but *internal* attention may also be broad or narrow. An example of *broad internal* attention would be reflecting on the situation during a break in play and reviewing agreed tactics and considering one's next move, or mentally rehearsing a corner before approaching the ball: the focus of broad internal attention is thought or (emotional) feeling. An example of *narrow internal* attention would be consciously letting go of tension for a moment or checking out the feel of an injury to gauge its seriousness: the focus of internal narrow attention is physical sensation.

Graham Roberts 'lost concentration' in the heat of the moment by allowing his attention to be stuck on the offending opponent. Tony Galvin's attention became stuck on the referee. In both cases, their attention was *narrow* and *external*. When I asked Graham what he might do to break his habit, he suggested that he fall down, holding the part of him that was injured until his anger subsided. This was a good suggestion since it could easily be allied to changing his focus of attention – from narrow external (the opponent) to narrow internal (the pain of his injury). Meantime, Tony came up with a different answer. I asked him what *happens* when the referee makes a strange decision and he said that sometimes players are surprised. So then I asked how he might profit from their surprise and he said he could see where his opponents were standing and run into a good defensive position. Tony's solution was therefore to change his attention from narrow external (the referee) to broad external (looking round at his opponents). Of course, in both cases, the logical left-brain decision to adopt a more fruitful response to disturbing occurrences during the match, was not enough. From that point on, the new response had to be practised, both in training sessions and by rehearsing it mentally each day. In both cases, the players worked at this mental training programme and achieved the change that they wanted.

Later I got a blackboard and drew the following diagram to explain to all the playing staff how conflict can affect concentration. Since it may be right to have one's attention in one of the four basic areas at one moment but not at the next, each area or 'box' is divided into a positive and a negative section. I then filled in examples as follows:

		BROAD	NARROW
INTERNAL	+	'What should I do now?' tactics	Mental rehearsal (before a corner or a free kick, after scoring a goal, etc) relaxation (only when you can do it in a few seconds).
INTERNAL	−	Worries Thinking about mistakes	Fatigue Pain
INTERNAL	+	'What options do I have?' Encouraging others Directing others	Shooting Closing down Distracting an opponent (pushing his attention into a negative box).
INTERNAL	−	Spectators (linesmen) Abusive opponents	Only seeing one option Shooting when it's better to pass. Ball-watching Spending too long distracting an opponent.

Distracting an opponent was Paul Miller of Tottenham's addition to the positive narrow external box. This prompted me to add 'spending too long distracting an opponent' to the *negative* narrow external box, as I suspected this was something that could happen to Paul. Knowing how to distract an opponent's attention from an appropriate to an inappropriate box, without being distracted oneself, is an art which John McEnroe was frequently accused of practising by his opponents. Mohammed Ali practiced it openly. He hired a loud-hailer, drove round to Sonny Liston's house in the middle of the night, before one of their fights, and called him names until Liston got out of bed, came out and fired his shot gun; and he taunted the 6'6" Ernie Terrell, as they fought in the Houston Astrodome in February 1967, with the words 'What's my name?' each time he unleashed a punch – forcing Terrell to register the fact that he, Mohammed Ali, was no longer called 'Cassius Clay'. In both cases he fatally distracted his opponents' attention from the task at hand.

Any distraction competes for the athlete's attention and is therefore a source of conflict. Zhu Jianhua, as high-jump world record holder, was about to make a vital jump in the 1984 Olympic Games in Los Angeles when Britain's Steve Ovett collapsed in the 1500m final. The reaction of the crowd pulled his attention from a narrow internal or external focus to an inappropriate broad external focus and his failure to clear the height lost him the gold medal. An athlete should *practise* coping with surprise, or rather he should establish such a strong ritual of attention shift sequences that challenges to his attention no longer have enough power to distract. Los Angeles Dodgers pitcher Orel Herisher IV describes just such an established sequence when he says 'When I rub the ball on the mound, all I stare at is the mound and the dirt in front of it. Then I slowly raise my eye level to the grass and home plate until I get to the catcher's glove.' (Jim Kaplan, *Sports Illustrated*, July 1984.)

I work this way with cricketers. Batsmen, in particular, frequently complain of lapses of concentration. Again, it helps to ask for an example of such lapse and then to see whether the batsman has any idea of where his attention went. The next stage is to ask him to recount exactly how he moves his attention when he is playing well and suggest that he establishes a ritual of shifts to come into play the moment the bowler starts walking back for his run-up. Such a sequence might be: (i) rehearse the previous shot if it was good or re-edit it if it was bad (broad internal); (ii) feel the bat in one's hands and tap the crease (narrow internal);

(iii) glance at the field placements (broad external); (iv) watch the bowler as he catches the ball from the captain and turns to begin his run-up (narrow external); (v) take a deeper breath and allow one's shoulders to relax (narrow internal); (vi) repeat some well-rehearsed affirmation to oneself (broad internal); and (vii) watch the ball (narrow external). The exact sequence would depend entirely on what feels right to the player concerned. He then practices it in training, makes any necessary adjustments and rehearses the sequence mentally each evening, whilst beginning to introduce it during matches.

Steve Rhodes, the young wicket-keeper who was kept out of the Yorkshire team by David Bairstow, joined Worcestershire in 1983 and had a brilliant tour for the England B team against Sri Lanka in 1985/86, told Dudley Doust of *The Sunday Times*: 'Concentration was the thing I worked on. I discovered I had to switch off when the bowler walked back.' 'His switch-off device was ingenious,' added Doust: 'Kapil Dev and Dipak Patel, from the slips, had taught him to count in Hindi.' (15 June 1986.) In this situation, then, Steve Rhodes switches from narrow internal (watching the player, wicket and ball directly in front of him) to broad internal (counting in Hindi).

If 'practice makes perfect' applies to technical skills, it applies equally to mental skills, in this case concentration. Brad Lewis, the manic part of the US 1984 Olympic Gold Medal winning double sculls, felt that his easy-going partner, Paul Enquist, needed to improve his concentration. Adopting a practice which had by then become routine in many sports, he arranged that their friends would try to distract them during training. His originality showed in his settling on an affirmation (see page 155), the sentence 'No-one beats us', and writing it out large on a blackboard which he placed in front of the ergometer, so that they could both think these words as they trained amongst the din. The practice of course was to strengthen their ability to switch their attention from the negative broad external square (shouting spectators) to positive narrow internal (silent repetition of an inspiring affirmation). Rod Dixon, interviewed on television immediately prior to winning the 1983 New York marathon, singled out concentration as something which he was still seeking to improve. 'The body needs the mind to discipline it,' he said. 'I'm not used to concentrating long periods of time.' Referring to potential inner as well as outer distractions, he added: 'Training must prepare you for the bad times.' In long distance running particularly, it is essential to learn to switch attention correctly from other competitors (broad and narrow external) to physical sensation, rhythm, etc (narrow internal) and back.

When practice has been assiduous, conflicting distractions are easily forgotten. American skater Katherine Adams fell over at the start of her free programme at the 1984 St Ivel competition and yet picked herself up and skated so well that she still managed to win. 'It didn't really affect me,' she said afterwards, 'because in practice if I have a fall I just get up and keep skating.' (BBC TV, 26 September 1984.) Ultimately the flow from one attentional shift to another becomes so perfectly established and so natural that incidents external to the correct and inspired performance don't register in the performer's awareness at all. 'It's a sort of hypnotic trance in which all the work that you have done before comes out of you,' explains Christopher Dean (*The Times*, 16 February 1984.)

Factors outside the competitive situation, as well as the behaviour of opponents, may distract a team athlete but the team itself must also deal positively with external challenge. Teams which are strife-ridden or just disorganised tactically are vulnerable to attack and the higher their reputation, the more ardent that attack is likely to be. In a way, Peter Caddy – co-founder of Findhorn – was referring to this principle when he said that places of 'light' attract the forces of 'darkness' and, equally, the Findhorn practice of forming a circle before starting any activity was to ensure that we met the challenge involved, purposefully and united. There are many parallels to this. King Arthur and his Knights of the Round Table were a synergetic team, the Round Table being as potent a source of their united strength as the magic of Merlin. In legend, science fiction and children's stories, to form a closed circle is to enlist protection as well as to discover the power of synergy. This was the meaning of all early circular dances, and the present-day huddles of American football, rugby and basketball teams have a similar function.

Protection can be *invoked* – called upon with power – by any team of people. The old-fashioned community singing (in Wales the singing of hymns) prior to a match could be described as a ritual dedication 'to the highest'. If the individual so wished, it could have been used as a conscious request for protection. Such a ritual can help each member of the crowd, group or team to retain access to a sense of self, whilst simultaneously experiencing oneness with all others. The hippy communes of the sixties infiltrated by drug peddlers, and the Liverpool supporters at the

Heysell stadium in Brussels in May 1985 influenced by a group set on violence, appear to have had no such defences. For the unprotected, like Black Orpheus at the Rio Carnival (in Marcel Camus' 1958 film), high experience can tumble to horror in only a moment.

2. *Challenging opponents*

One of the great spectator attractions of sport is the performer who finds the courage to attack a worthy opponent with real aggression. This is as true of the high-board diver, the golfer and the gymnast as of the track competitor and it is equally true of the striker who, in football, takes on a towering defence. By daring to attack such formidable barriers, the athlete risks spectacular failure yet can break through to a new level of performance altogether. One can say therefore that there is such a force as a creative aggression.

Gestalt theory views aggression in this positive way. It suggests that different kinds of relationship contain different degrees of 'joining' and 'distancing' energy. Affection as a form of relationship is four out of four parts 'joining' energy. Sexual activity is three parts 'joining' but one part 'distancing' (if one partner yields too easily, the other may lose interest). Teasing, or its extreme form sadism, is an equal mix of the two impulses. *Aggression* is three parts 'distancing' but contains the urge to contact the hostile object, whereas *defence*, the opposite to affection, is a 'distancing' force directed against any disturbing factor.

Steve Perryman, explaining some tactical move to me, once pointed out that forwards must be intuitive and creative but that his job, as a back, is mainly to destroy. In Gestalt terms, defenders must express four out of four parts 'distancing' energy but forwards one out of four parts 'joining' energy. In sports jargon, forwards must 'take on their opponents', whereas defenders must 'spoil'. Occasionally, though, the whole team can become excitingly aggressive. 'Sometimes you can win the game in the first ten minutes,' Tony Galvin, Tottenham's strong-running midfield player once told me, 'by pushing on and denying them the space to play. Defenders hate that when they haven't settled down.'

Tottenham defender Paul Miller, in a reflective mood before one important match, once said: 'I don't like the person I am on the pitch.' I could see his point. Paul was the modern professional who, by his own admission, would use any method available, including threats, insults and worse, to destroy an opposing striker's effectiveness. On occasion I've seen a Tottenham player commit a foul that made me freeze with embarrassment. I've also seen things done to Tottenham players that aroused my own deep anger. Tony Galvin hobbled into the Wembley dressing room at half-time in the 1982 Milk Cup Final against Liverpool with unbelievable bleeding stud marks down the length of one leg. Everyone knew who'd done it (except of course the referee) and everyone knew it had been done deliberately. When a player I now count as a friend 'got' the criminal on our next trip to Anfield, I felt my own idiot satisfaction. After every match, Mike Varney went round asking each player 'Any knocks?' as a matter of course and invariably two or three players had ice bound to one or other part of their anatomy for some time before getting bathed and changed. This is another aspect of football that is uncomfortably easy to compare to the army. Very often it does seem as if the players go out to a battlefield, rather than on to a football pitch. Courage is a prerequisite for the game.

Of course cricket isn't very different. Frank Keating reflected on this in relation to Malcolm Marshall's bowling – perhaps the fastest in the world – during the 1986 England tour of the West Indies. 'Purists at the old game of chivalry would say there is something sickening, even sadistic, about Marshall's bowling. He is confident about his defence: "Simply, I am a professional. I play to the rules. I am lucky to have my fitness and aggression but I do not lack sense. I am a fast bowler, this is my job; if I bowl dangerously and I'm told I intimidate, then the umpires are empowered to stop me. When they do I think of bowling differently: till then, I can only play to the best of my ability, such as it is."' (*Guardian*, 8 February 1986.)

A year earlier, Sidney Harris had written in the *Detroit Free Press*: 'Sporting contests were first devised to demonstrate merit within a rigid set of constraints. One of the most important restraints was sportsmanship – a concept that has all but disappeared from modern professional athletic events... (which make) the goal more important than the pursuit.' (20 August 1984.) This, of course, is the point. Many athletes and coaches believe that winning is everything. 'Winning is living,' said American football coach George Allen. 'Every time you win, you're reborn. When you lose, you die a little.' (Bill Shirley, *Los Angeles Times*, 9 November 1983.) John McEnroe once said: 'The American philosophy of win, win, win is ingrained in me. I don't apologise for that, but on occasion I've gone too far in my desire for success.' (ibid.) And perhaps the most famous quotation of all, widely attributed to American football coach Vince Lombardi but actually said earlier by Red Sanders of University of California at Los Angeles: 'Winning isn't everything; it's the *only* thing.' (ibid.) Not to do everything one can get away with doing is to reduce the chance of winning and, a professional manager might add, with no conscious cynicism, to reduce the chance of winning is to let the side down. Once he accepts that winning is all, the athlete soon discovers that actual conventions no longer match declared conventions and he competes according to the current unformalised rules.

This creates pressure, pressure which can be mercilessly increased by some factions of the media. US Alpine World Cup women's champion, Tamara McKinney, talked to Bob Lochner of the *Los Angeles Times*, prior to the giant slalom event of the 1984 Sarajevo Olympics. 'I don't want to sound like a flower child,' she began defensively, 'but if you don't realise that there can only be one No.1 and that it may not always be you, then you'll be disappointed a lot.' (16 February 1984.) When US skier Phil Mahre, at the same Olympics, expressed the opinion that it is competing rather than winning that counts and then failed to gain a medal in the first of his two events, Dan Barreiro wrote in the *Dallas Morning News*: 'The bad news is that Mahre gets another chance Sunday in the slalom. I hope he chokes again. Or that he doesn't even show up. Phil Mahre is America's best skier but he could do us all a favour by getting out of town. Right now.' (16 February 1984.) (However, it is unlikely that Mahre saw that particular story in Yugoslavia and – as it turned out – he won the slalom.)

In many contact team sports, upsetting, even hurting opponents has become an undeclared part of a defender's job. A defender who is not prepared to participate in this conventional game within a game may soon lose his place. Most coaches leave it to the game's administrators to close the gap between the formal and the undeclared sets of rules. Only when assaulting his opponent out of context of the flow of play or when getting distracted by his own actions, so that his assault is to the detriment of his own and the team's performance, is the defender told he is wrong. In my view, sport is debased by such cynicism and by any coach who overtly or covertly threatens a player who refuses to conform. True defence is admirable and exciting. The defender's role *is* to destroy the opposition's attack but by fair means

not foul. Paul Miller did err. That said, he also defended with
conviction and often with considerable courage. Aggressive
defence means challenging for '40–60' balls – balls which, as a
defender, you've only a forty per cent chance of winning – struggling to protect the team as a whole. As Peter Shreeve so often
said, Paul had lots of jam tart (heart).

Joe Louis once said of Tommy Farr, the British fighter who lost
to him narrowly on points, 'Heart is where you don't give up.'
(Nick Pitt, *Sunday Times*, 9 March 1986.) There were times when
Paul Miller's home crowd gave him 'endless stick' (Peter
Shreeve's term) and yet he was usually the last to falter. He was
totally committed and, if the cynical use of this word as applied
to defensive play was often appropriate and used by the players
themselves, the original positive sense of unflinching support
was equally so. Paul, with his captain Steve Perryman, was the
first to volunteer to represent the players at a charity event or to
include a visitor in on-going conversation. He was also the team
jester. If Mark Falco matched him for speed off the mark, it was
Paul who said moments after we'd beaten Liverpool at Anfield
on 16 March 1985, the first time Spurs had managed it since 1912
– the year (as the media pointed out annually) that the *Titanic*
went down – 'I bet the QE2 passengers will be s******g bricks this
evening then, eh?' Paul did his best to maintain a consistent and
total outfrontness when it was needed. However, once a match
was over, his instinctive method of complete withdrawal and re-
covery was to spend time with his baby daughter – a switch in relationship from four out of four destructiveness to four out of
four affection.

Of course, in competition, women athletes may also switch
from mellow withdrawal to forthright (and illegal) destruction.
At the age of thirty-seven, Barb Hardison, catcher of three-times
world champion soft-ball team Little Ceasars, told one journalist
that she wrote poetry, although she was inspired by the muse
'only when I am depressed'. However, she had also been a professional American football player in the late sixties, before the
American women's league folded and she missed the football. 'I
liked the contact,' she said. 'You could legitimately hit someone
and not look like a bad person.' (*Detroit Free Press*, 30 August
1984.)

Soccer defenders may be four out of four destructive, in relation to the opposing team but they score four out of four for
positive support of their own team, whereas strikers have to be
at least two out of four for themselves. It is the strikers who

demand service as if by right and the defenders who ensure it is provided. Strikers need an element of selfishness. Mark Falco once said in a mental training session, at a stage when goals wouldn't come, 'Maybe I'm doing too much work for others. I'm so far behind that I'm not in a position to score.' Whereas a couple of days earlier Clive Allen, his partner up front at that time, had been reflecting on a similar theme: 'When I'm in the 18 yard box, my own thing comes into play. It's my right to shoot. However, when I'm surrounded by a couple of players outside the box, I must learn to look for other players. That's when we need variation.'

This is to develop a keen 'selfishness' which has to be perfectly controlled. At the first hint of such selfishness being inappropriate, of it hurting rather than helping the team cause, conflict will flare *within* the team. When the manager in his playing days was a defender, as Keith Burkinshaw was, the flare-up happens very quickly and the offending striker can find himself isolated. Jason Tomas of *Sunday Times* recalls such an argument between Malcolm MacDonald and Don Howe at Arsenal FC: 'During a training session, MacDonald refused to adhere to Howe's instruction to go into wide positions to create scoring chances for other players: "I'm much more liable to score than they are," MacDonald reasoned.' (20 October 1985.)

So far we have only considered the direct challenge. There is a shadow side to such energy, even darker than the illegal assault. Fritz Perls says that, whereas 'the healthy character expresses his emotions and ideas, the paranoid character projects them'. Projection occurs when we refuse to recognise and express our own feelings, whilst becoming hypersensitive to the same feelings existing (to a much lesser degree) in someone else. If we don't express our aggressive feelings, they will re-emerge as feelings of guilt or of fear: either we'll be aggressive towards ourselves or we'll imagine someone else being aggressive towards us. In the war 'the frightfulness of the aggressor nation is increased by the same amount of aggression which the victim projects into them and it is decreased to its actual level when the victim refuses to be intimidated and makes use of his own aggression'. (*Ego, Hunger & Aggression.*)

In war, one acknowledges all the good traits of one's national character, coming to feel close to those with whom one would formerly not speak, and projecting all the negative divisive traits on to the enemy. Violence, often confused with aggression, is aroused by this projection. Sam Keen, interviewed by Scott

Ostler of the *Los Angeles Times*, explained that in the Second World War, 'American soldiers were pictured by [their] enemies as Chicago-style gangsters. Blacks were portrayed as quasi-gorillas despoiling the artistic achievements of European civilization.' This is now happening in sport. 'As in politics, we're suspicious of everything,' Keen continues. 'They [the Soviets] secretly use drugs or are brainwashed. It couldn't be that they [the Soviets] actually love sport or trained hard. Instead of being gracious or seeing competition as a way to be ennobling to all, we see it as pride at stake, national pride. Counting medals becomes vindictive. We put faces on the enemy. We make them seem like ugly people from a cold dark country, regimented athletes in almost concentration-like camps, programmed for the glory of the state. Their athletes are really professionals; ours are good clean boys from Kansas who never took a penny.'

Keen points out that the projection as all projections, has some truth – the Russians may well use steroids more effectively than the Americans and, in Ostler's words, 'the other guys do the same thing. American athletes are probably portrayed in the Soviet Union as cheating, dope-snorting, Commie-hating pseudo-amateurs whose motivation is a fat shoe-company contract and a TV announcing job'. Yet even in war there was once the idea of the 'honourable enemy'. '"In World War I, we saw some of that with the fighter pilots. The Red Baron respected by his enemies. Patten and Rommel had great respect for each other. You go back to the whole notion of chivalry, when you had an honourable opponent. Combat can be a noble and worthy thing. But in sport, to the degree that we demean our opponent, there isn't even joy in victory." ... Sport, the Olympics in particular, would be a lot more fun if we got back to the Greeks' original concept. "Their notion was that people were strengthened by wrestling, just like people were strengthened by philosophical dialogue. In any contest the Greeks believed both competitors learned. Out of the clash came something neither would be able to experience alone."' (Scott Ostler, *Los Angeles Times*, 13 February 1984.)

Coaches sometimes alarm their athletes by confusing war with sport, as the England national junior team coach who – not so long ago – insisted that his young charges stamp all over a German flag just prior to meeting Germany on the pitch. Such wild psyching up can push some players into a clumsy rage whilst isolating, offending and creating intense anxiety in others. Sometimes such a gross performance topples into absurdity at the risk of adding derision to the complexity of emotions evoked. When Derek Wyatt was first called to the England rugby team in March 1975, he was stunned by the behaviour and performance of the England coach, John Burgess. At the pre-match talk (before the players had lunch and moved off to Twickenham), he began an oration with such strength, force and commitment that by the time he had finished, he had removed all his clothes, bar his underwear.

I suspect that projection of any quality on to your opponents will restrict your team's ability to perform appropriately. Emotional arousal prior to a match should focus on your own positive qualities as a team, rather than on the imagined qualities of the opposition. In sport as in life, there is a time for carefully-planned behaviour, a time for aggressive behaviour and a time to withdraw – before, during and after a performance. Sports people need to appreciate and respond to this rhythm if they are to perform at their peak for long periods of time.

Destructiveness and aggression are both different to violence. Perls says: 'The role of aggression in the well-integrated personality is a means of coping with a situation – certain situations require aggression.' Yet sometimes aggression is motivated by hate. 'If you don't have any other way to cope, then you start to kill. . . Violence is the result of impotence.' (*Gestalt Therapy Verbatim.*) Many violent fouls occur when a player feels unable to achieve his end in any other way, when at some level he doubts his ability to cope. There are other explanations. In 1960, Danny Blanchflower was already saying 'You are inclined to take habits into your life and into your game or your music or whatever it is. Now this is an age of violence. I think that our football is becoming violent. It seems that way to me.' (Geoffrey Green (ed), *The Encyclopedia of Association Football.*)

Helping athletes to challenge their opponents
When you suspect that an athlete is too scared to attack or see that he attacks with crass violence, remember that he may be projecting his true aggressive feelings on to his opponent. His assumptions need to be challenged and I would then ask him 'What *are* these intimidating qualities you imagine your opponent to have?', 'What do you *see* that makes you imagine this?', 'What other explanation could there be for what you see?', 'How would it be for you to act like that yourself?'. This last question particularly would help your athlete to contact and express his own positive feelings of aggression. In Perls' words,

'the frightfulness' of his opponent is then 'decreased to its actual level' and he is able to welcome the challenge that his opponent offers and respond with excitement.

The athlete's true aggressive challenge to his opponent can be developed only with practice. However, since such practice carries the risk of injury, new managers are reluctant to encourage it during training. Richmond Rugby Club changed their training from Thursday to Wednesday nights, so that any injuries caused by all-out confrontation would have longer to heal before the Saturday match: when the training was on Thursday night, everyone held back. Tottenham, on the other hand, did not allow full-blooded challenges in training at all. This presented a problem to England player Gary Stevens, who knew he needed to develop a more aggressive heading technique, but it was solved when he began daily mental rehearsal of times in past matches when he had headed aggressively.

3. *When the individual experiences conflict within himself*

Part of your responsibility as a humanistic coach is to provide counselling for athletes who are discouraged, have difficulty making progress or are immobilised by indecision. In such cases, I will introduce the athlete to a variety of different mental training exercises (see page 9). Steve Archibald, who eventually left Tottenham in 1984 and began a sparkling new career with Barcelona FC, experienced some conflict in making his choice to move. Despite having been the focus of much recent unrest at his old club – as will be seen in the following chapters, three and four – there were still factors about staying in Britain which were attractive to him. At my suggestion, he did three mental training exercises – two 'left-brain' and one 'right-brain' – to help resolve his inner conflict. The first exercise was a Gestalt dialogue – an exercise described at greater length on pages 83 and 133 – where he acted out an imagined conversation between the Steve who wanted to go abroad and the Steve who wanted to stay in London, moving back and forth between two facing chairs as he did so, voicing and answering his own objections. The second was a writing exercise which required him to identify reasons for and against leaving England and then to decide on two or three steps he could take to reinforce the positive reasons and two or three more he could take to reduce the negative ones. (Professor Stuart Shapiro of the University of California at Santa Barbara has developed a complex form of this exercise, based on Kurt Lewin's work on change: see bibliography.)

The third exercise, the right-brain one, was a variation on the psychosynthesis Wise Old Person visualisation exercise. I asked Steve to close his eyes, relax and imagine himself sitting in a field, looking around. When he turned to look behind him, he saw a mountain and decided to climb it. He left the field, found a path and gradually made his way to the top of the mountain. There he saw some sort of shelter. He went in and inside was an old person that he knew to be wise. I suggested he ask the person whether he should leave England and listen carefully for the answer. He then left the shelter, walked back down the mountain, past the field to his car and drove home. When he opened his eyes, he told me that this exercise, like the other two, had reinforced his sense that it was right to leave England.

The great Reggie Jackson of the California Angels baseball team had a terrible season in 1983, having averaged a strike out every 2.8 at-bats compared to his previous career average of 3.9. Thirty-eight years old at the start of the following season, his seventeenth in major leagues, Jackson still wrestled with the problem of what was wrong and whether he should retire. 'I've got a mental fight on my hands now,' he said. 'I've changed some of the combinations trying to find the handle but I still don't know if I will, I still don't know if I'm through. I only wish God had a listed number so I could call him. He's the only one that knows for sure.' (Ross Newham, *Los Angeles Times*, 12 March 1984.)

Very often though, the Wise Old Person visualisation reveals that the answer is in the athlete himself. As Sebastian Coe points out: 'The coach, whose job it is to train both mind and body to simultaneous performance, can watch the results with objectivity, rather than the athlete himself. In the end, however, the true experience and the self-knowledge that goes with it belongs to the runner and to him alone.' (David Miller, *The Times*, 7 February 1986.)

4. *Conflict within the team*

The negative expression of internal conflict can usually be found in any organisation. In national institutions, major clubs or student bodies which have responsibility for the development of many different sports, or indeed commercial companies which have many different departments, such conflict can only be absent when the person or people in charge have an unfailingly appropriate style of leadership (see Epilogue). Where the person in charge is authoritarian, conflict may not be immediately evident but it will be there and may easily result in sub-groups or in different departments holding to incompatible routines, so that production suffers and morale is low. Obviously, conflict then has a negative rather than a creative effect. Hidden conflict inevitably results in a loss of creativity. This happens too within a single sports team, when there is a loss of trust or respect and antipathetic cliques emerge but in business particularly different departments can become so obsessed with their own goals, only to be gained at the expense of others, that it results in a state very much resembling war.

'Each group starts to see the other as the enemy and distorts perception of reality, recognising only their own strengths and the weaknesses of the other group.' As hostility increases communication decreases, which 'makes it easier to maintain negative feelings and more difficult to correct false perceptions. If the groups are forced to interact at the bargaining table, neither one really listens to the other but only listens for cues to support its arguments.' (P Hersey and K Blanchard, *Management of Organisational Behaviour.*)

A good manager has to be able to interpret silence at team meetings. It can arise from a lack of opinion or concern, it can sometimes be a result of shyness but it can also indicate that distinct and suspicious cliques have emerged. Instead of a frank and creative exchange of ideas, which on the surface may seem far more full of dissent, each clique may be deliberately withholding ideas and information, for fear that they be used to their own disadvantage by others. Wide-ranging divisions are unlikely to occur below the level of sports administration but most sports teams will have internal clashes, even between established members. Describing Somerset County Cricket Club, Peter Roebuck wrote: 'Brian Rose negotiates, runs our company and handles financial affairs. As for the cricket, he says we must all pull together. I suppose he could not very well suggest that we fight tooth and nail, spitting at each other in the corridor. But cricket teams rarely resemble the Magnificent Seven in unity, not with a dozen renegades vying for the available horses.' (Peter Roebuck, *Slices of Cricket.*)

Clashes usually result from personality differences or differences of perspective on viewing the team's own performance or the performance of future opponents. This can be demoralising. Peter Roebuck once said that if an established player continually runs down other players or the captain is out-of-sorts with the team, 'the team will only play to 85% of its ability'. Yet he added that, in the case of the running feud between Close and Trueman in the Yorkshire team of the sixties, or indeed of his own differences with his Cambridge University captain, the tension actually seemed to be creative.

It all depends how such differences are dealt with by the coach and by the players concerned. Properly handled, these internal conflicts can lead to improved team performance. Conflict that occurs both within the team and with opposing teams can therefore be either good or bad. If an argument at a team meeting ends with everyone feeling they've discovered something useful as a result, that argument has also strengthened team spirit. If a bad defeat provokes the team and the coach to re-examine their tactics and training methods, this is also constructive.

Conflict between team members, both on and off the field, is to some extent *necessary*. Peters and Waterman found that one sign of the 'excellent company was internal competition with peer pressure rather than orders from above being the main motivator to the development of new products. (Thomas Peters and Robert Waterman, *In Search of Excellence*.) Apart from conflict arising from developments on policy or tactics, a sports team has to cope with the basic fact that individual athletes must struggle against each other for selection. Peter Shreeve would refer cheerfully to the dour struggle for first team places amongst his large squad of Tottenham players as 'healthy competition'. Such competition can become a stimulus for improvement, provided that each player is told what and how to improve. At Tottenham, the pressure was unremitting. At the end of each season several players were discarded. No one could give up and settle for a reserve team place, even if they had a contract and wanted to. Those who failed to respond positively found that either change was imposed or that life became so unfulfilling that they were motivated to make the change themselves.

Dealing with conflict within the team
The conflict felt by the individual athlete, faced with a difficult decision is often more intense than that experienced by a team having to take a similar decision. The *team* decision-taking process is examined in more depth in appendix B (pages 215–221). However, when conflict within the team results from personality or behavioural clashes, there is much to be done before any decisions can be made.

A behaviourist and a humanist coach would deal with conflict between team members in different ways. Where the team had broken up into cliques, the behaviourist might seek or even invent an outside threat that is common to all factions so that, feeling their differences are less important than their common difference to the real or invented aggressor, the various cliques will re-unite. Somewhat more laudably but probably with less effect, he might remind the various cliques of the larger goal of the team, club or business of which they are all part, the goal which supposedly they hold in common. This is to trumpet the 'rah-rah-rah' brand of team spirit but he might then set tasks which ensure the need for all cliques to interact creatively.

A third way also more favoured by the behaviourist than the humanist is to see each group or disputing team member separately in his office. It is standard practice for a teacher, having identified a 'trouble maker', to take this student aside after class. Sometimes this is necessary. Sometimes it is easier to right a student's misapprehensions and make positive contact with him away from the classroom. However, the teacher not only risks drawing the trouble-maker's fire at himself but ignores the fact that the trouble-maker's behaviour may spring from the whole classroom situation (see chapter four). By holding the interview behind closed doors, the teacher loses the chance of creating team spirit out of a creative open discussion that involves the class as a whole.

Usually, the humanistic coach would organise such a discussion. If you have some valid criticism to make, dealing with the situation with the whole team often has the additional advantage that fellow-students or team-mates will voice that criticism themselves – but in a way that can be better appreciated by the individual concerned. An example of internal conflict being resolved in this way was reported as occurring in the British Olympic bronze-medal winning hockey team. Pat Rowley wrote in the *Guardian*: 'It is symptomatic of team unity that Taylor (the goal keeper) has bowed to the wishes of his team-mates and changed his style for defending corners.'

Conflict between team members, rather than between a team member and yourself – whether between individual athletes or between groups – can be resolved in one of two ways. *Occasionally*, the best thing is to ignore it. Efforts at persuasion by one side or another rarely resolve a conflict and, if a full discussion fails to prompt an acceptable solution, it may be necessary to agree to disagree.

As a coach, I have sometimes made the mistake of trying to force resolution of conflict between players, when in fact there was no need: the players concerned were able to live with the disagreement and the team's performance didn't suffer as a result. Some conflicts are resolved by circumstances, just as intense inter-school rivalry at primary level dissolves when the children find themselves at the same secondary school or when professional footballers leave one club to join another. The most heart-warming moment of my Tottenham experience was the unusual one of witnessing a player being welcomed by the supporters of the club he had left behind. Usually, once the change is made, the player is not only accepted and integrated amongst the erstwhile opponents he has now joined but he is treated as an enemy, if not a traitor, by the supporters of his previous club. Not so Ray Clemence, Tottenham's goal-keeper, on his return to Anfield for the first time since leaving Liverpool FC. When he came out on to the pitch after half time and ran to the goal under the Kop, there was the loudest roar of applause of the whole afternoon.

The rigidity that comes from personal investment in a particular outcome is responsible for most conflict. When the dispute is between current team members, the best starting point for the humanistic coach is to hold a team meeting and to encourage the expression of conflicting views without siding with one view or another. Any discussion designed to resolve such conflict is likely to become heated but gradually you can guide the open exchange of feelings towards increased understanding and respect. Eventually, you'll be able to prompt a brainstorming session on how else team members may satisfy their conflicting interests. The team meeting is probably the most effective way to develop team spirit. The process is described in more detail in the chapters on Relationships and Communication but for a full account of all the technical aspects of leading such a meeting, I would suggest you look at the companion volume to this book, *Sporting Body, Sporting Mind: An Athlete's Guide to Mental Training*.

One of the most effective ways to solve intellectual problems is lateral thinking (see page 219). The *emotional* clashes of personality and behaviour within a group or team may also be changed by a shift of viewpoint but by a shift 'upwards' rather than 'sideways'. As a teenager I was fortunate to know the economist Fritz Schumacher, who later wrote *Small is Beautiful* and *A Guide for the Perplexed*. He used to liken self-discovery to climbing a mountain at the top of which sits God. At the bottom of the mountain begin a number of different paths, each of which might lead upwards and each being the path of a different religion. 'The trouble is,' he said 'that we tend to waste years of our lives wandering around the bottom of the mountain, wondering which is the *right* path. At the bottom of the mountain we can't see very far, get terribly confused and argue a lot. It's only when we commit ourselves to one path and start to climb that we realise that all the paths lead to God.' When I remember this story, it helps me to be more tolerant and can remind me – after, if not always in the middle of an argument – that there is another dimension, from which I and my opponent can be viewed as 'one'.

This leads to an alternative view of conflict which is foreign to many team athletes in the West but is one which could only improve the quality of sport for athletes and spectators alike. It doesn't deny the intensity of conflict but it emphasises the dignity and creativity of the experience. In the East such a view has a tradition of centuries. Sadaharu Oh writes: 'In combat I learned to give up combat. I learned in fact that there were no enemies. An opponent was someone whose strength, joined to yours, created a certain result. Let someone call you an enemy and attack you and in that moment they lost the contest.'

This is a 'spiritual' view of competition. Religions emphasise the spiritual experience of life and it is natural that the Fritz Schumacher story is of God and a mountain. To aspire to a higher dimension of understanding and 'to call on God' is the process of *invocation*. The Findhorn practice of spending a moment in silence, 'attuning to' or invoking harmony and the 'highest good' for the group was spiritual but not religious. It certainly worked. In terms of conflict within the team, new insights and mutual understanding soon emerge once there is a shared willingness to look up from narrow self interest and aspire to the perfectly functioning unit.

The behaviourist team coach is vaguely aware of this when he trundles out all those platitudes about 'playing for the honour of the Club'. Where team spirit exists and has been securely rooted in shared effort, such invocation will not just ensure a tough mental attitude but will dissolve internal conflict. Where little investment has been made by players, coach or club, or where the coach has yet to make real contact with his players, such an invocation will only prompt cynical asides because there is little shared sense of the higher unifying nature of the Club. When Bill Beaumont joined the England rugby team in 1975, his coach used the catch phrase 'you're playing for me, you're playing for one another' repeatedly during his long pre-match talk. On the way to the ground, No. 8 player Andy Ripley pointed at some flowers on the verge and said to Bill, 'Hey, see those flowers? You're playing for them.'

Meditation is a discipline particularly well-adapted to stilling conflict or other turbulence within oneself. Attunement as practiced at Findhorn, which can quieten conflict within a group, is a form of group meditation. Roberto Assagioli, the Italian psychiatrist and father of psychosynthesis, describes how group meditation not only stills intra-group conflict but may also give rise to the experience of synergy: 'In group meditations there is a mutual integration of qualities and a mutual protection. There is also the great advantage of mutual checking and pooling of results. But there is more than that, a rather mysterious but very real factor exists which is due to the very nature of groups... Whereas the isolated individual often feels ineffective and consequently becomes despondent, many meditating on one theme multiply the power of each individual by an extra factor – that of the common purpose and concerted endeavour. An interplay of mental energy is set up, and strength is gathered in to the united effort by the diverse contributions each one makes – strength felt by each in the group.' (Assagioli, Roberto; see bibliography.)

It is unlikely that much of the rain break that allowed John Lloyd to recover from being a service break down in the fifth set against thirteenth seed Eliot Telscher in the 1985 Wimbledon tournament was spent by him in silence but as he, his wife Chris, David his brother and Bill Brett his coach sat together, I assume that an 'interplay of mental energy' was indeed set up and 'strength gathered in to the united effort' by the diverse contributions each one made. When the rain stopped and the court was uncovered, John Lloyd went out, broke back, broke again and won the match.

3

CONFORMITY

Symbols of conformity

A couple of weeks after the 1982 Cup Final, I received a letter from South Africa. Someone Christopher and I had met at Findhorn had seen us on television, walking on the pitch with the Tottenham players before the game, all of us wearing identically tailored grey suits. This was the climax of an adventurous and demanding season, our second season with Spurs. The Final was a draw but Tottenham won the replay and going back on the coach from Wembley, with the Cup we had won for the second year in succession, we sang all the way to White Hart Lane. When it came to 'We've got the best. . ., in the world, we've got the best. . ., in the world' each player's name was sung in turn. Right at the end Glenn looked around, saw us, and began singing 'We've got the two best psychos in the world, we've got the two best psychos in the world. . .,' and for a while I lived with the illusion that integration was complete.

My grey suit wasn't my first show of conformity. As a teenager, I had a school blazer with gold ribbon sewed around the edge to denote something or other and then there was national service. After that I swore I would never again wear anything that meant anything to anyone but me and disappeared to France and Algeria. However. I hadn't reckoned on volleyball catching me the way it did and a few years later I, the hitherto chronic non-conformist, had my first experience of *wanting* to conform. When I gained an Edinburgh University blue, one of the first two awarded for volleyball, I hurried to get a heavy blues scarf with the dates embroidered in the corner. Later, I acquired a Great Britain blazer with its standard British team badge of the Union Jack between the words 'Great Britain' and 'Volleyball'; but finally I bought my Scotland volleyball blazer which, Englishman though I am, I wore with the greatest pride of all.

At least one national coach has called his athletes 'a bloody disgrace' when they came to his first training session wearing denims and T-shirts. He insisted they all wore blazers and ties from then on. I couldn't have done that: funds were so low that each of the Scottish volleyball players had to buy his own blazer. However, I don't think I would have done it, anyway. Of course, it was great that nearly all players *decided* to get one. The blazer symbolised the spirit that was already there and we went off on our first tour abroad, shining both within and without.

John Madden, coach to the Los Angeles Raiders for ten remarkable years, is clear on the issue of uniforms: 'I never agreed with coaches who thought a coat and tie develop discipline, or with coaches who thought that rules against long hair, beards or sideburns developed discipline. To me, discipline in football occurs on the field not off it. . . I had only three rules on the Raiders – be on time, pay attention and play like hell when I tell you to.'

Uniforms can be an outward symbol of either positive or negative team spirit. They can be part of an inspiring ritual, a conscious affirmation of unity but they can also be used to enforce or (as in the case of T E Lawrence) to find anonymity. They can confer a group identity and are usually part of a complex of norms adopted to strengthen the group's ability to achieve its objective. National anthems can be inspiring or sinister, depending on the situation. Some English officials present disapproved of 'Scotland the Brave' being played as our national anthem by the Scottish volleyball team at international tournaments but it gave us a tremendous start – all the more for knowing the English were upset. Even *Australia II*'s symbol of the kangaroo in red boxing gloves knocking out an eagle was taken so seriously by the Americans in their 1984 defeat that they retaliated by designing their own symbol for the next race – a kangaroo tick biting a kangaroo.

When Maurice Bamford took the Great Britain rugby team to Lilleshall, in preparation for the first 1985 Test v New Zealand, he discussed motivation with his players. 'Some said they liked motivational music, others didn't – some said they would if it was the right music; and said they had found it hard to respond

to some of the things done with previous international squads.'
(*Open Rugby*, October 1985.) His players 'seemed unanimous'
that they adopt a giant lion mascot. I believe that team uniforms,
mascots and anthems only help to inspire unity if the unity has
been developed already. Only then can these things reflect or
bring such unity into focus at times of excitement or disarray. If
the players haven't already experienced a sense of integration
and belonging, such outward symbols of unity may even
distance them further.

Norms

All teams have *norms*. Norms are team agreements – usually unspoken – which shape the behaviour and attitudes of each
member. They help to make the life of the team orderly and predictable. Some norms are so static that they are really unstated
rules. Offend once and you get an immediate response. Coming
from an amateur sport and an academic background, I dressed in
open-necked shirt and jersey, the first time I attended a Tottenham match. Nobody said anything but neatly dressed in suits or
blazers, all the coaching staff and players looked at me in surprise – or so I imagined in my embarrassment.

It wasn't written anywhere that Tottenham players must
arrive in the dressing room by 6.50 pm for an 8.00 pm home
match kick-off but this norm was equally formal and static,
whereas the norm that a player should not answer back to a criticism made by the manager was less formal and one against
which players would occasionally offend. There were less
obvious, informal norms which were nonetheless quite static.
Riding on the coach to an away match, the four black players,
Garth Crooks, Chris Hughton, Danny Thomas and John Chie-
dozie used to sit together, whereas other established players had
undeclared seats that were 'theirs' and, indeed, the seating on
the entire coach was structured normatively. The coaching staff
sat in the front, the young and new players in the middle and the
senior players at the back. All these were norms of behaviour but
in any team there will also be norms that determine how members perceive what is around them, what they believe and even
how they feel about things. For instance, it would seem to be a
norm in the England men's cricket team that, as a fielder, the captain moves authoritively from one part of the pitch to another,
giving clear opinions and instructions. The press, the selectors
and perhaps one or two of the players read all sorts of con-

clusions into the fact that David Gower liked to put his hands in his pockets and, in June 1986 – although no doubt for many more consciously held reasons as well – he lost the captaincy. Such norms are often unspoken; taking time to discuss them openly increases team spirit, clearing away any unresolved friction that had been caused unconsciously. Because so many norms are unstated, it can otherwise be very difficult for a new member to realise what they are, which means that much time may pass before he is fully accepted.

When norms allow only a rigid code of behaviour, there will be conflict and when this happens at school it usually results in punishment. Most norms develop informally at first but if the majority of your team's norms are informal you are sure to find life difficult. Again, the answer must be to hold a meeting and come to some agreements or at least a mutual understanding of different points of view.

One of the reasons for a team or class member being dubbed a 'problem' by the coach or teacher (see page 50) is that, after time has been allowed for adjustment, he still doesn't adopt the group's norms. There can be many reasons for this, one of which is that the person concerned is continuing to conform to the standards of a previous group of his experience. 'If a certain pattern of behaviour brought the desired results or was comfortable in previous groups, he will tend to repeat that pattern.' (Malcolm and Hulda Knowles, *Introduction to Group Dynamics*.) Most players at Tottenham, feeling a sense of real or imagined injustice, would nonetheless choose to hold their peace. Steve Archibald did not conform. Such behaviour was against his nature but he may also have slid into arguments with the manager because he half suspected that the explosions he'd had with Alex Ferguson at his previous club, Aberdeen, had spurred him to his best performances. An account of his change to more appropriate norms is given in the next chapter.

The non-conformist

Despite frustrations caused by non-conformists, considerable tolerance was actually shown to them at Tottenham. They may not have been liked by the management but their spikiness was ignored in public. There was even a genuine attempt made to understand them or at least there was when they were obviously gifted. This was reflected in the freedom that most players had to express their individual talents on the pitch. Glenn Hoddle was always encouraged to roam freely by Tottenham, whereas Bobby Robson, the England manager, only began to consider allowing him the same freedom in June 1985. 'Some research suggests that when a situation permits a person to be himself, to act freely and with integrity, his behaviour will be the most constructive and creative of which he is capable. It is when he is under goading pressures to be something other than what he is, to be alienated from himself, that he is likely to become a problem personality.' (Knowles and Knowles.)

It takes considerable courage and an undiminished gift for cool appraisal under pressure to allow the freedom of expression which Tottenham allowed. For someone such as myself, quite lacking technical judgement of the game, this atmosphere was highly stimulating. Steve Archibald and Glenn Hoddle both *knew* they were good (which incidentally helped them to maintain their ability). Both at times were experienced as being difficult to manage but in the end they were nearly always selected. Steve Perryman says there came a day long ago when he made a conscious decision to give the ball to Glenn without the conditions he would have demanded normally in exchange. From that day on, he said, Glenn was able to show his worth.

Unfortunately there is no rule that says lesser players don't believe they are equally brilliant and due the same freedom. A successful manager is always in control and even when he appears to renounce control it is a conscious decision. Somehow he knows when a player will give *his* best only if his freedom is restricted. In the same way, he must be able to tell whether a thirty-two-year-old athlete playing poorly is in a slump or is over the hill. Personally, I believe that the best manager is the one who understands and respects the needs of the individual, be they for recognition, security, belonging or affection (see chapter six). He is also likely to be successful, for when these needs are met, the athlete will be fulfilled and give of his best.

John McEnroe as a member of the US Davis Cup team, gave Arthur Ashe some problems. McEnroe by all accounts was an intensely loyal team member but he was *not* a conformist. John Higgs in his *Guardian* 1985 Wimbledon preview contrasted 'the old school of conforming gentlemen' and 'the new breed of stormy individuals', referring to Gelett Burgess's 1907 distinction between 'bromides' and 'sulphites'. 'Bromides are all peas in the same conventional pod, living by rule and rote with habits of thought that are ready made, proper, sober, befitting the average man. Bromides conform to everything sanctioned by the majority, and may be depended upon to be trite, banal and arbitrary. Sulphites, on the contrary, are people who do their own thinking. They are independent and explosive and everything they do will be a direct and spontaneous manifestation of their own personalities... Of the tennis sulphites, John McEnroe is the most famous, perhaps the most famous athlete in the world.' Higgs speculates that McEnroe's refusal to sign a code of behaviour, demanded as a condition to being allowed to play Davis Cup tennis again, probably won him more friends than enemies. 'Wilful choice of conduct is one thing but behaviour requirement is another, smacking as it does of McCarthyism and the House of Un-American Activities Committee of the Fifties.'

Cultural conformity

Conformity is prized more highly in some countries than in others. American ex-Dodgers baseball player Jim Lefebvre returned from a spell playing in Japan talking about the Bushido code of ethics. 'They don't tolerate individualism, 'he explained. 'The nail that stands up is the nail that will be hammered down.' (*Los Angeles Times*, 1 March 1984.) For the Japanese athlete, both individual and team sports are akin to a spiritual discipline. Marathon runner Seko's coach K Nakamura says: 'The idea is to run with heart and spirit. Only when you have a pure heart can your body learn how to perform naturally and undisturbed by thoughts.' (Cliff Temple, *Sunday Times*, 12 August 1984).

Service and submission by the trainee to the master or the coach is expected and given as a matter of course. Sadaharu Oh relates that first-year baseball students were required to support the college team. 'Freshmen-year on the baseball team was for learning that the individual always subordinated himself to the team. The game as we knew it was incomprehensible otherwise.' He explains that in Japan 'it's impossible to play just for oneself... If you go against this, you also go against yourself'. A Japanese house has few and very thin walls, there is little privacy. This reflects 'the very traditional sense our people have of belonging to a group. In such a setting there are many verses but only one poem'. At the same time, the individual is expected to develop his individual strength and ability. 'Of course, Mr Kawakami stressed harmony among us ... but... Play with greed for victory, he taught, and this he most peculiarly emphasised as an individual thing... We had an obligation to the team but this obligation was best fulfilled by learning to use ourselves to the limit.'

The importance of the individual within the team

Whilst conformity is not required in British or North American culture as much as it is in Japan, some elements of the above stir memories of the British public school ethic. As a schoolboy *I* was required to stand on the touchline and cheer the first rugby team, when I would much rather have been playing something myself. At that time there was also an unstated double message given to young athletes that said 'do your damnedest but don't be seen to take things too seriously'. The athlete Harold Abrahams, already less than endeared to the British establishment by virtue of being Jewish, made matters worse by ignoring this national norm, when he hired the gifted Egyptian–Italian coach Sam Mussabini, to help him prepare for the 1924 Paris Olympics. (He did however become a hero when he won a gold medal.) Perhaps for this reason, my experience has been that in amateur team sports, other than at national level, athletes will train hard together but often not alone. That isn't quite always the case, however. Gus Leighton was one player in the Scottish volleyball squad when I was coach who maintained his place by relentless individual training and an unselfish positive attitude towards the team throughout training and matches. For me he remains an outstanding example of a player choosing to channel his considerable energy into the mould of a team, using its incentive and structure to achieve something he couldn't have reached with anything less than total commitment.

Many players fail to make such a choice. They work hard in training sessions, do their best in matches and yet in some way seem to drift along with events, without pushing their considerable ability to its limits, not hungry enough to explore. Bromides rather than sulphites. If you hold a meeting, how many and which members talk? At Tottenham, in a sport where admittedly there is no tradition of speaking out, gifted players such as Mike Hazard and Tony Galvin would rarely speak unless asked. Dr George Brown, Professor of Confluent Education at University of California at Santa Barbara, points out that as children we learn to avoid being centres of attention. It is the job of a good leader to help this to change. When I reviewed the 1984/85 season with Mark Falco and Gary Stevens, each said independently that the main gain they had made during the season was one of confidence. They had improved their ability to challenge on the field, 'felt bigger' and realised that this confidence carried through into other situations, such as team meetings where they would speak more frequently.

A team is a living organism. It is created, gains strength and maturity, undergoes changes, expresses itself and eventually falls apart. Individual team members should take part in forming the team, rather than be formed by it. This can easily be forgotten by a new member, for there will already be an intricate set of norms that he'll be expected to adopt. Yet the moment he joins, that team is no longer the same, his joining is an event in the life of the team and its potential is already different. He can either choose to express the qualities that he brings to the team or he can attempt to conform to the team as he imagines it to be. 'Many people dedicate their lives to actualising a concept of what they *should* be like, rather than actualising themselves,' says Perls in *Gestalt Therapy Verbatim*. When they do this they are more predictable and lack great flair. Considered harshly, such conformity is a kind of escapism, a settling for less than one might otherwise achieve, when one is faced with the challenge of a hard struggle, of being different, or the risk of failure. 'There is so much in our culture . . . that encourages us to remain ancient men,' writes Wendell Johnson, 'to view change as portentious and ominous and to value as wisdom a conservative preference for a future not different from the past.' (*Living with Change: The Semantics of Coping.*)

Often unconsciously, the athlete will label himself in some limiting way. Frank Keating described in the *Guardian* (26 April 1986) how Gareth Chilcott assumed that because he was a rugby prop forward, he had to be hard, fierce and dirty. After being banned for a year, he was finally selected for the national team: 'At Twickenham, that first day for England, what does he do? He not only clobbers the frail Aussie scrum half, Farr-Jones, but does it right in front of the Press box.' It was only in the face of the reaction of the public, the officials and above all his club team coach that he woke up and changed. When an athlete plays his assumed role successfully and consistently, he will reinforce that view of himself in the minds of others as well as himself, thereby limiting still further the team's potential and creativity, as a chain reaction of reciprocal role-playing occurs. Although most athletes are asked to fulfil a particular role. within the bounds of this role they should express their own originality, less concerned to please than to discover abilities hitherto unsuspected that are drawn from them by the challenge.

Only the authoritarian, manipulative leader has any use for total conformists. Conformists are 'less able to make decisions, more anxious and less spontaneous when compared with independents.' (Critchfield, R S; see bibliography.) They are more conventional, moralistic, dependent and passive in their personal relationships. They usually have 'pronounced feelings of inadequacy, low self-confidence and unrealistic pictures of themselves'. Few top-level sportspeople would fit this description but some of the more traditional sports do have such a top-heavy structure of rank and role that the participants must often make a conscious effort to retain a sense of being in charge of themselves.

Trevor Brooking, the West Ham and England footballer, once told Simon Barnes of *The Times*: 'Funnily enough, I think the thing that did more for my football than anything else was going into business. You see, in football, everything else is done for you. You never have to think. But through business, I learned to get on in the outside world and to have confidence in myself. I began to believe in myself and I reaped the benefit on the pitch.' (20 January 1984.) John Madden, speaking of his time at California Polytechnic, says 'As a coach, the class that helped me the most was child psychology. I learned that, as a group, football players react like children.' Keith Burkinshaw, in his forthright way, complained that some players didn't even know how to organise their own holidays. 'It amazes me how much advice they need. They're babied. We should ask them to think more for themselves.' In the Tottenham tradition and excited latterly by the Brazilian play he had seen in the Spanish World Cup, he continually asked for improvisation on the pitch. 'I want them to use their imagination, not be robots responding only to me.'

In many top football clubs, players are slotted more or less permanently into a set pattern to which they have to adapt. In the *short* term, this can be a useful experience, as Gary Stevens discovered, playing in Tony Galvin's position in left mid-field for Tottenham. He found that he hadn't realised before exactly what passes Tony preferred to receive. This served Gary well when he returned to playing in the back four. However, squeezing a player's natural talents into a role that is a different shape or size is more likely to restrict creativity than to develop it. Such was the experience of gifted winger Peter Barnes, before moving to Manchester United, after unsuccessful spells with a series of lesser clubs: 'Wingers need a lot of the ball,' he said, after a particularly good game for United, 'and the trouble playing with a poor team is that you do not get much of it. The managers at Leeds and Coventry saw this happening but their response was to try and change me. They tried to turn me into a hard-working midfield player, getting my foot in, running around and tackling people.' (*The Times*, 23 October 1985.)

Bobby Cox, manager of the highly successful Toronto Blue Jays baseball team, is known for taking on casualties of such foolishness. Adopting players who are discarded by other teams, he uses them according to their skill. Rana Mullinicks, for instance, he signed as a hitter not a shortstop and Dave Collins to hit lead off and play left-field but not hit home runs. Bobby Robson took a long time to compose the England 1986 World Cup Soccer team. Shortly before the event he compared the process of composition to painting: 'Once you have found the players, you then design the system that suits them. If you haven't got somebody to fill a certain role, there's no point in playing that formation. You'd be heading for disaster. You examine the individuals – the colours, if you like – and then you imagine the best picture that you can paint.' (Stuart Jones, *The Times*, 26 May 1986.) Keith Burkinshaw deplored the fact that even children at school are trained to play in one position and remain ignorant not just of other positions in the team but of their potential ability to express themselves better in one of those positions. Already, at the level of school competition, coaches are hooked on winning and dare not experiment.

One result of restricting expression in this way is that children decide they hate team sports and move determinedly to an individual sport as soon as they find themselves free to do so. In fact many an athlete is more conscious of the regimentation of team sports than of the inspirational experience of team spirit. This view is severely reinforced by such slogans as the time-honoured one of American college football 'There is no "I" in team!' It was certainly all too much for Arnold Schwartzenegger, who tried soccer before eventually becoming a world champion bodybuilder: 'I played soccer but I didn't like that too well because there I didn't get the credit alone if I did something special. I just avoided team sports from then on.' (Charles Gaines and George Butler, *Pumping Iron: The Art and Sport of Bodybuilding*.)

Some coaches don't want star players, believing that team spirit is based in equality. I think they are mistaken. The players may rightly be considered to be equal but equal in their diversity. To confuse equalness with sameness would be a mistake. You would lose team spirit by pursuing such a policy, in the act of trying to defend it. Modesty is considered becoming – how many soccer players interviewed after a match have said 'It's really all due to the lads, Brian'? – yet some athletes have a natural positive arrogance which is far more exciting and presents a challenge which can bring out the best in everyone.

In any case, if your sport is a national pastime and your team is a success, sooner or later the media's attention will focus on a particular athlete. Since being successful, implies a high level of integration and team spirit, its choice and its reasons may seem artificial and not be yours. More often than not it will be someone who shines in attack, even though you may know that the linchpin of the team is a defender. In football as in volleyball, all eyes and most of the applause is reserved for attacking play. Few people appreciate a full-back booting the ball high into the stand and there are far fewer photographs of back-court volleyball players diving for the ball than of spikers jumping at the net. Darryl Strawberry, the New York Knicks baseball player, refers to the contrasting prose and poetry of defence and attack, when he says 'Hitting is an art, defence is a skill. Home runs just happen.' (Darryl Strawberry with Don Castellano, *Darryl!*.)

Yet there's no reason why a defender can't be arrogant too. In most team sports, whether contact sports or not, each individual has an opponent with whom he fights a personal duel throughout a match as an integral part of the complete team effort. Players *can* be aggressive in defence and it is with creative movement and a forward-looking aggression that good defenders encourage those in attack. In fact, *any* member of the team who is not creative and searching to improve will soon find himself outplayed as every movement is anticipated by his opponent.

To attack, to dare to do something new, requires courage. The most dynamic team, educated by a leader who trusts the outcome to be right if unexpected, is the team whose creativity flows from the confidence and joy of team spirit. (Anyone seeing Andy Gray's delirious interview minutes after coming off the pitch having beaten Liverpool at the end of the 1984/85 season, will hardly quibble with the word 'joy' in this context.) The healthy hockey or soccer team is therefore one that does not get strung out, that attacks and defends as a unit, some in the front line, some in support.

Sadaharu Oh is keenly attuned to the delicate balance between the needs of working as a unit and retaining individual flair: 'In our game, ever so team-oriented, there is a high moment of drama reserved for that combat that takes place between one strong batter and a strong opposing pitcher. We give the name *shobu* to this moment, and it is as if the struggle of one team with the other is narrowed and intensified in this desperate and decisive surrogate combat. It is the highest kind of individual struggle but it bears with it the potential for victory or defeat for an entire team.' If there is a positive connotation to 'conformity', it is in this joyful sense of individual members becoming as one to achieve a shared goal. It is the opposite to a conformity that is imposed.

When any group, team or nation is involved in an external conflict, there is considerable pressure for conformity from within. It is a natural protective reaction and yet, at the same time, it can adversely restrict the freedom of individuals. In war, anyone acknowledging good qualities in the enemy, however just the observation, is regarded as a traitor. Even in sport, where the threat is of a different order, a team member heard to extol the ability and strength of an opponent can be criticised for not thinking positively. This may be justified if the message is simply 'They're too good, we'll be thrashed', but if a realistic appraisal is voiced with a view to setting realistic goals, it is the *criticism* which is negative.

Of course, just as there are real traitors in war-time, there are real saboteurs in the social context of a team. The hallmark of such individuals is the ability cleverly to dismantle the suggestions of others in the team without ever attempting to erect something in its place. This leaves a disrupted atmosphere of helpless exasperation which can only be cleared when the saboteur is helped to explore his need to destroy and find a more positive way of meeting this need. Very often a team meeting is the right place to do this, as long as time is set aside to do it properly. The player's negativity and hostility will be a function of the team's structure and exploring it together will help each individual and the team as a whole to unblock a closed source of energy and move forward.

Once this has been achieved, the healthy ebb and flow of dissent and conformity will be re-established. A day or two after a competition is the ideal time for review and for setting targets for the next occasion. At this stage, dissent and discussion is most productive. Then, once differences have been resolved, decisions made and new goals set, further dissent is best put to one side until the next competition is over.

Pressure to conform, despite a feeling that to do so is neither right for himself nor the team, first comes from within the individual. It is not easy to object in the face of impatience, as did Juror number eight, Henry Fonda's character, in Sidney Lumet's film *Twelve Angry Men*. One risks isolation, loss of respect, of caring and of power, and it may even be dangerous. Yet, such fears can be groundless and to that extent the pressure to conform is self-imposed. The more secure the athlete feels and the more aware he is of his own needs, his own 'boundary', the easier he will find it to take critical opinion at face value. Athletes who lose their sense of identity, in negative confluence with the team, (see page 25) are most likely to submit and conform to any opinion, unaware that it might not be their own. However, pressure to conform *can* come from the rest of the team. When a group's identity is threatened, or in some other emergency or, in the case of a sports team, before an important match, such pressure may be justified for a while. At other times it is an expression of negative team spirit, the group acting as a mob, rather than as a team. This happens when the leader is weak or when he is strongly authoritarian and then goes away.

The leader can use his position to press for conformity. An extreme example of this is described by Kurt Lewin (see bibliography) as 'the three phases of change', a behaviourist procedure that is followed when training people for military service. The first phase is called '*unfreezing*', where each individual is given the motivation to change. This is achieved (i) by removing them from their routines, outside information and their relationships; (ii) by undermining all social supports; (iii) by humiliation to show their old attitudes as unworthy; and (iv) by linking reward to willingness to change and punishment to unwillingness. The second phase is '*changing*' which consists of (i) identification with the new models of behaviour that are demonstrated each day; and (ii) internalisation of this behaviour, which is achieved by putting each individual in a situation where he *has* to use the new behaviour, if he is to cope. The final phase is '*refreezing*' which consists of continuous or intermittent reinforcement.

The fact that the individual goes through this extreme process together with a group of people he had never met before, makes the new group identity itself an agent for refreezing. This process is fast and effective but needs continual reinforcement if its effectiveness is not to wear off, although the hope is that the group's knowledge will grow and attitudes change as a result of the enforced change in behaviour. It is obviously a process that crushes all individual ability to create a unit.

There is at least one English soccer manager who has a reputation for using a watered-down version of this method, which Hersey and Blanchard call 'directive' as opposed to 'participative' change. Such leadership can have it merits with a dependent immature group but is always bad with a mature group. For it to have any chance of success, the manager must be in a position of power and have the support of his superiors. Change is achieved quickly but tends to be volatile, only maintained so long as the manager retains his positional power. Enforcing conformity excites animosity, hostility and attempts to undermine the leader and his objectives. If the leader *only* uses this method to achieve development or change in all situations, the staff or players either leave, fight or buckle under. It leaves 'the impression of an administration dominated by a rather narrow group of ministers, close in temperament and outlook to the Prime Minister' was the *Financial Times'* observation on Heseltine leaving Thatcher (10 January 1986).

Of course, such a leader or manager finds it much easier to act in this way if he has first stirred the imagination and won the confidence of the team. Apart from being able to impose severe penalties, dropping the offending player from the team or giving the non-conforming employee the sack, the leader has a powerful if ultimately double-edged weapon in his ability to deride or scold the offender publicly in front of the team. Being submitted to such behaviour can result in totally negative conformity. It could seriously harm the young or relatively immature team member, denying him that valuable sense of self and the athlete's peak experiences, and pushing him into negative confluence with the team.

Even viewed dispassionately from the leader's side, there are disadvantages inherent in such leadership. Elements of rebellion will simmer beneath the surface and the team may divide into cliques. Once the coach has decided this is the only way to impose his will, he will find himself issuing ultimatums – conform or leave – and the mature dissidents will go. If you don't allow your athletes to display their different ideas and abilities, to express themselves on and off the field of play, they will lose the will to be creative. There will be no synergistic interaction between yourself and them, no new ideas and no enjoyment.

Hersey and Blanchard, writing about the business world, point out that screening potential employees for compatibility 'can lead to organisational or management inbreeding which tends to stifle creativity and innovation... Organisations need

an open dialogue in which there is a certain amount of conflict
... to encourage new ideas and patterns of behaviour, so that
the organisation will not lose its ability to adjust to external competition'. As coach to the Scottish volleyball team, I stifled
creativity in some situations – not by disallowing open discussion but by failing to find a way to make contact with one or
two players who, with the confidence of a different coach placed
in them, would have developed further and faster than they did
with me. My mistake was not to appoint an assistant, someone
who would see the positive qualities in those players that my
own personality prevented me from seeing clearly myself.
'Ronnie and Roy can see some things on the pitch which maybe I
can't, but I'll see things they don't,' said Kenny Dalgliesh of
Liverpool FC's first team coaches Ronnie Moran and Roy Evans,
commenting on the fact that he was often on the pitch playing
himself. (*The Times*, 25 September 1985.)

Henry Ford I, a leader in the paternalistic style, had two very
different assistants to deal with the lower orders. One was a hard
'hatchet man', the other a 'sympathetic confidant'. When appointing a coaching or managerial team, ensure that they are *not*
all in the same mould as yourself, so long as there is a compatibility of expectations, an understanding of each other's roles and
a commitment to achieving a common goal. When people with
different viewpoints and skills pull together as a team, that team
is powerful. Donald Saunders of the *Daily Telegraph* interviewed
Kenny Dalgliesh when Liverpool had *won* the 1985/86 Championships. 'Dalgliesh, always the most modest of men, prefers to
see Liverpool's achievement as a team affair, involving the
famous "bootroom" and the boardroom as well as the dressing
room.' (5 May 1986.) This is perhaps Liverpool's secret. Instead
of maintaining a stiff military division between directors, coaching staff and players, with mistrust and ill feeling whispering in
the corridors, they appear to *profit* from the very different points
of view by ensuring that all departments dialogue together. This
comes back to the principle of *synergy*: such positive interaction
produces not just a high team spirit but also ideas of which no
one department could have thought alone.

The more a coach insists on conformity to his own ideas, the
less he will consult his coaching staff and captain. At Tottenham,
I suggested in one end-of-season report, that there should be
morning meetings of the coaching staff, to which captain Steve
Perryman would be invited. Peter Shreeve instituted these meetings as soon as he became manager and although they were de-

voted to discussions of form and selection, rather than the fostering of understanding and team spirit amongst the coaches, they were a step in the right direction. Steve Perryman was invited to attend initially but the idea wasn't followed through.

In some soccer clubs the manager overshadows his captain completely and a fund of intelligent observation is hardly tapped. Under Keith Burkinshaw at least Steve Perryman had the power to alter tactics in the middle of a match if he felt that the situation called for it. John Madden, when coach to the LA Raiders, allowed his quarterback similar freedom, to the benefit of the whole team's performance. 'I always suggested plays to my quarterback. After all, I was the coach. But mostly I believed in letting my quarterback call his own plays. He has a better feel for the situation on the field – his own players and the opposing players. If he knows he'll be calling his own plays, a quarterback will study films more, discuss the game plan with the coaches more. When the game starts a quarterback must be a leader, a field general. How can he be a field general if he's waiting for instructions from the bench before every play? That limits his control, limits his leadership. 'Many lesser coaches never conceive of leadership as a role. They consider themselves to *be* the sole leader all the time.

Some coaches easily brand a brash young player a 'problem athlete' as soon as he has objected to a couple of requests. This limits their chances of appreciating let alone getting the best from him. When Gerry Pimm was appointed Head Coach of the University of California at Santa Barbara at the start of the 1983/84 season, NBC announcer Dick Enburg was quoted in a highly complimentary *Los Angeles Times* article, listing Pimm's achievements as a college coach. 'The real key to coaching,' summarised Enburg, 'is taking a kid who was star of his high school team (and having to relate to that status) break it down in essence and have him come back the team player contributing his strengths.' (11 March 1984.) Hersey and Blanchard give the example of a young six-foot four basketball player, star of his high-school team where he was renowned for his jump shot. His new college team coach knew that the player should develop a hook shot, with which to beat the taller defenders he would now meet. Had the coach insisted on the young player abandoning his jump shot and learning the hook shot instead from the start, the player's energy would have been cut by disappointment or even resentment. Instead, the coach organised a practice where the young player had to shoot baskets against a six-foot-ten defender. The jump shot wouldn't work and eventually the young player was *asking* what he should do.

The player who is guided to discover things for himself will come to speak from experience and with a good sense of his own identity. He will also be less likely to slip into negative confluence with the team, whilst being a main-stay of positive team spirit, an inspiration to other team members. Malcolm and Hulda Knowles suggest that the best way to preserve individuality 'is to give every individual the knowledge and skills necessary to diagnose and withstand the forces towards conformity and at the same time to express his individuality constructively'. Fritz Schumacher pointed out that the difference between animals and mankind is that whereas both have life and consciousness, only mankind has self-awareness. When I had my first few days of leave from national service and described the sense of losing all control of my life, he encouraged me to become *aware* of what it is like to be 'an ant in a column of ants' and suggested I profit from the situation to develop my unique identity as the observer. Only through self-awareness, the process of watching and recording his patterns of behaviour in different situations, can an athlete begin to take charge of his experience and come to express the whole range of his ability in the embracing context of his team. He is then able to engage in a responsible 'I'/'we' relationship.

A good leader teaches and encourages team members to support each other in this process. At the same time, when a new member joins the group or an established member feels restricted and disinclined to conform, the rest of the team can show a willingness to work towards integration rather than insist on conformity at all cost. A team which wants to integrate a 'non-conformitist' will give that member space to explore his differences with the rest of them, setting aside time to do this together and being prepared to learn something. It may even be prepared to change accepted codes which the non-conformist is violating, when there seems to be good reason to do so.

4

RELATIONSHIPS

Whether or not athletes take part in a team sport to experience
the sense of belonging (see chapter one), their way of relating to
people will affect their performance. For many athletes the
reverse is also true: experience of team sport affects the way they
relate to people. 'Baseball,' says Sadaharu Oh, 'was more than a
game... For me, it had become everything. It contained all I
knew about personal relationships, all I knew about the world
outside baseball. I somehow was learning from baseball itself.'
Whilst the humanistic team coach will guide individuals towards
self-awareness between the fixed social boundaries of the team,
making sure that their experience is one of personal discovery,
similar to that described by Sadaharu Oh, his behaviourist coun-
terpart will explore ways and means that interpersonal relationships within the team can be manipulated to bring the team
success. That said, the athlete's own motivation for joining the
team is almost always related in part at least to a need for success. Certainly the degree of success enjoyed by the team will
affect his relationship to other team members.

Within any team there is a complex web of relationships, the
relationship between the coach and each individual player, the
relationship between players and the relationship between the
coach and the team as a whole. It is also worth considering the relationship that the team and its individual members has with
their opponents. These relationships are partly defined by the
objective and rules of the game and are partly emotional, reflecting the division between task and affiliation needs which motivate individuals to join the team in the first place.

71

The relationship between coach and individual

'They say that his players don't love him. That's a sure sign of a good manager,' wrote Bill James of Tony La Russa, manager of the top US baseball team, the Chicago White Sox (*Sport*, July 1984). I disagree with James' idea of a good manager, but I can see that many managers are relatively successful while keeping a distance from their athletes. This is partly a matter of temperament, but also, I suspect, the legacy of a belief that managers must at all times maintain control and of a lurking fear that something awful would happen if they ever let go. David Halberstam says of Harry Parker, the US rowing coach, 'His nature does not encourage intimacy. Intimacy diminished his power as the distance enhanced it. There were, as one oarsman said, veils of privacy around him and one did not lightly try to remove them.... He did not become buddies with his oarsmen, even after they graduated, yet his pride in them was immense.'

Some distance at some times is valuable and not contrary to humanistic principles. Even the most humanistic of family therapists (who are frequently in the role of group leader) has to establish a professional distance from his clients, although he will always takes pains to put new clients at ease. It is a question of finding the right distance. When Kenny Dalgliesh was appointed player-manager of Liverpool FC in 1985, he told *The Times*: 'One of the hardest parts of my new job will be to divorce myself from the lads.' I understand this. As a volleyball coach, I sometimes made wrong decisions through being too close to the players. No doubt this was partly why I felt that Keith Burkinshaw kept too great a distance from his Tottenham players and that a few more concerned questions and kind words at a suitably relaxed moment would have developed team spirit further. Keith didn't agree and said that not only did he feel uncomfortable to be closer but also felt it was wrong.

What is the correct answer? I now think that the key is to be quite clear what you want for yourself when coaching and what you do to get it. If, as suggested in chapter six, the primary motivators are 'security', 'power' and 'love' (see also *Sporting Body, Sporting Mind*), I can see that, as a coach, my needs fell initially into the category of 'love': even after becoming a coach, my main motivation was probably still a sense of belonging. This wasn't wrong. It helped me to create team spirit (and has indirectly helped me to write this book) but it carried the danger that I would suppress criticism and fail to take decisions clearly. Only when we recognise and accept our own needs are we entirely free to do what is best for the team. The most inspirational coaches are those who long ago came to terms with themselves. When Jock Stein, Scottish national team manager died, Archie McPherson said on BBC television (11 September 1985): 'Jock was interested in what made people tick, rather than in what made players play.' I think this catches that special combination of caring and distance which took me so long to achieve.

When Alan Jones, the Australian rugby union coach, was in England he told David Hands that he telephoned his leading players regularly from London, to maintain contact. 'The biggest weakness in the whole game,' he said, 'is communication. You must get the players to talk to you. In England no one has ever talked to the players... You have to work around your team people. You have to know them and be prepared to trust their judgement.' (*The Times*, 9 January 1986.) The message? Care, show that you care but know when to back off and allow the players to be responsible for their own experience.

'I never thought it was bad to let my players know I really liked them,' says John Madden. 'Once they knew that, it was easier to communicate with them. Knowing his coach likes him is more important to a player than anything else. To me, it was important to be able to chew out a player for screwing up and for him to accept it because he knew I liked him anyway. Some players actually like to be chewed out.' Simon Callow, the actor, writing as a 'player' as opposed to a coach, confirms the truth of this. Describing his time in *A Taste of Honey*, directed by Robert Walker, he says 'What was ... indispensable was Rob's capacity to create the amniotic fluid in which creativity can flourish.... It's wonderful to act for him, aware of his eyes open wide, hypnotised by what the actors are doing.... I never doubted for a moment that Rob loved my work, even when he criticised it fundamentally.' (*Being an Actor*.)

Madden makes a distinction between being friends and being friendly with his players, and this gives a clue to one way in which a coach may establish a comfortable and effective distance between himself and his players. 'Too many coaches want to be "one of the guys" but that's the worst thing a coach can be. Your players don't need another friend, your players have all the friends they need, sometimes too many.... That doesn't mean a coach shouldn't be friendly with his players. By being friendly I

mean talking to as many players as possible, each day if possible
. . . I tried to talk to each of them.'

In fact, your ability to assess players correctly is more important than obvious closeness to them. It's probably more important
than deciding on tactics for a particular match. Watching and
listening to your players, whether at training sessions, at team
meetings or at interviews in your office, is a prerequisite to and at
least as important as talking to them. 'As the Raiders' coach, I
never had to look at any player's numbers to know who he was. I
knew from the way he ran or the way he moved. I knew most of
the opposing players too,' says Madden. As a coach myself, I
could remember the feel of each player shaking my hand as I
watched him volley and visualise his volley whenever I shook
his hand, 'knowing' the connection without any need for analysis. Knowledge, both intuitive and analytical, acquired by watching one's players, is essential to the art of selection and
substitution. Watching can also develop understanding and concern. If you know how to sit back in your chair in a discussion
meeting (where you have placed the chairs, yours included, in a
circle) and divert direct requests for your opinion to other players
who haven't yet spoken, you have a great advantage. You are
then showing yourself as a part of the team, by being part of the
circle, whilst keeping the psychological distance of an observer –
the focus no longer being on you.

Ideally, you will have an assistant to take over this observer's
role when it is time for you to speak. If not, you should plan the
meeting with your captain and ask him to do the job. Afterwards, even if you have an assistant, invite the captain to join in
your review of the meeting, because he has a unique position in
the team. He is the spokesman for the players, when the players'
view has to be given to the coaching staff or directors of the club,
yet he also takes information back to the players. Being a player
himself, he can communicate to other players in a more direct
and acceptable way than even you are able to do. His position as
an associate member of your coaching staff should be firmly
established. The closer he is to you the better he will understand
and be able to convey your point of view. When appointing your
captain, you should choose someone with whom you can communicate easily and whom you can trust and yet he must also be
someone who is respected by other players. A captain who
doesn't stand firm for the players in times of difficulty is of no use
to you. Steve Perryman, a typical mature self-motivated athlete,
was held in high regard by everyone at Tottenham. When I

asked all the playing staff to fill in a questionnaire (on individual goal-setting) at the beginning of the 1984/85 season, with a final question 'Whose performance do you most admire (i) in the Club? (ii) in other clubs? (iii) in other sports?', four fifths of the players present wrote down Steve's name first. The next and last question was 'What do you admire in these players?' (which I would be able to follow at an individual session later on with the question 'Is this a quality you want to develop in your own game?'). The answers in relation to Steve were consistency, dedication, honesty, confidence, the will to win and all-round ability.

One of the best combinations of coach and captain in rugby union – at least according to the players and journalists who were there – was that of the Carwyn James and John Dawes British Lions team that toured New Zealand in 1971. The perfect understanding and respect each showed for the other allowed for considerable flexibility in day-to-day organisation (Barry John sometimes played soccer instead of training with the rest of the team) without any negative repercussions.

In cricket, the team captain may also *be* the coach, just as I was in the Edinburgh University volleyball team. Perhaps in cricket this works well enough. The one time that a cricketer is under intense pressure is when he is at the wicket, a lonely figure against eleven members of the opposition. For the rest of the time, he is relatively free to observe and, as captain, make decisions. In volleyball, it is different. Any team seeing the opposition coach come on court as a player may well concentrate their attack on him, putting him under pressure and knowing that if he falters and makes a couple of bad mistakes, cracks may appear in his team's united resolve. The player-coach will also then find it increasingly difficult to know when best to call time-outs and when and which substitutions to make. Any game in which the choice and timing of substitution has an important effect on the balance of play, should have a coach who is both physically and emotionally detached.

Personally, I believe that any team benefits from a coach, whether or not the rules provide for mid-competition talks, time-outs or substitution. In any competition, your main role is to watch and compose your observations into an acceptable form of feedback for your players whenever that is possible. If the rules *don't* allow for mid-competition substitution you have no choices to make that can affect the course of the game. You may still be emotionally involved, even worried that the result will reflect upon your own ability, but for the moment you can only sit back and watch and for that reason should be better able to make a detached assessment of your team's performance. The *disadvantage* of your position is that you really are more detached from your team and therefore may have to work harder to gain your players' attention and respect when it comes to planning tactics, selecting the team and training for the next match. This would particularly be the case if the captain were to disagree with your opinions.

Soccer and volleyball players may disagree sometimes vehemently with their coaches but there remains a closeness, an interconnexion, an awareness of the coach as one of the extended team whose decisions have a direct outcome on the course of the game. Tottenham's Peter Shreeve preferred to sit high up in the stand to watch the course of the game, only coming to the pitch when he wanted to make a substitution. At White Hart Lane, he had a telephone connection to the dug-out from his seat in the director's box but even when playing away from home he managed to build an invisible barrier around himself, which seemed to be at least as effective a way to remain attached to the team as the practice of those managers (Brian Clough amongst them) who put on the team strip and sat in the dug-out. Only at half-time, which lasts for fifteen minutes in a professional soccer match, is the manager alone with his players. His ability to help them to let go of individual preoccupations and re-experience themselves as a synergetic unit will then depend on the relationship he has evolved with them and the experiences they have shared together.

The roles of captain, trainer, coach, manager and head of delegation often overlap and the titles are used differently by different sports. As mentioned in the Introduction, the business leader is often called 'manager', as is the head coach in soccer, American football and baseball, where his assistants are called 'coaches'. In volleyball, the leader is the coach but when the Scottish team went abroad, Dougie Richardson, another member of the Scottish Volleyball Association Executive Committee, came to relieve me of all administrative tasks and attend the tournament's daily scheduling and business meetings. Dougie also played the invaluable roles of assistant coach and physiotherapist but was called 'team manager' or 'head of delegation'. This arrangement was essential, especially in the hours preceding a match, when I needed to give my whole attention to both the team's warm-up and my own.

In cricket and to a great extent rugby, the leader was long the captain. Cricket teams particularly have been slow to acknowledge the role of coach, the captain traditionally and in fact being totally responsible during the course of play. However, there are now signs of change, not just in cricket and rugby but also in tennis where, except in a rain-break or during the Davis Cup when the non-playing captain sits on court, no one can advise a player until the match is finished.

If you need to develop an especially close relationship with the captain, it's also the case that you may be engaged in an antithetical relationship with a 'problem athlete' (see page 57), who often appears to be unhappy and something of a loner. He is usually a top performer, if he weren't he would have disappeared into the reserve team long ago.

I sometimes became depressed at Tottenham as I listened to the coaching staff talk frustratedly about individuals who for them were undoubtedly 'problem players'. Quite wrongly, I sometimes allowed myself to be drawn into lending support to these negative thought forms, rather than defending the individual concerned by finding examples from my own experience with them to support a contrary view. This always happened when I'd make the mistake of wanting a player to adopt and achieve a particular goal, usually one which the manager would wish. Then I too was open to feelings of frustration. Instead, my objective more than anyone's should have been to help the individual to discover his ability and direction. When I begin a session with an objective in mind, I not only miss important cues from the athlete but close off my intuition. No synergy happens between us and the session achieves very little.

The phenomenon of the problem athlete is more common in wealthy professional teams than in amateur sides with the bare minimum of players turning out each Saturday afternoon, although emotional storms can break out quite easily in amateur sides too. This is not *just* because the professional team has a greater pool of players. It is also something to do with distance. An amateur team is often from a close-knit village community and may resemble it. The professional team usually has the less open atmosphere of a big city and is less easily experienced as a 'family'. Yet I believe that it is indeed in some important sociological sense a family and that the big club 'problem athlete' serves a function within that 'family', just as a 'problem child' does within his household.

That is to say that the problem athlete doesn't exist on his own but fits into a predetermined pattern. Despite the apparent 'distance' and guardedness, he is part of a whole and if he *does* leave the team, someone else will have to appear to fulfil his role. It is as if a 'problem player' is *needed* to keep some sort of balance. Sometimes in a two-child family one child is 'bad' and the other 'good'. If the 'bad' child shows signs of reforming, the 'good' child will taunt him until he succeeds in getting his sibling to revert to his former behaviour. If taunting fails, then usually the roles reverse and the formerly 'good' child becomes 'bad', ensuring that though the details are different, the pattern is the same.

Very often, the problem child is a function of the existing relationship between his parents. If the parents don't get on well together, one of them may be over-protective with their child and the child comes to focus on his fears. When these fears become chronic, the child is labelled a problem or is said to have a problem and is brought to a therapist to be cured. Twenty-five years ago, the child would be interviewed by the therapist alone, in an attempt to help him cope with his fears but with the advent of family therapy it is generally recognised that the family should be interviewed together and, when that happens, a skilled family therapist will solve the problem by getting the *other* parent to spend time with the child and ultimately by helping the parents to overcome their own difficulties and engage with each other rather than the child alone.

It is not always easy to discover how the 'problem person' serves the unit by being a problem, especially if as coach or manager you are personally and emotionally involved. (George and Judith Brown might suggest a 'disidentification' exercise. For instance, pretend that you are an observer from Mars... What would you see happening?) Certainly, where there is a constant pattern, where there is always *one* player who is felt to be a problem, it is worth looking very carefully at which group of people do the griping. Is it the players? Is it the coaching staff? Is it the directors? Do they just gripe within their own group or do they share their gripes with other groups? Above all, what are they *gaining* from griping in this way together? Does it divert attention from something more difficult to manage? Could it be that they need to be united to function well but don't much like each other? In this case, for instance, griping together about the problem athlete would afford them a sense of comparative warmth and closeness which would make working together much easier.

Nonetheless, there *will* be something about the athlete himself which needs attention. It's unlikely that he is chosen *randomly* to fulfil the problem athlete role. When the negative effects of the problem begin to outweigh the *benefit* of having a designated problem athlete and you have a real desire to 'solve' the problem, it is worth reflecting on the athlete's behaviour. Almost certainly, he will be 'asking' to be the problem. *How* is he asking? Going back to the example of Steve Archibald of Tottenham age 57), he 'asked' by not bothering to avoid arguments when felt provoked. He allowed this to happen because he half be- ed that a sense of injustice helped to fire him up for a match.

he first thing to notice about this is that Steve had not only clarity and courage to face what he sometimes felt to be a loss of sustained fierce aggression in his overall performance but the determination to put this right. A manager is inevitably tempted to start and finish by blaming such a player for his behaviour but the player should first be *complimented* on his effort to improve his game and then counselled towards finding an alternative solution to the problem he has identified and, in his own way, is dealing with.

When Steve first spoke of this pattern of behaviour, I asked him to get an image for his aggression. Steve, who has a highly vivid visual imagination, immediately saw a dangerous black bear. He then said that the bear seemed to rampage around in his life continually but suddenly to disappear when he went on to the field – this at a time when he felt he had lost the edge to his footballing aggression. As a result we built a practice whereby Steve would visualise the bear snarling behind bars in a short session prior to each match and then see someone open the cage. He *was* the bear in his imagination and ran out on to the field with all its aggression.

This is a remarkably similar use of imagery to that used by Mark Breland, when he won the welterweight boxing Gold Medal at the 1984 Olympics: 'I like to meditate before I fight,' he said after the final fight. 'I imagine a tiger, ready to let loose and sometimes feel myself turning into a tiger.' (ABC TV, 10 August 1984.) Both athletes were evoking and harnessing their aggression. At the end of the match, Steve would do another short visualisation, seeing the bear go back into the cage and the door being locked. He said later that not only did his play improve but that he suddenly noticed that his wife Maureen was driving faster than he was: that he was far more relaxed off the pitch as well as being more aggressive on it. Unfortunately, in his final season at Spurs, when neither Christopher nor I were there, a newspaper quoted Keith Burkinshaw as having accused Steve of 'cheating' (giving less than his best). Steve was so enraged that he reverted to his previous pattern and had a furious argument with his manager. Since this behaviour immediately resulted in a flood of goals, he wasn't motivated to change it again until after he had left the club.

Keith Burkinshaw and Peter Shreeve had always held the highest regard for Steve's ability on the field but in Barcelona Steve found a manager who appreciated him more holistically: 'He's a deep character,' Terry Venables observed in a conversation during the 1986 World Cup. 'If you are prepared to sit down and discuss something that involves him before you do it, he appreciates that and has intelligent things to say. Sometimes I'll say "You made a good point" and we'll go his way. He's played very very well for me. He is a strong character too and strong characters are normally selfish up front but Steve lends himself to the team completely. He gets into the six-yard box and creates space for others as much as for himself.' Just how much time a manager has to talk to his players individually depends on that manager's priorities and inclinations – there is always more demanding there attention than they can possibly have time to do. Yet a lesson to be drawn from this example is that making yourself available to your players, as do Alan Jones and Terry Venables (and as did John Madden) prevents many problems ever arising and to that extent obviates the need for using some of the more difficult counselling exercises. It also channels the intelligence of your players into the mainstream activity of building a team.

It should be clear that the term 'problem athlete' (as in 'that player over there is a problem and needs sorting out') is an emotional one. Indeed, as coach, you can take it that if you find yourself making repeated negative emotional comments about any player, you are yourself a part of the problem. At this stage, if you wish there to be a change you have only the option of expelling the athlete from your club or calling in someone else – your assistant captain or a sports psychologist – to conduct some kind of meeting between you and the athlete concerned. This type of problem is of a different order to one in which a player has lost his form. (Where you are *not* emotionally involved, you can indeed call the player to your office and, in certain situations, berate him. However, if instead you ask him what *he* thinks of his current performance, you may well prompt the very criticisms that you wanted to make.)

When a coach tells me that one of his players cheats, is scared, blames others for his faults, or doesn't try – all words that I've

heard – it's obvi⌐   ⌐o the
coach, as the person ⌐
cerned. However, the c⌐
ogist, to go and sort out t⌐
advance that the player will ⌐
best that I can do in response to ⌐
athlete a few discreet questions wh⌐
ify one of the claimed negative patterns ⌐
pattern he wants to change, ask how he m⌐
the solutions would involve making agree⌐
members of the team and this in turn might be ac⌐
athlete does not admit the alleged behaviour, the problem
remains the coach's and there is little I can do to help by talking
to the athlete alone.

The family therapist would never agree to such a situation in
the first place. For him, the question is not even 'Whose problem
is this?' but rather 'Who are the members of this problem?' and,
as already suggested, 'What function does the problem serve?'
and 'For whom?'. It's possible that the only 'members' of the
problem are the athlete and the manager or the athlete and the
coaching staff, in which case the best course of action would be to
conduct a meeting in a room other than the manager's office or, if
no other room was available, for me to sit in the manager's chair
and the manager to sit with the athlete on the other side of the
desk. Better still, we'd take the chair out from behind the desk
and push the desk back against the wall. I would then ask the
manager and athlete to discuss the manager's problem, whilst I
guide the discussion. The first thing would be to ensure that each
heard what the other had to say, asking them to repeat each
other's statements if I felt there was any doubt. Then, having encouraged them to speak their resentments and their demands of
each other and having examined how the needs behind the
demands might be met, I would lead the discussion around to an
expression of appreciation that each would certainly have for certain qualities of the other.

Such a scenario exists only in the realm of fantasy, in so far as
my work with a professional soccer club is concerned. However
stressed the manager might be by the perceived behaviour of his
'problem player', such a way of tackling the situation would be
immensely threatening as it would demand that he gave up his
control and be prepared to admit himself at fault. The nearest
that the manager might move towards such a situation (if he
could *see* that he was locked into a negative relationship with this

player and wanted to change), would be to conduct a conversation with the athlete in my presence and to allow me to comment afterwards. Alternatively, he just might agree to his assistant being a mediator, in the unlikely event that his assistant voiced an opinion different to his own.

That said, I have been able to conduct such a session within the Haringey Cricket College, also professional but run by a more progressive-minded coach as a programme for the young talented unemployed. The coach, Chris Gibson, has a fiery nature and clear demands which do not always seem logical or fair to his charges. Yet, faithful to the experimental nature of the scheme, he has enabled me to conduct encounters between himself and individual players along the lines outlined above.

Of course, when a Tottenham player experienced himself as having a problem with the manager, rather than the other way around, the same type of encounter would have been appropriate yet the chance of it happening was just as remote. The manager might have been more relaxed initially (although he certainly wouldn't vacate his chair), but eventually would have experienced the same threat. I was therefore again reduced to working with the player alone, asking him to state his perception of the situation and to suggest ways in which he felt he might come to resolve it. If the player was upset or depressed, I would often suggest that he act out his feelings by doing the Gestalt dialogue exercise, already mentioned in chapter two (page 46) and described in more detail in chapters six and seven (pages 133 and 152), placing a second chair opposite him and asking him to imagine that the manager was sitting on it and to speak his thoughts to the imagined manager.

Once he had expressed all his feelings, I'd ask him to stop, change chairs and then to *become* the manager and respond to all the accusations and questions he had voiced. By conducting both sides of this conversation himself and responding in one role or the other to questions I interposed, he would usually come to a calmer sense of the situation and find it easier to take decisions and move forwards. Sometimes, I would attempt to prepare the way, without admitting this was my objective, by speaking to the manager informally later on. Of course, our talks, in the sense that I never *worked* with him, were always informal, whereas Chris Gibson was prepared to jump in at the deep end, take part, and see what happened. Admittedly, Chris had less to lose and no tradition to overturn, the scheme itself being an exciting experiment.

The relationship between coach and team

If it's true that you need to maintain some kind of a distance from your players, so that you may act and guide and generally do your job efficiently – if you need to maintain a sense of self and avoid slipping into a negative form of confluence with your players – you can and indeed should seek to be totally confluent in the *positive* sense with the 'Group Being' (see pages 110 and 140), the ideal manifestation of the team. It helps to regard this ideal as already being on its way to actualisation, already having a discernible character (see page 219). As the manager you, more than any other member of the team, should aspire to ground this ideal in reality: you should represent and affirm this view of the team without wavering. By identifying yourself with this ideal view, your knowledge of what the team may become, you are better able to see irregularities in the pattern of relationships between team members and help to re-establish harmony and strengthen team spirit.

Steve Archibald's original way of meeting his needs was inappropriate, not because it upset the manager – the manager has the power to chose how he responds and to help the player towards a different solution – but because of the damage that it caused to the smooth functioning of the team: it inhibited team spirit, as players inevitably slid into taking sides. Even if every player were to have felt that Archie was in the wrong, there would still be a division in the team between himself and the rest. Inevitably, he stirred Steve Perryman's frustration and, in his book, *A Man for all Seasons*, Steve writes: 'Steve Archibald was always a loner at Spurs, and individualist on the field and never part of the group off it. There were times when I'd go months without talking to him, not because I didn't want to but because we both felt we had better things to do than try to understand each other.' Archie was upset by this and felt it wasn't true but Steve replies that he meant 'didn't talk seriously', his way of captaincy being to foster relationships with each player. Feeling that Archie wasn't interested, he let this relationship slide and, despite some misgivings later on, still asserts 'I worry about people I can *help*', not those out of reach.

Again, it is irrelevant to pronounce one or other player to be 'right' and the other 'wrong'. In such a context, each athlete has valid reasons for his behaviour and the situation is demonstrably part of the larger context of the team as a whole, manager and coaching staff included. The point of concern is that the team is unable to reach its full potential: for whatever reason, it is not in good health.

Fritz Perls defined 'neurosis' as a disturbance in development, an educational rather than a medical question. In this sense we all have our neuroses, ways in which we prevent ourselves 'from growing, from going further ahead'. (*Gestalt Therapy Verbatim*.) Somewhere in *most* teams, people – coaching staff and players – interact in a way which blocks development of the team as a whole and of certain individual team members specifically. Real communication is then minimal. The more distance you put between yourself and your players, the more difficult it will be for the team to move past the blocks that impede its progress. If you only appear in the dressing room to speak to your players as a group without allowing discussion and feedback, or only summon them individually to your office on matters of discipline, you cannot succeed beyond certain limits.

Apart from anything else, the tension that you feel, faced with the antics of your 'problem athlete', can become unbearable. What was a conflict develops into a damaging relationship. Your judgement becomes clouded and a rift begins to appear between different factions of the team. By then it is too late for discussion in your office and the only way to put yourself, your player, the rest of the team and your coaching staff back on speaking terms is to hold a special discussion meeting. This is not a solution that comes easily to any coach, hence Simon Callow's fascination when David Hare of the Joint Stock Theatre Group explained 'We're trying to break away from the dishonesty of rehearsals where actors go to the pub and slag the director off behind his back, while he and the writer sit and bitch about the actors. This is both dishonest and counterproductive.'

Setting up a meeting to heal bruised relationships needs some forethought. You must decide, in advance, how long you want to spend on the matter. Get clear of your own resentments, demands and appreciations, *vis-à-vis* your problem player and ask your captain to be prepared to lead the discussion if need be. Everyone, yourself included, should sit in a circle and anyone involved in the dispute should be encouraged to state their view of an incident which illustrates the problematic pattern of behaviour. You as coach should take part in the meeting but, if you are emotionally involved, someone else – your captain (if not involved personally himself) or a neutral counsellor – should lead the meeting. Once the motives of each side are brought to light, the team can brainstorm on ways in which these needs may be met in a less destructive fashion.

As in any discussion meeting, there should be a blackboard on which someone may record the main points as they are made. At this meeting it may mean listing gripes, listing demands, listing appreciations or recording decisions. Should you lead the discussion yourself, do so as you would any other discussion, sitting back and encouraging team members to make statements rather than ask questions. If direct questions are asked, backed by statements which have already been discussed at length by the team, respond honestly. Bring the discussion to an end by listing decisions on the blackboard. Ultimately the decision *could* be to follow a course of action which is unpopular with the team but this can be accompanied with a promise to re-examine the issue at a precise future date, in the light of events arising from the decision you have taken. In the end the decisions themselves are less important than the process by which they are made.

When the meeting is over, review it with your captain and coaching staff but also alone. How far did you meet your objective? What did you gain from the encounter? What did you learn? There will probably be much there of value, especially if you have managed to allow honest comment from the players on your own actions. Then ask: 'What is my next step?'. If you want to gain maximum benefit from the exercise, write down these thoughts in some sort of training log book and keep them for future reference. Chart *your* progress.

As coach, I found that writing down my reflections on any meeting or training session – though not something I did at all regularly – invariably gave me new insights. Before long I'd then be composing a letter to all the national squad, for them to think about too, before our next training session. I'd do this sometimes with my club team as well, even though we were already meeting twice a week.

If the prospect of holding such a meeting is untenable, as you imagine it ending in insurrection, reflect a moment. The more likely that seems, the more important the issue involving your 'problem athlete' probably is. If it's really the case that the whole team will gang up on you, given half a chance, what pressures are you creating? How likely is the team to reach its chosen objective? What changes could you make to divert this tension into creative channels? Is your real objective different to that of your team members? If so, is there a way in which both may be satisfied?

If your players are unhappy and frustrated, they are unlikely to perform to anything nearing their potential. The aim of discussion meetings is not just to reach decisions but to increase understanding, in the spirit of Wendell Johnson's comment that 'if we really understand someone, we understand how he differs from us'. The synthesis that is borne of team spirit is one that respects individuality. When a player is able to be himself, he adds to the competitive effectiveness of the team and is a source of inspiration. Let down your own guard just a little and the rewards will be great. The night the Tottenham team returned from an away match to White Hart Lane and Keith Burkinshaw held an impromptu party in his office did more for team spirit than anything that had happened in weeks. John Warren, one of the Australian soccer team, in Scotland for a World Cup qualifying match, told a *Daily Mail* reporter that his coach Frank Arok had finally agreed to have a night out with the team, after years of 'isolationism': 'There was some straight talking and, the next day, Frank admitted he had learned more about his players in one night than in the previous eighteen months.' (*Daily Mail*, 19 November 1985.)

Once this contact with the heart of the team is made, even the most rabid behaviourist coach finds a humanist stirring within him. Perhaps for the first time, he gets a sense of the team as an entity, rather than as a group of people that he has to mould into a functioning unit. As he begins to let go a little, the questions *'Who* is this team?' and 'What is it seeking to become?' may occur to him, together with the realisation that the team has indeed a unique potential and personality of its own, waiting to become fully grounded.

The relationship between the players

As mentioned earlier, some athletes believe that a first class performance can be achieved without team members liking each other and Sadaharu Oh suggests that respect (for team-mates *and* opponents) allows a greater clarity of perception. There are however many recorded instances of individual team members who liked each other and felt that this contributed to their performance. Indeed after the 1985 Ryder Cup Severiano Ballesteros said that one of the reasons why he and Manuel Pinero played so well in the foursomes was precisely because they do like each other. The actor Simon Callow describes the development of his performance in *As You Like It*: 'I met Sara Kestelman, Rosalind. I liked her immediately. What I didn't realise was that as actors we'd have the instant rapport that is such a God-sent bonus. The moment we started working together we became an ensemble of two, the Kestelman-Callow company. It's a matter of unquestioning trust and immediate sub-textual communication. We knew each other intimately as actors long before we knew each other as friends; when this is the case acting becomes jazz. The extraordinary thing is that this can exist between actors who don't like each other very much at all, and not exist between the closest of friends. When the two come together, chemistry and camaraderie, it's the best thing in the world.'

There is one interesting mode of classification that goes some way towards resolving this paradox. Making the distinction (see page 18) between *co-acting* and *reactive/proactive* teams on the one hand (such as baseball, cricket and more especially swimming, rowing or sailing squads, where individuals compete separately in the same competition) and *interacting* teams such as basketball, soccer and indeed theatre companies, where one player's action depends on and determines another's – it suggests that interpersonal rivalry helps co-acting teams towards success, whilst greater co-operation helps interacting teams towards success. Although friendship may rarely survive the pressures of rivalry and not always be present in co-operation, respect is essential to a good performance in either case. British canoeist Jeremy West, speaking to journalist Simon Barnes of his Olympic partner Andy Sheriff, said 'It is important to believe in the other person in a two-man boat. If you can't then you're wasting your time. You get to know each other so that you do not need to communicate verbally in a race. You just know when the other person is pushing. You both know when to give everything, you can feel when the other person is doing the same.' (*The Times*, 15 June 1984.)

Respect tends to bring in its wake honesty of effort and expression and the recognition, within a team context, that it is not only technical skill and physical ability that count but also strength of character. All teams have star players that thrill the crowd with their poise, power, strength or control. At Tottenham, it was Glenn Hoddle and Ossie Ardiles on his day. Someone like Tony Galvin rarely got a profile in the press and said little in the dressing room or at team meetings, yet after Steve Perryman he was probably the most respected player in the team.

During the 1985 Tour de France, Britain's Paul Sherwen was

the subject of a long Charles Burgess article in *The Guardian* because he was 158th out of 158, as the Tour entered its final week. Sherwen described how his position was of no importance, since his job as a member of La Redoute team was to help his team leader Stephen Roche towards victory. This meant shielding Roche from the wind, helping him stay as near to the main bunch as possible, changing Roche's wheel or giving away his own bike if Roche got a puncture, in fact doing everything that his job's name (*'domestique'*, meaning 'servant') implies. Such a job would be untenable were it not for the respect which it commands within the team. Indeed there is a respect between domestiques of rival teams as they help each other to complete the challenging hill stages within the allotted time, riding together in a bunch and lending each other their water bottles.

Respect and appreciation are born from understanding and grow from an atmosphere of security and trust. The first step towards establishing such an atmosphere is for you as coach to be clear and reliable in your demands and judgements, that you avoid speaking badly of players outside their hearing and insist on similar behaviour from your staff and from players themselves. If a player is dropped, he should not only know why but also what he needs to achieve in order to get back into the team.

The second step is to create space for discussion, not just of tactics but also of relationships within the team, of the mood and spirit of the team. The first type of discussion is called *task* discussion and the second *maintenance* discussion. The balance between the two must be right. A team that talks endlessly about matters related to team spirit will be ill-prepared for the mechanics of effective competition, though Alvin Zander points out that 'more group talk stimulates more enthusiasm' for what needs to be done by a group' (see bibliography.) A team that never discusses relationships and never allows expression of personal feelings will lack the elements of respect and intuition which can lead to greatness. Peters and Waterman report that Japanese companies give more attention to 'maintenance' (informal personal discussion) than do American ones and have a much stronger team spirit as a result. This reflects the Japanese reverence for the family, whereas Americans have always championed the individual: the Bill of Rights refers to the rights of the individual.

A tour boosts an amateur club's team spirit because the strangeness of situations and surroundings tends to fill out the perceptions which players have of each other. They gradually display opinions, feelings and skills related to other areas of their lives than sport. Edinburgh University Volleyball Club's first visit to Oslo and the Scottish national men's team's tour of West Germany both gave birth to a powerful folklore, catch phrases remembered and photographs still kept twenty years after the event. As coach you can devise meetings and training sessions so that such revelations occur during the normal run of the season as well. After a careful introduction it can become a norm for players to express themselves more fully. This will demand some adjustment in relationships but the energy available for joint action will be vastly increased. George Brown says: 'When you change to being who you are instead of being caught up in who you should be, there's more of you in the relationship and therefore the relationship will change.' The ills of conformity and negative confluence melt away. Individuals stand out more clearly, are suprising and appreciated.

Maintenance or 'team spirit' meetings allow for norms to be developed in a way that reinforces team spirit, precisely because it is the athletes who establish them. This has been observed in a school setting: 'Open sharing allows for widening the range of alternatives for perceptions, cognitions, feelings and behaviours. Also, public sharing of norms produces greater social support for the agreement eventually decided upon. Changes in methods of working in the group are brought about more effectively when students are involved in planning the changes. Imposed alterations often bring about resistance and the development of counter productive norms that may impede the class's group processes.' (*Group Processes in the Classroom.*)

As you sit back, diverting appeals to your judgement, you should watch the pattern of participation, perhaps for a while, even chart the exchanges across the circle on a sheet of paper (how does the result correspond to interchanges required during competition?) with a view to inviting comments from individual team-members at a later date. Everyone should be encouraged to speak: 'the broader the participation among members of a group, the deeper the interest and involvement will be'. (Malcolm and Hulda Knowles.) Yet this can be difficult for younger or less experienced team members and in this case the formation of smaller supportive groups, whether pairs of older and younger athletes or groups that interact tactically during competition, should be reinforced. The process of encouraging pairs of players to appreciate each other's performance and to express what additional needs they have of one another, satisfies both task and maintenance needs and strengthens the intuitive bond between them. Steve Perryman, sitting in on a session I once led with Mark Falco and Clive Allen, said to them 'Two strikers being devious together are more effective than each being devious alone.'

All team sports have famous pairings. Alan Knott and Derek Underwood, the Kent and England wicketkeeper/spin bowler pair had a legendary understanding, despite the difficulty a wicketkeeper normally has in keeping for a bowler whose very art is deception. 'He seems to know instinctively what I'm going to bowl before I do,' Underwood once said of Knott. (*Sunday Times*, 17 June 1984.) Alan Trammell and Louis Whitaker, 'Sweet Lou' and 'Tram' of Detroit Tigers baseball team, the best combination of middle infield players, have a similar understanding. Robert Goldberg writes: 'At the end of the game, the first thing they do is shake hands ... They don't talk a whole lot, they're just comfortable around each other ... Whitaker is black and Trammell white. Whitaker bats left and Trammell right. Whitaker is reserved (the team ghost) and Trammell outgoing (the team agitator). But somehow, on the field, you have a hard time telling them apart. It's synchronicity. Trammell says simply "Lou's my partner ... We've come across a lot of different balls. I don't have to talk to him. When the ball is hit – we know." When one excels so does the other. Their career stats are practically interchangeable.' (*Sport*, July 85.)

Such understanding usually takes years to develop but it is possible to speed the process by fostering it deliberately. Pairings between older and younger players in practice and in meetings can be of great importance, in the development of a player's resilience. Tony Parks had some hard times at Tottenham whilst I was there, disappointed by his inability to gain a permanent place in the First Team. Yet for several seasons he was sustained by and responded warmly to Ray Clemence's friendship and encouragement, Ray being the vastly experienced goalkeeper he was trying to replace. It was the commitment that both players made to this relationship that made it so easy for Ray to calm Tony prior to the penalty shoot-out at the 1984 UEFA Cup Final. As coach it's worth remembering that a young player will usually learn more from an older player he admires and spends time with than he will ever from you, even though you tell him the same things. East Europeans have long practiced such pairing. We introduced this on a formal basis at Tottenham, together with the idea of positionally-divided small group meetings, during the run-up to the 1982 Cup Final. Peter Shreeve called it 'the buddy system' then but, like some other experiments that worked well at the time, it wasn't sustained.

Being on the side-lines is never easy: 'Understudying is a soul-destroyer,' says Simon Callow. 'It's the upstairs–downstairs feeling that is so hateful. Understudies ... have a creative contribution to make which is on the whole subordinated to their cloning function.' A substitute has to fill in for the player he replaces and, like a small part actor, he has 'to come to the stage warmed up. Leading characters have a comfortable stretch in which to get the engine ticking over; the small-part player must be glowing from the first moment.' Boudewijn Castelijn, the Dutch coach to the USA women's field hockey team, talked to me about this problem when Christopher and I started working with him in April 1986. 'I want a squad in which *every* player has a unique part to play,' he said, 'One in which a player sits on the bench knowing that she is as important to the team as the players on the field, ready to make her special contribution the instant it is required.' Such an ideal will take time to materialise but it is worth continuous experimentation and discussion with the players.

Chris Hughton of Tottenham, recovered from injury but unable to regain his place in the team, spoke of Gary Mabbutt who was keeping him on the side-line for the second leg of an important Cup tie. 'He's one of my best friends but I'm wanting Gary to have a bad game. If he's doing well you get disappointed.' In a game with substitutes or a club with a reserve team, this is a sentiment that is easily understood. The fact that Chris, on this occasion the substitute, could express it was to his credit and a significant step forward. Having recognised his attitude and expressed it, he was soon able to 'create change'. Towards the end of the session, I asked 'So what is your objective today?' to get the response 'to be prepared for whatever I have to do'. Then he added: 'I shall wish everyone best of luck, just as if I'm playing. I'll give Mabbsie advice based on what I learnt in the first leg. All the little disappointments I can get back to next time.'

If you coach a large club you will not only need to show you are interested and aware of progress made by substitutes and reserve team players – helping them to feel part of the larger unit – but should encourage contact between players of the club's different teams. This speeds the progress of reserve players and ensures easier integration when they move into the first team.

Simply watching first team matches will help, just as it helps injured first-team players. When Gordon Cowans broke his leg, he was out of football for one year. 'In situations like mine, you do sit back and compare yourself with other players, more than when you're actually playing. Watching Bryan Robson has brought it home to me that I could score more goals. I've been fascinated by the timing of his runs into scoring positions . . . the way he hangs back and starts his run while the men in front are in the middle or reaching the end of theirs.' (*Sunday Times*, 26 August 1984.) Such observations would probably be of interest to other members of the club, both those who attack in Robson's position and those who have to defend against such an attack. They might even be of interest to Robson himself, or at least would prompt him to make some additional comment of his own. The occasional post-match review that allows substitutes, reserve team and injured players to add their observations can therefore generate new ideas but, just as important, it will also develop team spirit beyond the narrow bounds of current first team players.

As coach or manager you should be aware of the special relationship that an injured player has with the rest of the team. Very often there is a softness and warmth that allows more meaningful encouragement than anyone else can give. At Tottenham, injured first team players were encouraged to be in the dressing room before a home match, although too often they were not invited to team meetings at the training ground, where their detached yet fully cognisant views would have been of considerable importance. As a volleyball coach, I found that an injured member of the squad was a great support during a match. At time-outs he'd bring the water bottle to the side-line and add a quiet word of support and advice to one or other player. When I made a substitution, he'd help the player who'd been replaced to warm down emotionally (by encouraging him to talk) and then to tune in again to what was happening on court, so he'd be ready to return if the occasion arose.

The interaction between injured player and other team members has two-way benefits. By remaining in the family atmosphere of a synergetic team, an injured player maintains the relationship so that he slides back into his allotted place more easily when he regains fitness. It is also possible that he recovers faster, as if this positive atmosphere has the power to promote healing.

At a meeting, when you divide the team into small groups,

always bring them back to a team circle at the end of a set period of time. Encourage each group to share its process with the team as a whole. Sometimes you may ask each group to say what it needs from the others and what it is able to offer. Teams within teams are a strength, provided they are all focused on the good of the whole. Where one small group is at odds with the rest, encourage the team to explore the conflict together, with a prospect of discovering some valuable new insight.

Form your small groups thoughtfully. Left to themselves, young players may drift into a support group of their own which gives out no energy to the team as a whole. I saw this happen in Madrid with a group of Tottenham substitutes. No ill is intended but this kind of support avoids rather than makes contact and is a form of negative confluence. Perls said that 'our sense of union depends paradoxically on a heightened sense of separateness': unless we retain a sense of our separate identity within the team, we have no chance of experiencing that sense of positive merging with each other that is team spirit. Instead of an increased awareness, we 'check out' into an unconscious state. Card games that go on until late at night, played endlessly by young, dissenting or substitute players who are unable to drag themselves away are the epitome of negative confluence.

Whenever the participants of a small group within the team fail to provoke each other to new discoveries and hold themselves apart from the rest of the players, that group is likely to be a negatively confluent clique. It is the exact opposite to the relationship that exists between team members when they improvise with sweet intuition to lift their team towards its goal. Denise McCluggage, in her perennially exciting book, *The Centred Skier*, describes her experience of seeing 'bright cords ... a network of visible energy' connecting members of the Golden State Warriors basketball team on a night when they thrashed the New York Knicks. 'The lines all emanated from Rick Barry ... (who) was glowingly, obviously the hub of the team that night ... In contrast ... the evening's visitors were disconnected. A few feeble lines extended from Bill Bradley to two other teammates but Walt Frazier moved in his own cocoon ...'. This is remarkably akin to Sadaharu Oh's experience of baseball. The relationship of team spirit is of a very high order, spiritual if not psychic: 'What you do on a team has consequences for everyone else, not just for yourself. ... Ties are created between players that are deep and lasting.'

The relationship between players and their opponents

In the theatre it is the public, in business one's competitors and in sport one's opponents who present the challenge. Without 'opponents' and therefore without challenge, a team will not be stirred to produce their best. One's opponents are to be valued as the wind that fans the flame of one's own team spirit. For a healthy team with clear realistic aspirations, the opposition provides a renewed impetus to unity and creative achievement (see chapter two). Hence the respect for opponents which is traditional in the martial arts and many amateur sports. John Biglow, the USA Olympic rower, believed that because 'your adversaries had subjected themselves to virtually the same regimen that you did, you respected them as much as you respected yourself'. (Halberstam.) Sports do vary, however, in this respect.

The attitude of rugby players towards their opponents can be wild on the pitch and raucously matey off it. The episode of George Crawford, the referee who walked off mid-match saying he was sick of the violence prompted Peter Corrigan of the *Observer* to write: 'The right of rugby forwards to punch, kick, gouge, bite and generally discomfort each other has gone unchallenged for so long it has become deeply embedded into the game's traditions and the solution will require major excavation work... Many rugby forwards have feuds more long-standing than you'll find in most Italian villages and it is part of their machismo to risk an early bath in pursuit of them... It is quite amazing considering the size of the men involved and their general demeanor that they reserve their dislike of each other to the field of play ... They seem content to swap a few punches, take whatever punishment the referee deems appropriate and later leave the field arm-in-arm, get drunk, pour beer into each other's pockets and indulge in their favourite hobby of hotel alterations.' (22 September 1985.) To which might be added Peter Dobereiner's wry comment: 'We ... have standards – or hypocrisy as the purists have it. Thus the drunken wrecking of a hotel may be condoned as youthful high spirits (rugby), as yobbish hooliganism (football) or as a national scandal (cricket). On balance, we want our sportsmen to perform like hard bastards while conveying the impression of gentlemanly unconcern and off the field we insist that they behave with the decorum of ambassadors. The ideal of the gifted amateur, Eton and Christnose, dies hard.' (*Observer*, 2 September 1984.)

First Division soccer players are rigidly isolated from their opponents until they meet in the tunnel to go out on the pitch. Peter Shreeve would mention one or two individual opposing players in his team talk but with little emphasis and no display of emotion whatever. On the pitch there is unremitting verbal abuse. 'Divorce yourselves!' Peter commanded tersely, one half-time when the temperature was rising. Yet many players regard abuse as a legitimate skill which they search to perfect. After the match both sides meet in the home team's players' lounge, in some cases amicably enough but occasionally grudges are stored away for next time.

I believe that this approach may be improved, in two respects. Before a match it does help an athlete to know his likely opponent and to visualise his response to that opponent's best moves. When John Madden emphasised to George Beuhler the need to control the Chargers' 300-pound defensive tackle, number 74, Louie Kelcher, another player taped a large '74' on to the Coke machine and Beuhler slammed into it. He later played his best game. Fred Perry, the British player who won the Wimbledon singles title three years in a row in the thirties, also believed in the importance of watching his opponent but didn't bother to analyse tactics or technique. 'I was never interested in what a player could do on court. I was interested in his mannerisms, his idiosyncrasies, his nervous motions. Jack Crawford had one trick I used to watch for. He used to wipe his hands like every other player does, down the side of his pants but when he got a bit nervous he'd wipe his hands across his shirt and wiping a wet hand on a wet shirt doesn't do much good. I knew then that I'd got him.' (*Sportsworld*, December 1973.) The other improvement is more subtle but involves distinguishing an opponent's imagined personality and his actual skills. However good the opponent is, whatever he or she does, there is a correct move for the athlete to make in response. The greater the pressure, the more important it is to focus on this correct move. Hence Peter's call: 'Divorce yourselves!'

The only visitor I ever saw in the Tottenham dressing room on a match day was a friend of one of the directors. Even the directors only appeared briefly before one or two vital matches each season. Cricket is different. When I arrived in Canterbury one day to meet Peter Roebuck, I was surprised to be asked into the Somerset dressing room but astonished when a couple of the Kent team came in and joked with their opponents as they asked them to sign bats during a break for rain. A month earlier, I had travelled with Haringey Cricket College to a London cup match, to find that the dressing-room in which we were intending to hold our team talk was shared by the opposition but at County level I'd expected complete separation. In reviewing the 1985 season, Peter Roebuck had this to say about the superior value of the three-day game: 'To a cricketer the longer game is the only serious test of his skill. In it he is an employee protecting his contract and a craftsman using his skill. The game is a series of private duels, with each player expressing his character on the field ... Since it is a private duel the players feel, as might warring soldiers, that they are as much in harmony as in opposition. If a spectator is rude, someone will murmur sympathetically that "your dad has arrived". It is your on-drive against his slower ball, a comparison of notes...' (*Sunday Times*, 22 September 1985.) Despite the ferocity of bouncers and apparent unequalness of eleven versus one, it would seem that for some at least cricket is still a comparatively civilised game.

Yet if post-performance custom varies from sport to sport, most athletes know all about gamesmanship. Footballer Paul Miller used to direct such prolonged attention on attempts to psyche out his opponents that he sometimes failed to notice their attack building up in time. Mark Falco once said that he sometimes tells an opponent how *well* he is playing, finding that this disturbs concentration just as well as abuse; whilst Steve Perryman has a story of playing against Leeds as a youngster, injuring a player unintentionally and being intimidated by hearing Billy Bremner and John Giles calling his name from player to player.

I tried a similar psyche-out technique in volleyball, standing at the net as a blocker, watching the ball coming to the setter and calling out the direction into which the setter was shaping to pass the ball. Gamesmanship is a long-established code of practice. The fact that it so often backfires on the perpetrator makes it a little easier to accept: not only can the 'gamesman' get his own attention stuck on his indulgence in gamesmanship but he can fire his opponent to greater determination to beat him. Gamesmanship as practiced by Mohammed Ali or Bobby Riggs is an art that is enjoyed by spectators – despite themselves – but equally enjoyed is the sight of an athlete responding to attempts to distract him with irate but controlled power. This was how Kevin Curren brushed John McEnroe aside in the 1985 Wimbledon semi-final.

Gamesmanship is designed either to distract one's opponent's attention or to raise his pitch of arousal beyond the optimum level, into the sphere of blinkered anger or anxiety. Concentration and maintaining arousal at a suitable pitch are two mental skills which all athletes need to learn. It's the fact that not many athletes consciously train to deal with feelings of anger (though more do spend time learning how to cope with anxiety) that makes many a tough football player susceptible to the psyche-out. Pam Shriver's response to the oft-repeated question 'How is it for you to play singles against Martina Navratilova, your doubles partner and friend?' is 'It's harder to play someone you dislike because you want to beat them so badly.' (*Psychology Today*, July 1984.) This leads us back to Sadaharu Oh's distinction between opponents and enemies, already quoted on page 52. 'In combat I learned to give up combat. I learned in fact there were no enemies. An opponent was someone whose strength, joined to yours, created a certain result. Let someone call you an enemy and attack you and in that moment they lost the contest.' If an athlete habitually loses his cool and lashes out in anger, he needs help to build a new physical response, as did Tony Galvin and Graham Roberts (chapter two). This is sometimes called an individual mental as opposed to a tactical game plan.

Finally there is a more subtle example of psyching out which is known instinctively by all good players of any game in which one side initiates play by serving, bowling or pitching the ball to an opponent. This is of sensing what can only be called the attention or readiness of the opponent and initiating play either before his attention is focused or the moment it wavers. The same happens in the martial arts and again Sadaharu Oh, referring to his experience of combatting such attempts to psyche him out, describes the process best: 'To train one's entire being to hold back from the tricks and feints of a pitcher, no less than from an enemy with a sword, is finally the single most important step in harmonising one's *ki* with the opponent's. *Ma*, the interval or distance between you, is eventually that which you rather than the other create by the strength of your waiting.'

5

COMMUNICATION

Good relationships within the team depend on good communication, although the communication may not always be verbal. 'Communication,' says Wendell Johnson, 'is the stuff of co-operation, of group effort, of social living. What we cannot do ourselves, we can through communication do together ... People need people.' The *domestique* and the star cyclist team leader work together with sparse efficiency that only a clear-cut pre-established pattern of communication will allow. There are good and bad patterns of communication. Either can become established as a norm. Manager and athletes all operate within an accepted pattern yet, with careful planning, open discussion and patience, this pattern can be improved towards greater efficiency and a higher level of team spirit.

Leading guest groups at Findhorn, especially the daily feedback sessions, Carol O'Connor and I began to make the distinction between *talk* and *chat*. We noticed that whatever the subject, when someone began to express what he was feeling, he immediately had the attention of the rest of the group. On the other hand, when he began to tell stories about other people's alleged experiences in a time past, everyone else soon became bored. We would then point out the difference, allow time for discussion and suggest that as far as possible the group adopt the norm of talk rather than chat. From that point on the norm was usually reinforced by group members and the feeling of vitality and team spirit would grow.

Judith Brown, in her book *The Happily Ever After Factor*, says that 'communication is sharing your experience'. Both athletes and coach have to learn this skill. Athletes particularly may fear being judged negatively if they voice their feelings and opinions. The tendency is to start sentences with the pronouns 'One...', 'We...' or 'The team...', rather than with 'I...'. It's less scary to say 'We've lost confidence and have no team spirit', than to say 'I've lost confidence and feel isolated'. Yet it is much easier to work towards change with the second sentence. When the first is spoken, someone has to ask 'Who do you imagine has lost confidence and lacks team spirit?', 'What makes you imagine that? Check it out with the person concerned', and, above all, 'Have you lost confidence?', 'Do you feel part of the team?', 'How would you score yourself out of ten on confidence and team spirit?' On the other hand, when someone says 'I've lost confidence and feel isolated' you can start helping straight away, with 'When does this happen?', 'When does the opposite happen?', and 'Who in the team here could do something to allow your attitude to change? What would that be? Tell him'.

Taking responsibility for one's feelings in this way only comes with practice and in an atmosphere of trust. If, as coach, you learn and adopt this way of speaking yourself, in your interaction with individual athletes and the team as a whole, you will be well on your way to creating such an atmosphere. In order to explore the process further, let's look at three different channels of communication that exist within the overall pattern. These are communication between yourself and the athlete, communication between yourself and the team, and communication between the athletes.

Communication between coach and athlete

The effective coach works hard and happily at creating broad lines of communication between himself and each of his athletes. John Madden, as we've seen, made sure his players knew he liked them. 'I tried to talk to each of them,' he explains. 'Sometimes it was merely a quick 'How ya doin''. Sometimes it was a conversation. But by talking to them every day, they didn't feel something was up when I would stop to talk to them.' This is one way to develop trust. It also helps if you have learnt to express the personal needs that lie behind what might otherwise sometimes be experienced by your athletes as an unreasonable demand. When you have to take issue with an athlete, 'chew him out' as Madden would say, there is always the possibility of removing blocks to his collaboration and overall effectiveness if you show what motivates you personally. 'Undeclared, unsatis-

fied wants of others lead to us being threatened or frustrated . . .
Unless I know the unspoken needs or hungers lying behind your
demand . . . I can only accept or resist on the basis of its impact
on me.' (Craig and Craig.) The coach who, for once, says: 'Look,
I've had a hard time with the administrators this morning and
am in no mood for chat right now,' will find that his players
respond readily enough. If he keeps the morning's frustrations
entirely to himself, he is almost sure to clash unnecessarily with
at least one player during the afternoon.

If your needs as coach seem to be partially blocked by your athlete's performance and you want him to change, spend time
thinking about your meeting with him in advance. Be clear on
your objectives and on how you would like to achieve them, as
you would before any meeting, but be flexible and prepared for
him to surprise you with a new view on the situation. In the final
analysis, the only effective communication is two-way. The behaviourist coach who never listens won't have enough information to know how to get the best from his players.
'Communication between a coach and his players,' Madden continues, 'was being able to say good things, bad things and
average things. Conversely, it's being able to listen to good, bad
and average things. Both ways, communication is also being able
to do it with the same attitude.' Having explained the wider context of your personal needs, the team context, invite your athlete
to give his own opinion of his current performance and of his relationship with you and the rest of the team. As he speaks, watch
as well as listen and allow yourself to pick up the information
about his thoughts and feelings that are given by his posture, expression and gestures. Sometimes these signals will be at
variance with his words and often they are of greater importance. By the end of his story you may find you are thinking along
new lines or that he has suggested the change in his performance
that you were wanting to suggest originally.

In business, workers have been found to respond best when
allowed to speak freely rather than being required to answer a
rigid set of questions. Business subordinates, like athletes, need
the space to express their feelings about their job and often just
the fact that the manager is prepared to listen, produces an
'increase in productivity'. Madden tells the story of his defensive
end, Ben Davidson, who bumped a quarter-back's arm in training, only two plays after Madden had shouted at Ike Lassiter for
the same thing. Asked why, Davidson said 'You got mad at Ike
and I wanted you to get mad at me.' 'Even at 6'8" and 280

pounds, Big Ben wanted to be noticed, whether it was doing something good or bad,' Madden concludes. This need to be noticed was dramatically demonstrated in the twenties, when a team of efficiency experts were called to the Hawthorne Illinois plant of the Western Electric Company to see whether improved lighting would improve productivity. In the experiment that followed, not only the group working under improved lighting improved productivity but the *control* group, working under normal lighting, did too. Further research showed that the increase in productivity arose simply from the increased level of communication between management and workers. Fifty years later, Peters and Waterman found that in 'excellent companies' communication was characterised by informality and simplicity: the managing director would frequently leave his office to talk to his employees and, where information had to be conveyed in writing, no directive would be longer than one side of a sheet of paper.

Andrew Gove, president and chief operating officer of Intel Corporation, a large American manufacturer of microprocessors and computer memory devices, *prefers* to meet his subordinates in their offices. 'A supervisor can learn a lot by simply going to a subordinate's office,' he says. 'Is he organised or not? Does he repeatedly have to spend time looking for a document he wants? Does he get interrupted all the time? Never? And, in general, how does the subordinate approach his work?' (Robert Tucker, see bibliography.) With no other objective than to tune in better to the person I was working with and with whom I needed to communicate, I did the same thing with the Scottish national volleyball team, visiting them in their homes from time to time, enjoying their hospitality. Too often a football manager will cling to the protection of his intimidating office and huge desk. Not John Madden, who made a point of going to the players, talking to them in the locker room or the trainer's room, where they felt at ease. Steve Perryman said the dressing room is the player's territory and that anyone else is regarded as a visitor. It is always best to tailor your behaviour as well as your language to those of the person with whom you want to communicate. Meeting that person on their home ground is already a step in that direction. (I also found it a very pleasurable experience.)

A French journalist talking to Brian Glanville of the 'outstandingly successful' Gerard Houllier, manager of Paris St Germain Football Club, said 'I think Houllier has given the players confidence. Peyroche, the last manager, didn't talk to them at all. It's very important to talk to them, even if they are stars. Which they are but they're still kids ... Houllier knows how to approach each one according to his personality.' (*Sunday Times*, 2 February 1986.) John Bertrand, captain of the *Australia II*, even asked Laurie Hayden to give his crew a personality test that would help him to adapt his form of communication to suit the person he was approaching. Hayden told him that one man was methodical and could only cope with one instruction at a time, another loved pressure and could cope with five or six instructions, a third was so aggressive and willing that he should never be given any instruction he might not be able to accomplish in case he killed himself trying and that a fourth would never crack and should always be told everything straight. Hayden also said that Bertrand himself was too much of a perfectionist in his decision-making and didn't compliment his crew enough. Such tests can be very threatening to the athlete and are bound to be mis-used by a behaviourist coach. On the other hand, John Bertrand was exceptional and clearly loved his crew. In his hands they were a valuable adjunct to his training.

Keith Burkinshaw, often reserved and distant from his players, nevertheless knew how to communicate clearly whenever he wanted. A few days before he left Tottenham, I was preparing an article on leadership and he let me ask him a string of questions. When I'd finished, he said 'You know it's a funny thing but I've found, if you want to get through to people, touching them is all-important. When I was coaching in Zambia many years ago, I noticed that black men walked down the street holding hands. At first I thought "There's a lot of that type here" but later I realised this was their way of communicating. Soon I learned to touch their hands myself, if I wasn't being understood and it always worked like a charm.' Keith's popularity with the media and indeed with his office staff was, I suspect, much to do with this ability to reach out *figuratively* to people when he chose and his willingness to listen. The value of the correct use of touch as a means of communication is mentioned in the best-seller business book *The One-Minute Manager*. Authors Blanchard and Johnson suggest that when the good manager 'sees you have done something right, he comes over and makes contact with you. That often includes putting his hand on your shoulder or briefly touching you in a friendly way'. The difference between a behaviourist and a humanist communicating by touch (and I suspect that *The One-Minute Manager* is aimed at the behaviourist) is that the behaviourist will use reaching out to persuade the recipient to do something, whereas the humanist expresses the impulse to show his support.

Sometimes, as in cricket when the captain speaks to the bowler, giving a player advice during a match can be a major boost to the team as a whole. If it's done the right way, the captain or coach can give the impression he has a plan and is in control of the situation, even if he isn't. However, if your sport is one in which you shout instructions to your team during the course of play, you should make a detailed agreement with your players as to what you are likely to shout and how you are going to express it. For a manager or his assistant to shout 'Let's start getting the ball in again, Glenn!' when 30,000 people are shouting something else and Glenn is in the middle of the field, is worse than useless: it only succeeds in distracting any of the players who hear part of the message. Such a message should be shortened to 'Glenn! Get it in!' and only shouted when Glenn is within easy ear-shot.

Last minute instructions before the match can also be confusing but when they are necessary, keep them as short as possible and then, as I've already suggested, ask the player concerned to get an image for the instruction, based on some past experience in which he did what you are asking him to do now. If he spends a moment remembering what it felt like to play in this way, there's a chance that he'll remember and reproduce the action in the coming match. The procedure though will need practice.

As coach, you should also be clear and direct during training. Instead of asking 'Isn't your left elbow too low?' (which can evoke a defensive 'No it isn't' response), say 'I notice that your elbow is lower than Richard's. How is that for you? Play a few more balls and see for yourself what's happening'. This gives the player reassurance of firm support, whilst encouraging him to discover what is right himself.

Communication between coach and team

As coach, you largely determine the quality of communication that exists between yourself and your team. The more methodically you work at being honest and up front yourself and at making it easier for your athletes to do the same, the better communication will be. Such understanding is built over a period of time.

The 'Johari Window' is a diagram developed by Luft and Ingham and used by Hersey and Blanchard to describe leadership personality and to show the degree of openness that exists between the manager and those under him. It is based on the fact that some of a manger's behaviour patterns and attitudes are known to him alone (these are private perceptions), some are known to his subordinates alone (to these he is blind), some are perceived by both (these are 'public') and some by neither (these are 'unknown'). The 'window' therefore looks like this:

	Known to self	Unknown to self
Known to others	public	blind
Unknown to others	private	unknown

When the manager discloses how he feels about certain matters relating to the business or his team, he is increasing the 'public' square at the expense of the 'private':

Disclosure	Known to self	Unknown to self
Known to others	public	blind
Unknown to others	private	unknown

On the other hand, when team members give the manager feedback on how his behaviour and attitudes are perceived by them and he is willing to listen, then the 'public' square increases at the expense of the 'blind':

Feedback	Known to self	Unknown to self
Known to others	public	blind
Unknown to others	private	unknown

When the manager is prepared to show his response to things relating to the team *and* to accept feedback on his behaviour and
attitudes from his athletes or subordinates, the 'public' sector of
his leadership personality will grow at the expense not just of the
'blind' and 'private' sectors but also of the 'unknown'. The
increase in self-awareness will be experienced with excitement as
a new dimension of confident ability:

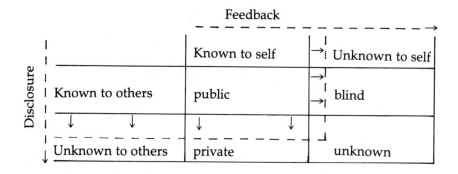

It requires considerable self-confidence, trust and curiosity for a
coach or manager to listen sympathetically to feedback or to
allow his athletes or subordinates to know his own feelings and
way that he relates to his job. Yet it is generally the case that the
smaller the 'public square', the less effective is his management.
Managers, for instance, who angrily bite off feedback from their
athletes will operate from an increasingly isolated position and
'will develop significant blind areas that will eventually damage
their effectiveness'. (Hersey and Blanchard.) Feedback, in fact,
should be encouraged. Actually, it *can* be encouraged fearlessly,
once you realise that feedback is an expression of feelings, *other
people*'s feelings for which *they* are responsible, not you. If they
are upset, in the end it is they who choose to be upset, rather
than bored or patient or cheerful. In the last analysis you can't
make them feel anything. (Should that seem ruthless, see how
positive the sentence becomes when you change the pronouns
around.)

If I tell you 'You're quite wrong to select that player for this
match', you may well reply angrily that I don't know what I'm
talking about. If on the other hand I say 'I feel worried by your
selection of that player', you cannot contradict me because it's
obvious that only I can know my own feelings. This is the point

at which the *insecure* manager will still snap back 'I'm not interested in your opinion' and isolate himself further from information which may be relevant and help him to do his job better.

There are obviously constrictions of time and appropriateness on the *discussion* of feelings but then a person's feelings can often be acknowledged without any need for discussion. As long as athletes or subordinates feel free to express their feelings, know there will be times set aside for a 'maintenance' discussion (see page 88) or review and can see that you are being open about your approach to your job, a strong team spirit is developed and your efforts are successful.

Three further points need to be made about the Johari window:

(i) Note that 'disclosure' only relates to team or business affairs unless outside matters are affecting your work. In four years of working at Tottenham, I only found myself engaged in anything remotely resembling straight counselling work, as opposed to sports mental training, on a handful of occasions and, on each occasion, the topic was directly related to the player's performance. Apart from anything else, there is little time for such sharing, unless it's to be in such informal situations as a long journey.

(ii) Occasionally you, as coach, may deliberately and rightly chose to isolate yourself from some person or group related to your job. This is simply done by starving the people concerned of disclosure and building a barrier to their unwanted feedback.

(iii) The Johari window of your relationship with individual athletes may not be the same as it is for the group. I am particularly aware of this phenomenon when I lead a Sporting Bodymind course with Christopher Connolly. These courses are designed to give a practical experience of the way we work with athletes, to both coaches and athletes who want to learn what they can of the techniques, in the space of two days. Generally speaking, my 'public square' is quite large during the course, maybe larger than Christopher's: I tend to give gut reactions without much thought and am concerned to know how people are reacting to the presentation as it progresses, whilst he is a little more guarded, thinking longer before he speaks and preferring to stick to the timetable than to have a great deal of group feedback. In the intervals, however, I spend more time alone and, if with individual course members, I'm more closed, tending to have my attention on the next part of the course and the group as a whole. Meantime, Christopher is sympathetic, genuinely interested in individual feedback and sharing his own response – to the point where I usually need to remind him when it's time to start the next session.

The way that you prepare and open a team meeting, whether a talk or a discussion, will have a considerable effect on the type and level of communication you achieve. As far as possible, you should choose a room where there will be a minimum of distractions – a room that is quiet, that is not cluttered with unnecessary furniture and yet which is comfortable. At Tottenham, even when training sessions were at White Hart Lane rather than the training ground at Cheshunt (where there was but one bare room) discussions used to be held in the changing room. Eventually, I managed to get the point across that a real discussion, one in which players actually spoke freely to each other, dividing into small groups for part of the time to do so, was best conducted upstairs in the player's lounge. Not only was this comfortably furnished with armchairs that could be moved around but it was isolated from the daily noise and hurly-burly of the maintenance, grounds and cleaning staff.

Once you have chosen a suitable room, make sure that everyone else in the building knows that you will be there and shouldn't be interrupted. If the room has a phone, ask that calls be intercepted, saying that you won't be available for a certain period of time. Then, some time before the athletes arrive, arrange the chairs suitably. Generally speaking, if this is to be a discussion meeting, you'll put them into a circle. If it is to be a talk, they can be put in rows facing you.

One experiment on patterns of communication compared the effectiveness of communication which was achieved in a circle, where individuals are only permitted to talk to people on either side of them and communication that can be achieved in a star formation, where people on the outside may only communicate with the person sitting in the middle.

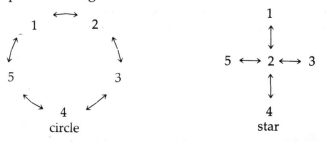

It was found that a problem is solved faster by a group where every communication is made through a leader (the star formation) but that this formation resulted in poor morale. In an emergency, the circle group pulled together and did better. (Hersey and Blanchard.) Irrespective of the actual positioning of the chairs, if you consciously or unconsciously foster the norm by which every comment that is made in a discussion meeting is made to and answered by you, you are operating according to the star system. This usually happens when players are lined up in a row facing you but has still to be guarded against when the chairs are arranged in a circle. If morale is to be strengthened by players being taught to exchange views with other players, (whether in fact those next to them *or* across the circle is immaterial), you must deflect questions that are directed at you until you are ready to sum up.

Even when you have a suggestion to make or some information to give to the athletes, if it is a discussion meeting, provoke them with questions to come up with an idea themselves. Apart from the fact that some new and far better plan might be sparked off, the actual involvement of all the players is increasing their reserves of commitment which will be available to them in a tight match situation. According to Fritz Perls, 'immediate gratification' (eg by giving all your answers and ideas straight out) 'doesn't produce a memory' (*Ego, Hunger and Aggression*), whereas the process of discussion and contribution to that discussion not only brings the athletes a clarity of purpose but also inspires the energy to go for it when the competition starts.

'The autocratic "star" pattern is appropriate where followers have low commitment, motivation and ability to take responsibility but it frustrates and lowers the morale of the high responsibility ability group.' (Hersey and Blanchard.) The circle pattern is used by the humanistic coach who believes the input of his athletes is important, when deciding on objectives or change. It is a slower process but it 'develops involvement and commitment'. The star pattern is used by the autocratic behaviourist coach anu decisions are reached sooner but it 'develops resentment and hostility'. Whatever your preference, when you are first appointed, you should take account of the existing communication pattern. Introducing a 'circle' pattern in a group used to a 'star' pattern of communication would create confusion – members being used to being dependent and 'closed'. In point of fact though, even a humanistic coach will use a star pattern of communication in certain situations, such as at a time-out or a pre-match talk.

John Bertrand paid acute attention to communication patterns amongst his crew when preparing *Australia II* for the America's Cup. First he broke down any tendency to insularity inherent in the necessity for specialist crew members' by 'asking the port winch grinder what he thought of the shape of the sails' or 'shouting to the starboard trimmer about the windshifts' and by 'asking key questions of people who were not reasonably qualified to know the answer and who were operating in an entirely separate area. The answers were irrelevant, but it made people *feel* great. Above all, it made them think and it made them keep thinking all of the time. And ten people who are racking their brains together are likely to be a lot more useful than three'. In other sports the ability to understand and empathise with the view of other members of the team is essential. 'Every great player knows not only what he does on a play but he also knows what everybody on the team is supposed to do,' says John Madden of American football. 'Any time a tackle tells me "I'm the tackle, I don't know what the guard does", then he doesn't really know what *he* does. It's the same way in business. When a salesman tells me "I don't know how this thing works, I just sell it", I look for a salesman who does know how it works'.

The next step John Bertrand took was to get rid of superfluous remarks by having competitions in which the person who spoke first out at sea had to buy a round of beer on their return. On other days he'd tell his crew to report everything they noticed, to say anything on their minds to one of two most experienced members and get those two to filter back the most important information to him. To develop awareness, he began by spending the first half hour yelling questions, 'demanding that they tell me their thoughts. In time, it would become second nature to be aware, not to be nervous, to communicate to Hughey and me anything that seemed significant. This type of communication therapy has major advantages. It gives us the combined strength of 11 brains rather than one and it also breeds a powerful camaraderie, somehow making each person feel that it was up to him, that to fail would be to let everyone else down. I've seen skippers try to force out this feeling by bullying, but you cannot do it that way. Team spirit is a one-way street. It evolves only when people *want* to fight for each other'.

This reminds me of my brief excursion into coaching women's volleyball. I was ill at ease, feeling that there was no feedback from the women at all. I assumed that the women didn't enjoy my coaching style, although I later discovered that wasn't the case. Either way, my coaching was comparatively poor, since without apparent feedback, there was no stimulus to me having new and creative ideas. Thinking back, I realise I should have used some of these techniques described by Bertrand.

Preparation for a team meeting ends when the athletes arrive and you all take your seats. The blackboard should be somewhere near you or your assistant. Don't begin the meeting until everyone has arrived, unless you are really short of time and then only after making the position clear to everyone there. Family therapists always allow an initial time for adjustment, a period of inconsequential conversation. Thereafter, a moment of silence – in the unlikely event of it ever being accepted as a norm – would allow individual team members to tune in to themselves, to their reason for being there and to a common positive experience of their 'Group Being'. This would also be a particularly effective way to start a meeting where controversial difficult decisions have to be made. If the team begins the meeting as a unit, fierce argument can expand the team's awareness without anyone being alienated.

Deal with unavoidable noise from outside by emphasising the sense of unity inside, as you open the meeting. Refer to it as a challenge to your focus as a group. When Tottenham arrived at the stadium to play a European Cup match in Prague in 1985, the noise of the crowd beyond the dressing room was unbelievable. Peter Shreeve soon overcame this by speaking emphatically and making lots of eye contact as he gave his pre-match talk. I might have begun by letting players focus on the noise for a moment, it being a distraction anyway, and then comment on the contrast provided by our own quiet unity. In a storm like this it would be precisely this quality that would carry the team through.

A training session should also have a clear beginning. Trainers who stand watching players jump around, wondering whether or not the last couple of them are going to turn up and then finally say in a subdued voice 'Well, perhaps we should begin' do not inspire a positive united performance. Similarly, a coach who keeps athletes behind with 'just one more' practice, long after the scheduled end of the session, soon lets slip any sense of committed team spirit that he might have stirred. At Findhorn, we had a 'tuning-out' attunement as well as a 'tuning-in' – a renewed affirmation of our fellowship and purpose.

Communication between players

Team spirit determines the level of communication there is between players during a match and the level of communication can determine the outcome of that match. Communication will be both verbal and non-verbal and can be developed in training, in full team meetings and in the meetings of pairs and small groups.

Meetings develop the mutual understanding of players (which, in a match can be more important than words) if attention is paid to the way they speak to each other. Taking a back role in a discussion allows you to look out for a variety of significant exchanges, some of which are described in *Sporting Body, Sporting Mind*. Encourage everyone to take part. You may divide the team into smaller groups to make things easier but eventually it is by speaking to the whole team for the first time that a player gains a sense of his own power. He then often feels a rush of warmth, excitement and connectedness, a greater appreciation of team spirit. Later you can teach him to change judgements, impersonal comments or repeated 'chat' to an expression of his feelings. It will probably be emotion that leads him to speak in the first place and once he learns to acknowledge his emotion, everyone else will be able to respond to his statement more easily. In fact expressive behaviour raises the awareness of the team and helps to move it away from blocks and into action.

Make sure that the longer-standing players don't leave out new members by using language or referring to situations they can't understand. Schoolchildren can do this deliberately in a school classroom to isolate an unpopular classmate. Very often a member of a class will be so unpopular that everything that he does is interpreted negatively by his classmates. (This can also happen not just within a team but between the coach and the player he designates as a 'problem'.) A good captain may well pre-empt your stepping in as interpreter and himself ask that a term be explained which he realises a new player hasn't understood. He might also demand that underlying ill-feeling be expressed and dealt with openly so that misunderstandings be cleared and appreciation of differences increased. However, he shouldn't speak too early in a discussion either and, when he does speak, should build on points made by other team members, referring to previous speakers by name. If he sees that someone's attention has drifted away, having made a point which got lost in the ensuing discussion, the captain can refer to this point and draw the player back into contact with the team. The more important the captain's role during competition, the more important it is to coach him to take this role in discussion meetings.

Sometimes as you listen to the discussion, you'll notice that a certain word or sentence is repeated by several players over a period of time. Ask yourself as you prepare to bring the discussion to a close (or indeed ask the team) 'If there was to be one word or sentence that sums up what we have discovered in this discussion, what would it be?' If a word or sentence is found (one week, prior to an important Cup match at Tottenham, the word was 'battling'), write it large on the blackboard, beneath the list of decisions that have been taken and let it be an *evocative word* that carries team spirit into the next contest.

Sometimes two players avoid responding to each other, or show, without voicing it, their disagreement. If this pattern is repeated in their relationship in training and if their interaction during competition could be improved, their mutual understanding and communication may be developed by inviting them to speak to each other without the rest of the team being there. One would have to prompt them with questions but having managed to get them to talk about the way they related to each other during a match, I'd see whether they appeared to be listening to each other. If in doubt, I'd ask. Very often two players who've been in the same team for a while and do not get along easily, will have acquired a set of negative thought forms about each other so that as soon as one speaks, the other tunes out, already thinking of what he wants to say in reply. I'd call them on this. What are they imagining about each other? Almost certainly they are each talking to an image of the other that is of their own making. The task is to help them to see and hear each other anew.

Each of them will have needs that they would like the other to meet. They may be in touch with them and express them as demands but the demands themselves are usually based on unstated problems and resentments. In fact, only good can come from helping them to express these resentments. As they do so, they begin to wake up a little to the reality of each other. By the time they can say 'I need this from you' they are in touch with themselves, with their own feelings and from that point they are able to speak directly to the other. They are also now able to hear each other. They are paying attention. As Judith Brown says, 'paying attention is an essential part of communication'. You don't even 'have to do anything about what you see and hear, at that moment'.

Eventually, when they have expressed their resentments, made their demands and shown their needs, they can be led to expressing appreciations: 'So what is it about each other that you appreciate?'. And, if the pace of the transition is right, understanding will move towards genuine respect.

Of course, when working with players with an *immediate* view to improving their interaction in competition, where there are no resentments but where there has been a lack of observation and intuition, I would ask the question 'What do you appreciate about each other?' early on. Moving beyond habitual reticence heightens awareness, good feeling and interest in each other. In this case, the question then *leads* to 'So what do you need from each other?' or 'So how can he help you more?'. Even two players who work well together benefit from taking part in this sort of structured conversation. (A more detailed account of how I would facilitate such an exchange is given in chapter seven, page 171.) Reticence is a social convention of much value. It is possible though that a player – because he appreciates some team-mate's overall performance – accepts and makes the best of some habit which hampers his own. Accepting this difficult behaviour may itself have become such a habit that he only realises improvement is possible when he is *asked* to find something his team-mate could do to help him. No improvement will be made until he does ask. As often as not his team-mate is unaware of his own trying behaviour. An ally who is only given part of the picture cannot give of his best.

Whether dealing with players who don't get on well together or with those, as in this case, who do, there will always be a tendency for each to answer my questions in the third person: 'What do you appreciate about him?' gets the answer 'He takes his time and has great calmness'. When this happens, I come in quickly with 'Tell *him*!' and after he's changed his observation to 'You take your time and I appreciate your calmness' I'll probably need to ask them to turn their chairs to face each other rather than facing me.

So far, I've only suggested that small groups and pairs should comprise players who interact closely during competition and those who appear not to get on with each other too well. Occasionally it is worth grouping those players who *don't* normally interact. In soccer, it would be good to have some tactical discussion in small groups, where you pair strikers and backs. Each has much to learn from the other, since strikers are continually trying to fool backs and backs have the job of disconcerting and dispossessing forwards. Players on the same side should pool all their knowledge, perceptions and tricks.

For a period of time I worked with Chris Hughton on improving his communication. Keith Burkinshaw and later John Pratt always tended to shout more than ever when the team were playing from right to left in front of the dugout at White Hart Lane: Chris and Tony Galvin were known as the deaf and dumb school, there on the left wing. It seemed as if Keith and John were trying to make up for the lack of communication on the pitch. Before one match against Nottingham Forest, I asked Chris what his objectives were and he itemised three ways in which he was going to focus on improved communications, especially with Tony. The first was to help other players to make movement, the second was to shout to them and the third was to make movement or runs himself – 'Me doing something wakes up their minds'. Until that moment I'd only been thinking of verbal communication and, if I'd thought of non-verbal communication at all, it would have been hand signals as are sometimes made in volleyball but in soccer would be virtually useless. Chris, of course, was right. When he had the ball, he could tell Tony what he wanted him to do by moving himself in a certain direction. When he hadn't got the ball, he could still run into space to get Tony to pass the ball to him or he could draw a defender to allow Tony to move into space.

Eamon Dunphy, in his extraordinary book *Only a Game: The Diary of a Professional Football Player*, describes the way in which a perfect system of non-verbal communication can develop between two players who play beside each other: 'When you share a job with somebody in football, a relationship develops between you, an understanding that you do not have with players doing a totally different job. If you are just knocking a ball between you, on a training ground, a relationship develops between you. It's a form of expression – you are communicating as much as if you are making love to somebody. If you take two players who work together in midfield, say, they will know each other through football as intimately as any two lovers ... It's a very close relationship you build up when you are resolving problems together, trying to create situations together. It's an unspoken relationship, but your movements speak, your game speaks. The kind of ball you give each other, the kind of passes you give each other, the kind of situations you set up together, speak for you. You don't necessarily become closer in a social sense, but you develop a close unspoken understanding.'

As for verbal communication, there are at least four different types: criticism, questions, demands or instructions and encouragement.

Criticism

Negative criticism is detrimental to team spirit and therefore to performance, even when it might seem to be justified. For a player struggling to lose this particular habit the best advice is for him to express his *feelings* rather than his judgements. Since the two are so closely linked, this is not so difficult. The language may still be violent but it is no longer directed against a team-mate. One way to help him make this change is to ask him to review a recent occasion when he did criticise sharply and to ill-effect. After leading a relaxation, I'd take him through a mental rehearsal of the incident, asking him to notice as much as he could about how he felt *physically* at that time. Then, I'd go through the visual re-editing technique described on page 162 and in *Sporting Body, Sporting Mind*. I'd ask him to go back to the beginning of the incident, start to play it through and, at the moment where he is about to shout abuse at his team-mate, imagine himself expressing his physical and emotional feelings instead, in a way that helps rather than hinders the team's performance. This new version should be rehearsed for a few minutes each day for about a week; and for the next three or four weeks he should review each training session and match, preferably with you his coach, paying particular regard to his communication with other players. If any player or players have been upset by his criticism, they might be brought in on the review sessions to contribute their feedback on his performance. The more conscious each athlete is of the current objectives of each of his team-mates, the more each can help and encourage the others, thereby making a positive source of inspiration out of what might originally have been a negative factor.

Questions

The only possible time for brief conversation in the midst of interacting sports is during a time-out, half-time or a break for injury. In a reactive/proactive sport (see page 18) such as cricket, there are more opportunities. An athlete usually asks a question to clarify a particular tactical situation. Should he be covering a particular player or is it someone else's reponsibility? A question may also be intended to clarify or correct some action of the ath-

lete to whom it is being asked and very often is a lot more acceptable than a statement or directive which might be construed as a
criticism but which anyway requires the person asked to do some
translation into visual and kinaesthetic thought.

Instructions

I've already suggested that last minute instructions in the changing room – 'Don't forget to keep it simple!', 'Don't give player X
an inch of space!', 'Be sure to bend your legs as you dig!' – require
translation into kinaesthetic imagery, into the language of physical feeling, if they are to have a significant effect on the player's
game. The player must remember or imagine what it *feels* like to
do what is being asked. Usually he doesn't make the translation
and either forgets the instruction, only being aware of the
warmth and encouragement of his team-mate's attention, or he
carries the instruction into the game in its verbal form, where it is
used by his (left-brain) chattering mind to distract him, tense him
up and disrupt his performance.

Instructions relating to technique particularly but also to tactical movement are therefore best conveyed either by his team-
mate reminding him of a specific time when he did what he
should be doing now – 'Remember how that felt?' – or, if there's
time, in the middle of a competition, by asking him the 'How
much/how far' type of question. This question is designed to
bring his attention to the technical or tactical movement that the
questioner feels needs adjusting. Instead of shouting 'Keep it
simple, for Chrissake!' or 'Bend your ******* knees!' which
engages the athlete's negative emotions and his left-brain chattering mind, it would be far better to ask the question 'On a scale
of one to ten, how simple do you feel that tactical move you did
was?' or 'Do you think you are bending your knees very little, a
fair amount or fully, as you dig?' which directs his attention back
to physical sensation (which in turn leads to a natural adjustment) and avoids arousing any emotional response.

All tactical information that is new and that relates to the way
that the competition is developing must be given clearly and directly. Information that relates to overall tactics comes either
from the coach or captain. At Tottenham, in a game where
instructions are not meant to be given from the sideline but invariably are, the manager in the stand, phoned the assistant
manager in the dug-out who then shouted information to the
player nearest to him. (If that player happened to be Tony

Galvin, nothing much happened, Tony's attention being totally on the flow of play.) In cricket, the captain of the fielding team constantly consults his bowler. Story has it that Brian Close, at least when captain of Somerset, used to get his outfielders to move ten times in half an hour, in the apparent belief that they might otherwise fall asleep. The batsmen are usually left to their own devices, the captain rarely signalling from the balcony. In emergency instructions might be smuggled to the crease when the 12th man takes out drinks or equipment.

In an interacting sport all players can help by drawing attention to some movement of the opposition that a team-mate might not have seen and by directing him to make the correct response. In soccer or hockey this role often falls to the backs as they follow the build-up of the opposition attack, although it can also be filled by the forwards after they have been passed. In some matches, this kind of direction is the goal-keeper's main function. Dave Sexton, chief coach of the Football Association school at Lilleshall, said of England's goal-keeper Peter Shilton: 'His voice and personality influence the whole defence and the midfield as well. You can be good between the posts but that is not taking charge – which is even more important than goalkeeping in the way it protects the goal.' (David Miller, *The Times*, 21 June 1986.) Forwards and wing players will also call for the ball when their defenders have dispossessed the opposition, trying at the same time to create the space into which it can be passed.

In volleyball calling is essential, at least at lower levels of the game, to avoid confusion as to who takes the ball as it is served over the net. (Only the call 'Mine!' is allowed, 'Yours!' leading almost inevitably to the ball falling between two players.) Volleyball spikers will also call for the ball to distract the opposition blockers. If they can get the blockers to commit themselves whilst their own setter still has control, the setter will pass the ball elsewhere. When players at the net succeed in blocking the opposition spiker, the whole team shouts in triumph. In a typical exchange, where the blockers' team has first served and the receiving team's attack has been blocked, this means a point and the right to serve again. The shout here is again designed to affect their opponents adversely, to disconcert them, to encourage them to fragment into expressing criticism of each other and, above all, to get them on the run by establishing a fast rhythm that prevents their opponents from re-orienting themselves. Often such a momentum can only be broken up by the opposing coach calling for a time-out but, if no time-out is left and if the captain is unable to make psychological contact with his players and slow things down, the shouting blockers will sweep their team to victory, at least of that set.

This form of shouting, is really a message to one's opponents as much as it is a form of intra-team communication. The same is true, I suspect, of the elaborate ritual that greets a goal by one of a soccer team's players, although I doubt whether it has anything like the same effect, if only because it is done when the ball is dead. There is a common belief that the minute after a team has scored a goal is when it's especially vulnerable to a goal being scored against it: the celebration can distract the team more than it does its opponents. Certainly this form of communication is neither critical, questioning, directive nor even encouragement.

Encouragement

Encouragement is essential in team games, both pro-active/reactive and interacting (see page 18) and in fact is best regarded as a skill that needs to be learnt and practised. Encouragement is a lot more than 'Cheer up, old son!', though there is sometimes a place for that too. Certainly the pat on the back that accompanies such an expression is a lot more helpful than the leaping about that follows the scoring of a goal. Encouragement after a mistake is effective to the extent that it (i) deflects the athlete's attention from a 'broad internal negative' focus (i.e. negative thoughts and images, see page 36); and (ii) reconnects the athlete with his positive emotional experience of team spirit. It is not akin to the brand of comfort that focuses on, even whilst minimising, a misfortune. Since the prime aim is to distract attention from a broad internal focus, the receipt of a pat on the back (experienced through *narrow* internal attention, see page 36) is bound to help. A player who angrily shrugs off encouragement of this kind may have his own preferred way of changing his focus of attention but, since it doesn't include acknowledgement of the team, it could be improved.

One way that a soccer team can make this improvement is described in the chapter on Confidence. At the end of a training session, instead of playing the usual fifteen minute game, play a game in which every player who is dispossessed or makes a mistake, *himself* encourages another player in the team. If he fails to do so, the other team gains a point, these points counting instead of goals. This drill trains players to make a positive gain out of an otherwise negative event. Not only does it teach them to prevent *themselves* from getting stuck in a negative broad internal focus of attention after making a mistake but it also ensures that someone else whose attention was flagging is pulled back into awareness of the team. Team spirit is a bit like the laces on an old pair of shoes: every so often it can do with a sharp tightening yank.

Disappointment, self-recrimination and brooding on mistakes all occur in the sphere of broad internal negative attention. So does anxiety, which again can be counteracted by the 'distraction' of encouragement, pulling the athlete's attention back to an external focus. Injury and pain, where neither is bad enough to require immediate care, distract attention to a *narrow* internal negative focus. A pat on the back can shift attention to a narrow internal *positive* focus, a smiling face or a wry look can shift it to a narrow external positive focus. Again, encouragement helps. I once heard Peter Shreeve, in his pre-match dressing room talk, say: 'Don't say "You ****!" to milk the crowd. *Encourage* those who make mistakes!' Certainly mistakes of one player can depress and isolate the rest of the team and as soon as an athlete recognises this response in himself, he too should force his attention outwards by giving encouragement. ('... to milk the crowd'? ... 'Surely not,' I thought, but apparently it used to happen.)

One of the best doubles tennis matches I saw in 1985 was the Australian pair Pat Cash and John Fitzgerald against ex-South Africans Kevin Curren and Johan Kriek. At one moment when all four players were in the service courts, Curren lifted a ball over the Australians and, as they turned, instantly seeing whose ball it was, Fitzgerald was on his way. Nevertheless I'm convinced that it was the warm urgency of Cash's cry 'Go on! Go on!' that got Fitzgerald the last couple of yards to the ball, enabling him to lob their opponents in turn and win the point.

A month later, reading the *Observer* report of the catch that enabled John Lever to take his 100th wicket of the season, I came across the words '... and Gladwin at mid-off, who probably did not require loud cries of "Catch it!" to spur him on, dived full length...'. My guess is that, if the shout was timed correctly, it almost certainly *did* make the catch easier. The Japanese take encouragement of this sort so seriously that the novice baseball players of the Giants team, at least in the time of Sadaharu Oh, had as their first lesson the requirement to attend and chant slogans at first team matches. Until this element of the game has been learnt, no technical coaching was given at all.

I first saw the Japanese men's volleyball team training for a tournament in the late sixties. What impressed me most were the pressure drills, which I've mentioned elsewhere. Ostensibly, these were exercises in a particular technique, often diving or rolling defence, where one player would be fed a fast succession of balls. Having dived to his left to save one, he had to get straight off the floor and dive to his right for the next. The drill is exhausting and attention and strength soon begin to drain but the rest of the team is standing around shouting continual encouragement and it becomes quite clear that this enables the player to keep going long after he would otherwise have stopped. When I returned to Scotland and began to include pressure drills in the national men's team's weekend training sessions, I divided the squad into threes: one player working, one player feeding the balls from side to side, and the third player chasing after the loose balls to keep the feeder supplied. It seemed a waste of valuable time *not* to have five people (in five different groups of three) practicing defence at the same time.

It was only later that I realised the point of the drill was just as much to train players in the art of encouragement as it was to train them to dive and roll. Encouragement too is a skill. The exercise was designed to improve team spirit and the decision to have only one player in fifteen practicing defence whilst the others shouted was deliberate.

6

MOTIVATION

What is motivation?

Motivation is need, most often the need to avoid, to possess, to achieve or to discover. In general parlance, a motivated athlete is one who has a powerful need that is satisfied through performing his sport to the very best of his ability. A motivated athlete is committed to his performance, although his motivation may gradually change. His motivation for taking up his sport may be satisfied early or never at all but if it is satisfied early new needs will emerge and if it is not satisfied at all he will eventually seek its satisfaction in more promising circumstances.

Since needs can be created, the coach has the power to manipulate the behaviour of his athletes. If he does this he is termed a 'behaviourist' and, when he chooses to create or reinforce a need for his athletes to perform well, he is said to be motivating them. In this sense, motivation may be from outside as well as from within the athlete. A perceptive behaviourist striving for a successful performance may choose to reinforce needs which he has already observed within his athlete or team but he may also introduce an entirely new element, which develops into an equally strong need. If he is a team coach, he will discover that effective manipulation requires considerable skill and sensitivity precisely because each member of his team may be motivated by different needs.

There are two ways around this. The straightforward behaviourist approach is to standardise the needs of individual players. The second way is to create an environment in which individual players may become a synergistic team with aspirations of its own which incorporate or satisfy the needs of its individual members. No out-and-out behaviourist could choose this solution, because it could well oblige him to let go of his own needs. Derek Wyatt, a long-time fan of Bobby Robson and Ipswich Football Club, says Bobby Robson chose the first solution, encouraging his players to get married early and transferring those who answered him back. Alan Jones, the Australian rugby union national coach, showed his preference for the second, when he began a diatribe on motivation with the words 'Group discussion is important...'. (David Hands, *The Times*, 9 January 1986.)

Occasionally an athlete makes the startling discovery that his predominantly behaviourist coach is fired by needs of his own and is therefore equally open to manipulation. A grimly entertaining and complicated dance may then ensue.

In our (Sporting Bodymind) experience, the three primary needs are for security, power and love. Other needs have been identified but in the sporting context, these three are inclusive. Initially, an athlete needs the *security* of a place on the team, the reliability of his coach and, if he is a professional, a contract, a home and an income. He needs the *power* of confidence in his ability to perform effectively, power to influence his team-mates, fame, status or attention and material goods. He needs the *love* that is expressed in recognition and approval of coach, team-mates, family and friends. Two common reasons for an athlete joining a club in the first place are for good fellowship, and to have his own beliefs confirmed. When the athlete feels that any of these three prime needs can only be satisfied by sources outside himself, he is not in control of the situation and is open to manipulation.

However, as time goes by, an athlete may gradually discover an *inner* sense of security, power and love and escape from the treadmill of need for external gratification. A curious change then takes place: instead of *seeking* security, he *offers* it; instead of grasping for power, his joy is to share the power that he finds in himself; instead of needing recognition and approval, he gives it to others and in doing so becomes a fount of team spirit. From day to day he will give advice to younger players, will agree to attend charity events, will take responsibility for the decisions he makes during competition, will risk making a mistake at appropriate moments, and will place the team before himself. Such an athlete is said to be self-motivated. In my time at Tottenham, players such as Ray Clemence, Tony Galvin and Steve Perryman were outstanding examples.

Motivation is linked to maturity. As an athlete becomes mature in some aspect of his understanding and performance, he moves into self-motivation. I believe the value of sport lies in providing a structure within which this process may occur. Ultimately, the coach reaches his own level of maturity and, ceasing to fear for the opinion of others or even the loss of his job, will find deep excitement and pleasure in the task of leading his athletes towards self-motivation. However, in an educational, if not a results-oriented context, each stage of development for coach as much as athlete has a validity of its own in relation to the growth of the team. Even a coach's lack of maturity may provide the impetus for some of his more experienced players to acquire a sense of their own responsibility, to help less experienced team members and, in doing so, to become self-motivated.

Since not only each athlete but also the coach may be operating from different levels of maturity, the following questions are often asked: (i) How can I as coach motivate an athlete? (ii) How can I motivate my team? (iii) How can an athlete motivate himself? (iv) How may an athlete be helped towards self-motivation? and (v) How can I as coach help my team towards self-motivation? As a *humanistic* sports psychologist, I feel very strongly that a coach should *not* seek to motivate his athletes and should focus instead on the last three questions. The behaviourist coach, wishing to make full use of manipulative techniques to achieve a specific result, will not agree, so I answer the first two questions from *his* point of view.

How can I motivate an athlete?

The question 'how can I motivate an athlete?' is usually lurking behind another question Christopher and I are often asked – 'What about motivation?' The fact is that many coaches believe that motivation is a key part of their job and that (largely behaviourist) measures are essential to 'get the athletes going'. In asking such questions, they suggest that there must be an all-purpose recipe, a set routine to be instituted, without which no athlete will ever leave the dressing room. Professional coaches in particular *do* have complex systems of reward and punishment designed to ensure that the athletes push for the goals they've been set. These are usually backed up by the traditional team talk prior to competition. The idea that some athletes may be less motivated than others is not explored beyond the moment of team selection, when certain players are automatic choices, or at post-match coaching staff discussions, where one player or another may be designated as a 'problem athlete'. Normally, an athlete who seems not to be motivated will, in these circles, be dropped. Only when he happens to be a star or when the pool of reserves is so depleted that there is no replacement for that particular tactical position, will the question 'How can I motivate *this* athlete?' be asked.

The question assumes that the athlete concerned is less than anxious to achieve an objective that a behaviourist coach has set. This may be an objective that he has never wanted to achieve, one that he wanted to achieve once but does not want to achieve now or one about which he is ambivalent, part wanting to achieve it and part not. It may also be that he wants to achieve the objective but does not relish the prospect of the steps that need to be taken for this to happen.

Even as a coach inclined to a behaviourist approach, the first step towards the solution is to discover which of these possibilities is the case. For the first time, perhaps, it will be necessary for either the coach or his assistant to sit down with the athlete and prompt him to talk. It is impossible for the coach, however scheming, to find the way to effective manipulation without knowing what it is about this athlete that makes him unresponsive to the all-purpose techniques that are being applied to the team as a whole.

The strictly behaviourist approach to motivation, used by so many professional coaches, is based on a system of rewards and punishment. The coach, the teacher and the business manager are all in situations of considerable power. The coach can reward a player by re-selection or punish him by leaving him out of the team. He can reward him by allowing him to do some drill that he particularly enjoys or punish him by long demanding and repetitive physical exercises. He can reward him by speaking well of him, holding him up as an example of desired behaviour at a team meeting and punish him by holding him up to ridicule in front of his colleagues. In the case of professional players, an increase of salary or a bonus are often rewards, whereas fines, refusing pay-rises or dismissal are common punishments.

A business manager has a similar range of powers to which may be added techniques such as that of McDonald's, the hamburger chain, who nominate a 'server of the month' or Beechams who name the salesman who gains the highest number of orders. Even the teacher can institute a system of points or token rewards as well as being able to reward with high marks or grades and praise, and punish with ridicule and detention.

A behaviourist coach will soon realise that rewards and punishments can be tailored to the individual athlete for a maximum motivating effect, once it has been discovered what motivates the athlete concerned. If security is a dominant need, then the threat of dropping him or the promise of taking him on tour will be effective. If power is a dominant need, then a promise of a rise in salary or the threat of a string of negative comments to the press will work; and if the most dominant need seems to come in the category of 'love', the behaviourist manager might show willingness to spend time with him (as a reward) or the readiness to pour scorn on him in a team meeting (as a punishment).

Any coach adopting a behaviourist approach will punish such actions as repeatedly playing out of position, ignoring instructions or arguing with the referee and hope that the punishment will repress such behaviour. Hersey and Blanchard list certain conditions which must be observed if punishment is to be effective: (i) when it is meted out, only enough emotion should be shown to gain attention; (ii) it should be clear that a distinction is being made between the individual as a person and that individual's behaviour; (iii) it should be clear what the punishment is for; (iv) punishment should be given as soon after the offence as possible; (v) punishment should be awarded consistently; (vi) there should be no threat of punishment once the system has been made clear; (vii) it should be applied fairly; and (viii) care should be taken that the punishment doesn't begin to *reinforce* the poor behaviour.

To these, Oxendine adds that punishment must (i) be infrequent and (ii) be specific rather than general. (J B Oxendine, *Psychology of Motor Learning*.) Furthermore, since punishment only shows the athlete what he must *not* do and not what *should* be done, the punisher must make sure that the *desired* behaviour is completely clear. Yet, even following all these conditions, punishment can only repress bad behaviour and, at least in the school classroom, it is sometimes observed that *ignoring* it works better. Here the theory is that 'bad' behaviour is itself an attempt to get attention and often other tangible benefits as well. When the behaviour is ignored, the child supposedly finds there is nothing to be gained by continuing in this way and searches a different perhaps more acceptable course to meet his needs.

The punishment and reward system of motivation has other

pitfalls. If a child's good behaviour is ignored, whilst his bad behaviour is punished, the bad behaviour is actually reinforced whilst the good behaviour fades away. In a behaviourist's view, people seldom continue to do things that do not receive positive reinforcement. Singer points out that rewards tend to be more effective than punishment but they have serveral drawbacks: (i) after a while rewards lose their potency, so that the price keeps going up; (ii) in business at least and to some extent in a sports team, a uniform reward does not improve performance, whereas a reward that is given to some members and not others is a potential source of rivalry, detrimental to team spirit; (iii) rewards (in school situations often *praise*) also develop dependence on outside rather than inside motivation and an interest in rewards rather than the activity itself; (iv) a reward system often means that the persons most likely to win them are those who need them least, their enthusiasm already being high. (R N Singer, *Motor Learning and Human Performance*.)

Both behaviourist and humanistic commentators on motivation stress the importance of goal-setting, though still with the difference that for the behaviourist it is an effective way for the coach to achieve his objective whilst, for the humanist, it can lead the athlete to discover best his inherent ability. Carron (see bibliography) points out that when the athlete's performance is evaluated on its own terms, realistic goals lead to success in attaining them, which in turn provides motivation to continue. Goals have to be chosen carefully. If there is only a fifty-fifty chance of them being achieved, motivation slackens and it is almost absent when either failure or success are assured. Motivation is highest, according to Carron, when there is a high probability of failure and a low probability of success. When the chance of success rises to fifty per cent, it is 'time to increase the difficulty of the task, to choose more difficult opponents, to increase goals or to establish more stringent criteria.' Carron also suggests that when an athlete feels he has no chance, his coach should point out the weaknesses of his opponents, relative to the athlete's own strengths and show how these can be exploited.

Obviously, where complacency is a danger, the reverse procedure, stressing the opponents' strength in relation to one's own team's weakness, could also be effective. Some stress motivates, too much inhibits. Carron goes on to point out that performance consequences can be manipulated by (i) establishing criteria; (ii) choice of opponents; (iii) choice of task; (iv) assistance in goal-setting; and (v) evaluation of performance. Precise feedback is an essential step in setting goals for the next performance. In terms of physical practice, it is important to learn new skills in private, away from the stress of evaluation.

Very often, motivating older players is more difficult. They have heard exhortations many times before and, if something has happened to distract their attention or to blunt their enthusiasm, a new tack may be necessary. This could simply be demanding more from them. Hersey and Blanchard write that 'after people reach a certain age, they seldom achieve more than they think they can because they do not attempt things they think they cannot achieve'. Some coaches maintain that older players who are not self-motivated also tend to practice only those things they already do well.

How can I motivate my team?

This is the second behaviourist question. At first sight it would seem that such a coach must find it more challenging to motivate a team than to motivate athletes practising individual sports. We've already said that a uniform reward does not improve performance, whereas a reward that is given to some members and not others is a potential source of rivalry. (Most professional soccer teams in Britain combine a uniform system of bonuses for a match won with widely different salaries for each player, the sum dependent on the player's assessed level of skill.) However, the greatest challenge to the team coach thinking in terms of reward and punishment is that 'what motivates one person may not motivate another nor the same person at another time'. (Hersey and Blanchard.)

Not only will some team members have predominantly 'security' needs, some 'power' needs and some 'love' needs but some members will have progressed to the stage where they are looking primarily for 'self-actualisation', a sense of self-discovery and an increasing meaningfulness in life. A coach who seeks to motivate his team simply with promises and threats relating to money, will find that some athletes respond, others are indifferent and that others, perhaps his key players, are outraged and disaffected by the suggestion. Irish footballer Liam Brady, commenting on his years in Italian football said: 'People are bound to scoff when I say I didn't come here for the money but truthfully there was a hell of a lot more to it. I really was concerned with reaching for my limits. I didn't come to snatch the cash and run. Football is my main means of expressing what's in me and I wanted to find out how much was there.' (Hugh McIlvanney, the *Observer*, 14 October 1984.)

If the coach continues unwaveringly to use the same blanket form of motivation, several players will leave until he has only a group whose needs are primarily for security. Such a squad is likely to be young and immature, responsive to their coach but incapable of improvisation. The coach will have discarded all possibility of true synergy, of reaching a new level of under-standing and skill through the internal conflict of perceptions and ideas, and the team will succeed or fail according to his abil-ity alone. They will probably also become dependent on him and fall apart as a team when he leaves.

This situation will, of course, meet the individual power needs of the coach and, within a narrow framework, will produce a smoothly operating unit. Eventually, though, he may come to trust that his power needs will be met, experience an internal sense of power and, from that point on, begin to perceive the relative lifelessness of his team and seek to make changes. The same applies to the totally authoritarian teacher or business man-ager who eventually feels uneasy with the automatic agreement and lack of joy expressed by his class or department.

In my view, there is only one way out of this dilemma and that is to trust that helping the team towards self-motivation will also result in the kind of success to which the coach is personally attracted. If his job depends on measurable success and he has yet to reach a stage where the excitement of discovery is more ap-pealing than sitting tight, the leap is exceedingly difficult to take. Many a manager makes an occasional foray into the new terri-tory, only to return to familiar ground when disaster threatens. Deciding for safety often means opting for moderate rather than outstanding success. Professional players are professional in the prosaic sense that, at the bottom line, their involvement with the team is a job for which they are paid. Few people in this world opt for enjoyment and adventure at the risk of losing all security. If the coach is repressive, the players will still appear to be doing their best and may well believe that they are. Unfortunately there will be little happening to prod them towards the discovery that their best is much more than they imagine.

Meantime, the amateur coach has less at stake personally and may find that many of his players *demand* enjoyment and adven-ture as motivating elements in their playing for the club. His job is easier but still complex and demanding. He will still have a team of individuals who joined the club to meet differing needs and the character and degree of success of the team will still reflect his own motivation in becoming coach. In search of success he may attempt to motivate the team but first the team has to be created from the group of individuals who are potentially its members. Until this is done, any stated team objective will be deserted by any individual whose personal motivation conflicts with it.

Obtaining support for a team objective is always harder in a sport such as baseball or cricket where there is a minimum of interaction between players during the game. Players in these sports may temperamentally tend to be more individualistic than their counterparts in a game such as basketball or volleyball, where an intuitive connection on the court is a prerequisite for success. Basketball, volleyball, hockey and soccer players inevitably spend time tuning in to each other in training and when warming up, in order to prepare for the demands of the competitive situation. Here professionals have an advantage over amateurs: generally speaking they spend more time in each others' company, have more training sessions and more opportunities for meetings at which team spirit can be built.

If players are to feel motivated during competition, their coach must help them to become acquainted with the feeling during training. To this end, he should make sure that his exercises and drills are imaginative. Even the best drill should not be repeated too often: it's better to introduce one that is less good occasionally, just for variety. Towards the end of the season, when skill practice is less important, a coach can give his football team a game of volleyball or his volleyball team a game of hockey. Incentive is also increased if the reason for the drill is made clear, especially if the reason relates directly to the tactics to be adopted at the next match.

Zander found that strong groups, groups who sit close together, are addressed by name by the leader and choose a group name, will choose challenging goals more often that 'weak' groups, who sit randomly, are addressed as 'you' by the leader and don't choose a group name. Goals tend to be raised after success and lowered after failure. The more individuals perceive their actions to be significant in the group's attempt to reach its goal, and the more individuals are attracted to membership of the group, the more consonant will be group and individual goals. (Alvin Zander, see bibliography.)

Satisfaction of a desire for *group* success is attained equally by the superstars and the substitutes of a team, once that desire has been created or has evolved. Zander showed that 'groups with a strong desire for group success will prefer challenging group goals, whereas groups with a strong desire to avoid failure will prefer either very easy or very hard group goals'. When a team meets repeated failure, it once again becomes difficult to rouse a desire for group success. New easier targets have to be set. The Findhorn volleyball team almost disintegrated in face of a string of defeats. Only a newly adopted objective to put a certain tactic into effect at all cost, during a match, rekindled the desire to achieve as a team.

The one advantage that even the behaviourist team coach has over the coach of an individual athlete is the opportunity to perform, to project himself and inspire through the medium of a team talk. A team talk is, by definition, a monologue. If the coach is a good orator, a good actor or even a good comedian and able to show feeling, he can psyche up players effectively without any real concern for their individual needs. The flamboyant, the unexpected, the astute comments and actions will all raise the tempo. The bravado of George Allen, when coaching the Arizona Wranglers ('We're not going to lose, I won't allow it. It won't happen. We're going to win') (*Los Angeles Times* 24 February 1984) is matched by the subtlety of ex-UCLA basketball coach, John Wooden before the 1964 NCAA final v Duke University ('Does anyone remember which team finished second in the NCAA two years ago?') and the simplicity of the Iowa wrestling team coach who just played the theme tune from *Rocky*. That said, the team coach, like the individual coach, has to be aware (i) that less psyching up is needed for a difficult task; and (ii) that he'll lose much of his effect if he hasn't discovered which athletes tend to be anxious prior to a match and ensure that they have time and space to calm down. Derek Wyatt, ex-England wing three-quarter, when first coaching rugby at Richmond Football Club felt that his pre-match talks weren't evoking the response he expected. Eventually his captain interrupted him: 'Derek, you assume so much about the way us forwards think... Now, as far as the forwards are concerned...' and proceeded to give a completely different talk. Derek's had been low-key, his captain's was 'hype'.

The pre-match talk should constitute the team's emotional, as opposed to mental (and of course physical) warm-up. This is not the time to introduce new information, new tactics or new ideas, nor even to give a complicated account of tactics that were discussed earlier in the week. That constitutes mental preparation and mental preparation should be done a few days before the match. The team talk should be short and to the point. The tactical content should be a clear minimal summary of earlier agreements which had already been summarised into short slogans. If some unexpected or unavoidable event has made a last minute change of personnel or of tactics necessary, the coach should work out in advance how to explain this change in language as simple and uncomplicated as possible. Even the most mature players are unable to absorb intellectual left-brain ideas at this stage, although the coach can help the process considerably by asking them to translate any instruction into a visual and kinaesthetic memory. If the instruction is 'make aggressive runs at the opposition for the first ten minutes', the coach should add 'remember the match against so-and-so where we did exactly that? Take a minute all of you to remember how it *felt* to start the match that way'. Christopher Connolly calls this 'priming the pump'. Remembering the kinaesthetic feeling of something you are about to do prepares the body to do it.

The coach should avoid getting into discussion, unless he has really slipped up and finds several players are confused about the same point. In this case, the resulting chorus of questions should be interrupted by a short clear statement. If anyone still doesn't understand or is obviously worried, the coach speaks to that athlete alone later on, or together with a second athlete who *does* understand and can communicate that understanding both before and during the match.

The talk should be given standing up, the players sitting on one side of the dressing-room. This will come naturally to any behaviourist coach. Each player should be watched and the emotional build-up paced according to what is seen – or rather, according to how what is seen is interpreted, the coach trusting that his interpretation is correct. The preparation for this moment should have been done much earlier and over a long period of time. The coach should know his players and know how to arouse them to a suitable pitch. Which style would be more appropriate? Neil Campbell's exhortation to his Cambridge University crew 'What I mean by beat is beat them so bad that they hang up their oars and never want to row again' (*Guardian*, 2 February 1985), – Australian rugby coach Alan Jones' 'In my view, in life, there are four things which never come back: the arrow which is fired; the spoken word; time spent; and neglected opportunity. Today we have the opportunity to be either a foot-note or a headline in rugby history.' (David Hands, *The Times*, 9

January 1986.) The main challenge will be to give confidence to the anxious, whilst exciting the laid-back, a task for which the behaviourist is less well equipped than the humanistic coach.

It should be added that mid-game talks – at half-time in soccer, at time-outs in volleyball – more often need to calm the athletes down than excite them, and so should be composed of one or two clear instructions with only a final sentence of emotional lift. Peter Shreeve used to excel here, where many other managers or coaches are so excited themselves that they can hardly speak. Peter kept it simple, yet had a vivid choice of words: 'I'm *insisting* that you do a support run to take pressure off the player who has just the goalie to beat', 'I'm *sure* that if you're on the right, being rushed at and turn to play it that way but play it to the left, you'll be successful', or just 'do this and I'll carry the can if we lose at the end.' Since rugby and hockey players only have three or four minutes' break and their coach is not allowed to talk to them, he had best nominate or hope the players choose a cool-headed tactical team member as captain. It is also advisable to decide the routine for those few minutes and practice it in advance. Is the talk going to precede or follow tightening laces and checking for knocks?

How can an athlete motivate himself?

During the summer of 1985, I had a session with Sandy Baruah, one of the Haringey Cricket College team, who said he was depressed about his batting. 'What's wrong?' I asked. 'I can't concentrate, I'm asleep, not ready,' he replied and it gradually became clear that he really *was* asleep: that he was staying up till six in the morning on the night before each match, playing cards.

The interesting thing was that he'd chosen to consider his behaviour a problem and to discuss it with me. In essence his question was 'How do I motivate myself to play cricket as well as I can?' When I asked if he had any suggestions, his first was that he go to bed earlier but I asked him to put that aside for a moment. 'Anything else?' 'Well, I could have a cold shower before my innings and I could probably use mental rehearsal to help change this habit I have of cutting a ball pitched on the leg stump.'

This was uncomplicated and something he was clearly prepared to do, so we set up and went over a mental rehearsal (in which he dealt correctly with a ball pitched on the leg stump) which he would practise each evening when he got home. Then it was time to return to the suggestion that he should go to bed early the night before a match.

The important thing for him to recognise was that there were two Sandys: one who wanted to bat well and another who wanted to play cards until six in the morning. It wouldn't help for the Sandy who wanted to bat well to dictate to the other Sandy that he went to bed early. The card-playing Sandy would inevitably sabotage the scheme. Instead, I suggested that the Sandy in front of me discover more about the needs of his card-playing self. What were those needs and could they be satisfied in any other way, which would allow him to go to bed early on Friday night?

One way for an athlete to combat the sense that he lacks motivation is to do the Gestalt acting exercise already mentioned on pages 46 and 82. This begins by him asking himself 'What is stopping me from being motivated?'. Having got an answer, he should then allow the 'stopping' part to become so real that he can get it to sit on a chair in front him and can *speak* to it. He must be the self that wants to be more motivated and talk to the self that is holding him back, then change chairs, *become* the one that's holding him back and reply. This is important because he does in fact have a perfectly good reason for sabotaging his own motivation, which he doesn't normally allow himself to examine. If he allows himself to act out the exercise with feeling, he will probably find a resolution, a way in which all needs can be met without a conflict of interests. Sandy, for instance, found that his main need was to focus on something totally other than cricket, the evening before an important match. Staying up until six in the morning happened because he was with friends who wanted to do that. He soon found that playing and listening to music, sometimes alone and sometimes with different friends, provided the required change of focus, without leading to late Friday nights.

Often the solution to a lack of motivation will involve setting *intermediate* goals. Perhaps the athlete discovers that strong anxiety is a factor which inhibits his motivation. In that case, he must think of a step towards his ultimate goal which would be challenging to him but not scary – a step that he would mark, on a scale of one to ten, as only four or five degrees scary rather than nine or ten. He then makes that step his next objective.

The idea of the athlete acting out a dialogue between himself and the part of him that impedes his motivation or enjoyment may seem strange, yet most athletes experience some such conflict at some stage of their career. John McEnroe said after his on-court outbursts at the 1983 Paris Open 'I'm two different people. To describe me as Jekyll and Hyde is overstretching the point but I react to situations in a manner which is completely inexplicable. I don't have control and later I can't work out why my emotions ran away. I want to win so much that I do things I'm sorry for later... Some fans tell me they love it when I get angry. But there's another side of me – the nice guy. Maybe it doesn't show too much. I want the two to mesh together and for people to understand the part of me that honours commitments, that is integrity.' (Frank Burcombe, *News of the World*, 19 June 1983.) The *Gestalt dialogue* exercise and the subsequent *intermediate goal-setting* is one way to get two conflicting 'selves' to mesh together. Other Sporting Bodymind exercises which can be used to improve motivation are *setting priorities* (see page 191), *mental rehearsal* (page 157) of a time when the athlete did feel motivated, and *affirmations* (page 155) arising from that mental rehearsal.

How may an athlete be helped towards self-motivation?

This is a humanist's question. Carron points out to the behaviourist coach that 'the athlete's personality, aspiration level and intrinsic interest ... [are] a source of motivation which is largely independent on the actions of the coach'. For this reason, he suggests that the coach would do well to take into account the individual player's character. The humanistic coach will *also* seek out as much information about each of his players as he can but instead of doing so to manipulate the athlete's behaviour and to serve his own ends, his objective is to help the athlete discover and delight in the expression of his ability, trusting that this will also meet some of his own objectives and lead the team to a better overall performance. David Davies has described how Welsh rugby coach Carwyn James would always speak to each player individually prior to a match. 'James was a genius of a rugby man and nowhere was it more evident than in his pre-match talk. A smile, a wink, a clenched fist, a quiet word, an exhortation. He sent them on to the pitch fervent... When Carwyn did the rounds of the 1971 Lions team in New Zealand he left one man till last. To Barry John, James contented himself with: "Look after yourself, King."' (*Guardian*, 13 September 1985.) Certainly the encouragement given along these lines will help the athlete towards self-motivation. To adapt Carron, self-motivation serves to energise, select and direct performance.

The self-motivated athlete is not hard to recognise. Keith Burkinshaw had little use for any other kind. 'The driving force for the true player,' he told me a few days before leaving Tottenham, 'is (i) that he loves playing soccer; (ii) pride in himself, in his team and in his club; and (iii) last and *least*, the money. Look at Mike Hazard, at Ossie Ardiles (he's thirty-one now), their faces light up when they see a soccer ball, and Steve Perryman, he's played 760 odd games yet comes alive the moment he gets on to the pitch.' Martin Bell, British ski champion, said 'I'm motivated by the experience, quite apart from winning or losing. The speed is always a surprise. All the thrill never wears off.' (*Today*, 9 March 1986.) A sudden inability to deal with pressure (we look at this in chapter eight) can take this all away. Chris Lightbown of *The Sunday Times* evoked the most wistful of observations from winger Chris Waddle, soon after he moved from Newcastle FC to Tottenham: 'The football side's great, but some mornings you think of all the extra pressures, and wonder whether you'll be able to cope. But then I remember Kevin Keegan at Newcastle. He had a great thing whereby every morning he got up, and he looked forward to it.'

Self-motivators are 'more concerned with personal achievement than with rewards of success'. (Hersey and Blanchard.) For them, participation itself is rewarding. Typically, they seek precise assessment of their performance afterwards so that they can adjust their goals and tactics for the next occasion. This contrasts with the attitude of athletes who are still externally motivated and whose first concern is how people feel about their performance. Self-motivators also take responsibility for their performance, whereas the externally motivated athlete often blames a poor result on bad luck. 'With self-actualising people, managers need to worry less about being considerate to them and more about how to enrich their jobs and make them more challenging and meaningful. Managers become facilitators rather than motivators and controllers.' Hersey and Blanchard are speaking of business managers but what they say applies equally well to coaches and teachers.

Dorothy Harris makes a distinction between *intrinsically* and *extrinsically* motivated athletes. She says intrinsically motivated athletes are like children. Both naturally experience a sense of 'flow' which she describes as (i) a merging of action and awareness; (ii) a narrowing of the field of attention; (iii) heightened body awareness; (iv) control of action and environment; (v) coherent and non-contradictory demands for action; and (vi) an intrinsic reward system. (Dorothy Harris, see bibliography.)

This is the experience of the artist, of photographer Alfred Fisenstaedt, who said that when he first used a Leica camera, 'the camera short-circuited my brain and I could literally think through my eye and fingers'. (*The Times*, 29 June 1984.) It was also the experience of footballer Alan Ball: 'My greatest natural ability has always been ... I don't know, a kind of awareness. I see things on a football field long before they actually happen. I can see dangers, or openings. A sixth sense. Something I really can't explain at all, I was just able to see.' (*The Times*, 22 June 1983.)

The athlete who experiences this sense of 'flow' incidentally inspires the best in sports journalism. When McEnroe beat Connors in the 1984 Wimbledon final, David Irvine wrote in the *Guardian*: 'McEnroe seemed to have so much more time. At the net his racquet snaked out like a lizard's tongue to snap up a few returns Connors could muster', (9 July 1984), whilst Rex Bellamy wrote in *The Times*: 'His anticipations are so fast that he seems to make time stand still. On yesterday's evidence he is also a mind-reader (the mind being Connors') and can be in two places at once. An example of the latter quality occurred when McEnroe fell when advancing to the net. Connors popped the ball into the open court. Just a formality. But McEnroe was waiting – a perfect facsimile of the McEnroe who was lying on the ground yards away – and hit a winner down the line.' (9 July 1984.)

It is a fair bet, that at this stage of his life at least, McEnroe was 'intrinsically' motivated. Dorothy Harris goes on to define extrinsically motivated athletes as those who have been distracted by external rewards. When an athlete focuses on external rewards, his performance is directed towards what happens *afterwards* and he loses his sense of flow.

Perhaps my favourite newspaper article of 1985 was Dudley Doust's profile of snooker star Hurricane Higgins, 'Portrait of a legend in his bad year'. In it Higgins, left by his wife and children in his large empty house, describes how enjoyment and 'flow' can slip away hand in hand. 'The Hurricane, as usual, looked pale, drawn, vulnerable, flaky, rat-smart and exhausted. "I haven't enjoyed snooker in a long long time. I haven't gone cruising in the last five years, maybe more," he said in his frail lilting Ulster accent. "Cruising? That's the moment when suddenly everything goes silky-smooth without trying. It's golden. It's magic. It hasn't happened because the travel, the family, have taken too much out of me. I didn't feed my talent and I was slowly going down and down, slowly but surely." He inhaled again, drawing himself deeper into despair. "I don't want to go down. I want to start fighting. I want to keep at it – practice, practice – until the enjoyment returns. Snooker is all I've got left in my life." In reply the house fell silent.' (*Sunday Times*, 24 November 1985.)

Cruising, being in the Zone, having a sense of 'flow' or a 'peak experience' are all similar and have a strong element of the kinaesthetic awareness that we help the athlete to recreate when he comes to a Sporting Bodymind session. Gestaltists, as already mentioned, have little use for questions that begin with 'Why?...'. Instead we tend to ask 'What?...' or 'How?...': '*What* are you doing?' or '*How* do you experience that?', rather than 'Why do you do it?'. In directing the athlete's attention to what he is actually doing, you are helping him to make fine adjustments that he might not otherwise make. Similarly, in terms of motivation, don't ask *why* an athlete is motivated by financial rewards but how is that for him? Answering the 'how' question will lead him to greater understanding and eventually to confidence and self-motivation.

When Carlos Lopes was questioned about his training programme, after winning the marathon at the 1984 Olympics, he said 'The keys are endurance and happiness.' (*Los Angeles Times*, 13 August 1984.) Daley Thompson told Cliff Temple how he came to enjoy training for his weakest event, the 1500 metres. 'I saw Jurgen [Jurgen Hingsen, his only true rival at the time] in September and he told me that if ever we got to the state in the decathalon where he had to beat me by ten seconds in the final event, the 1500 m, in order to win, then he could murder me. And ever since that conversation, I've run every single day, even if I didn't feel like it. I just recall that remark and it gets me out of the house. He'll never learn, that Hingsen, never learn. That's what I like about him!' (*Sunday Times*, 29 December 1985.)

If enjoyment is associated with self-motivation, the well-used instruction 'Just go out and enjoy yourself' must be along the right lines. However, it has to be recognised that the instruction can be interpreted in different ways. One athlete, whose needs are for respect or adulation, may then feel entitled to 'play to the crowd' and give a display of bravura when the situation demands patience and care. Another, whose needs are for financial reward, may play cautiously in an attempt to win by amassing a higher score than anyone else, when the team needs

him to open out and take more risks. Both might enjoy their performance as they experience or look forward to experiencing the
rewards they seek. So the instruction 'Just enjoy yourself' must
be tied down to enjoyment of the kinaesthetic sense of playing
well. Such encouragement not only guides the athlete towards a
better performance but also helps him towards the experience of
self-motivation.

When I guide an athlete through a mental rehearsal of a
specific skill, one which he performed particularly well on a particular past occasion, I usually ask at some point 'And how does
that feel?'. Invariably with eyes still closed, the answer is 'Great!'
or 'Good!' and a large smile. I might then ask '*Where* does it feel
good? What's happening in your body just now?'. The athlete is
then in touch with the sensation and motivating force of his own
enjoyment. The instruction to treat himself to this memory for
five minutes each day is no great hardship and if, after our initial
practice of the rehearsal, we look at what exactly he was doing
then (in a technical, physical and psychological sense), which he
may not be doing consistently now, a set of logical steps can be
mapped out which will lead to the athlete recapturing that form.

Where an athlete admits to a lack of motivation, either directly
or indirectly, I follow the procedure I followed with Sandy. I first
ask him about his current needs and how far he is able to satisfy
them by performing his sport. I'd probably ask what led him to
join the club or start training and whether the needs he had then
are the same as those he has now. Together we explore what
changes he might make in order to satisfy his current needs,
whilst allowing himself to regain his appetite for his sport. This
may well develop into another role-playing exercise. I could also
introduce some of the other exercises suggested as profitable for
the athlete who wants to motivate *himself*.

How can I as coach help my team towards self-motivation?

It has long been established in the world of business that involvement in the decision-making process gives a sense of mastery
over job and work environment and that this leads to feelings of
competence, increased motivation and increased production. It
is a general rule that commitment increases when people are
involved in their own goal-setting and 'in organisations where
cohesive work groups have developed goals paralleling organisational goals, there is high productivity and people come to work

gladly because work is inherently satisfying'. (Hersey and Blanchard.)

The process of guiding an athlete towards self-motivation is akin to guiding him towards maturity. One of the changes that occur along this path is that of the athlete depending less on appropriate goals being set for him, until he reaches the point where he feels he knows best and wants to set his own 'potentially achievable' goals. If, at this stage, athletes feel that goals are imposed upon them which they feel to be restrictive or inappropriate, they will become dissatisfied and either physically or psychologically begin to withdraw, failing to turn up, complaining of injury and saying less and less in team meetings.

Even if, as a humanistic coach, you have a team of young relatively immature athletes, you won't stand up and rant at them. Instead, you'll begin the process of guiding them to maturity by asking their opinion before giving your own. At least, you'll do this at a discussion meeting, where the previous performance is reviewed and the next one in line is planned. And if you sense that some young athletes are reluctant to speak their opinion in front of the team as a whole, you will divide the team into random groups of three or according to tactical placements, and ask that everyone expresses their opinion on one or two specific questions, before calling the team back together for a general discussion. If the topic therefore is the next team goal and how to reach it, everyone is encouraged to think and express an opinion before a final decision is made. Even if you decide to implement a decision other than those suggested by your young players, the exercise will have been valuable. Having considered the question in some depth themselves, they will be better able to appreciate your viewpoint, when you express it at the end.

Dividing the team into small groups allows individuals within the team to learn from each other. When we first started small-group meetings at Tottenham, in the run-up to the 1982 FA Cup victory, Keith Burkinshaw felt he should monitor the meetings as much as possible, showing his interest and encouragement. However, it soon became clear that when he joined one of the groups his interest inhibited free expression, except by senior players, and thereby negated the point of the division. As coach or manager, you do best to encourage your athletes to strengthen the ties between each other, creating as many possibilities for this to happen as you can. If your division into smaller groups or into pairs is wise and well-thought out, you discover that the team can indeed motivate itself in ways that are beyond your own influence. The pairing of mature with immature, self-motivated with externally-motivated players in itself does much to foster self-motivation within the team.

The boost to confidence and motivation given by small groups happens too when the group of athletes is a small informal team. The young male Swedish players on the international tennis circuit – Mats Wilander, Joakim Nyström, Stefan Edberg, Anders Jarryd and Hendrik Sundstrom – have formed such a group. As Sundstrom put it: 'We are all really a team, we always watch each other's matches whenever possible, we hang around together a lot during tennis tournaments and we also like speaking Swedish together. It's a language few people on the circuit understand.' (*Tennis Magazine*, August 1985.)

Your dressing room talk prior to the match is similar in form to that given by the behaviourist coach. Not only will you now stand in front of your seated players but, in this case you may even rant a little, if ranting is going to be appreciated as an act. You have however two clear advantages. The first is that your players have already had a hand in deciding the goal and tactics to be employed in the coming competition: now you have only to re-evoke the spirit of the decision-making process, voicing the decision itself as a slogan to re-arouse the spirit of group effort. The second is that you can both give confidence to the anxious athlete and excite the laid-back athlete, whilst addressing the team as a whole – something that is very difficult for a behaviourist coach to achieve. This will be in part because the laid-back players will easily be persuaded to pair off with the over-aroused (if they haven't done so already) so that a positive median is attained by all. The other factor is that, once your team works synergetically, it acquires a 'Group Being' (see page 83), a unique personality, and, by addressing this 'Being' appropriately, you will be addressing all the diverse individual members appropriately as well.

Here admittedly you could be said to be motivating the team, rather than helping the team to motivate itself. However, the humanistic coach is very much more an integrated part of the team, albeit with a function (of leadership) quite distinct from that of other members. Neil Campbell says all his crews have been 'families', of which he becomes a part. In this sort of team, each person does his bit. 'The greatest asset a coach can have,' says Campbell, 'is to motivate. To be able to motivate, *they* (the crew) have got to be able to motivate *you*. It's a two-way street.' (Christopher Dodd, *Guardian*, 2 February 1985.)

Your authority now stems from acceptance rather than impo-
sition. You respond to a situation rather than initiate, believing
there is more to be expressed than that which would fit into a
mould of your own making. Above all, you question rather than
tell and, if you do tell, it is because that is part of the agreement
you have with the player or players concerned. A question provokes thought, even when there is no space allowed for a reply.
Even a pre-match talk can be full of rhetorical or actual questions,
as long as they are designed to remind players of previously
reached agreements and are not allowed to prompt an unnecessary discussion. Peter Shreeve's first words 'Are we clear then of
our play today?' served to focus attention on the match at hand.
They were immediately followed by the rest of his talk, with no
space for a voiced response.

However, many sports teams, even professional teams, do not
have any kind of ritual pep-talk or emotional warm-up prior to
performance. Even Harry Parker, before one Olympic final, only
said: 'Well, there are a lot of good crews out there today, so if you
want to win, you'll really have to dig in and get it.' (Halberstam.)
Personally, I believe that such a low-key approach must fail to
draw the best from the team. It is frequently adopted where athletes feel they 'know each other well enough' and that 'anyway,
many team members prefer to prepare in their own way' – ignoring the fact that a change and intensifying of focus should occur
just prior to a match. Peter Roebuck suggests that this often happens in first class cricket. Not only do players spend weeks away
on tour together and hours at a time playing a match but cricket is
a sport where interaction between team members is more limited
than most. On the fielding side the slips, wicket-keeper and
bowler are a team within a team, maintain close contact and
cheer each other on but the outfielders, whilst supporting this
inner group and rushing in to hug its members whenever a
wicket is taken, *are* physically outside the magic circle and relatively alone. As for the batting side, every man experiences the
pressure to score and, as with football strikers, this pressure
tends to make the player think 'me first', however team-
conscious he might be.

Perhaps as a result of the game's dynamic, more players than
usual are likely to prefer spending time on their own, rather than
warming-up as a group. There is also the fact that the 'leader' is
usually the captain, a playing member of the team. The more his
inclination is towards preparing himself emotionally alone, the
less he is likely to call players together for a team talk – besides, if

he *is* to give a talk, when would he give it? No one knows until ten minutes before the game starts, which side is to bat and which to field. It could be that, having had a rousing team talk, the side discovers it is to bat. Only two members of the team then go out to play, whereas, as often as not, the others settle down to play cards.

This can make life hard for a young player, in a game where there is usually a wide range of ages and experience within the team. It can also keep life relatively joyless for the older cynical player whose too often expressed flippancy drives the enthusiasm and excitement of young players back inside themselves, where it can all too easily turn into anxiety.

In such team sports, the need is for ritual, a norm to be established whereby every member of the team can unaffectedly touch into the experience of team spirit. If the man in charge has no fluency and little easy sense of humour, he should condense his talk into a matter of three sentences, knowing that providing a moment's focus is the main aspect of his job. At Findhorn, I began meetings with twenty seconds of total silence, followed by a single reflection on our group identity or purpose. Yes, the fact of arriving together in a changing room *does* orientate us towards the match we are about to play but, if nothing is said, the chance of touching into the unique motivating power of team spirit is lost. Even the academic is strongly in favour of the team talk: Zander's advice is to 'emphasise the unity of the group, the score as a product of team effort, and the perception that all members are within the group's boundary'.

I prefer the words of an unknown enthusiast, writing the record sleeve blurb to *Preservation Hall Jazz Band, Vol. 1*, and describing the traditional music of New Orlean's most famous band: 'In this style of music, where the musicians strive to help each other rather than grab the spotlight, it is natural for improvised choruses to be a feature. Working together harmoniously can generate a feeling of power. The ensemble often builds with cumulative effect and surging momentum to thrilling climaxes.' This perfectly describes the visible motivating force that the performance of one European player had on another, orchestrated by the echoing applause of vast crowds in all corners of the Belfry Golf course, during the final day of the 1985 Ryder Cup competition. Cricketers can do this too by showing courage at the crease but, if there has been no attunement prior to the innings and things are going badly, many players in the team will disappear from the balcony and join the dressing-room game of cards.

This isn't *wrong*. It just fails to make use of the emotional energy available and leaves each individual batsman to play a truly solo performance.

Whether in team meetings, during training sessions or at other times when with the players, the humanistic coach's main task is to help individual team members to discover, respect and meet the needs of each other. As the individual discovers how much other team members depend on him reaching his goals, the more important those goals will be to him. The coach must demonstrate that no individual can achieve success unless the team does also, helping team members to become as involved in the team performance as a whole as he is in his own contribution. The aforementioned Ryder Cup team gave a fine demonstration of this as those members who had completed their rounds, joined Tony Jacklin and walked back down the course to encourage the remaining members over the last few holes.

7

CONFIDENCE

There are bound to be misunderstandings between a humanistic sports psychologist and a predominantly behaviourist coach. If Keith Burkinshaw and Peter Shreeve sometimes thought me naive, I was occasionally shocked by their cynicism. Every athlete has some habitual responses, attitudes and patterns of thought which limit his performance in some way. These are 'games' that he plays and, as he becomes more aware of them and better understands their logic, he is already taking a step towards positive change. My job is to watch, to listen and to reflect to the athlete what I notice. I will also prompt him to identify his objectives whatever they may be and help him to decide how to reach them. I am not there to be convinced, to believe or disbelieve. This is open to misunderstanding by both the athlete, if he has been *required* to see me, and by the coach, if he wants to coerce his athlete into producing a performance to meet his own requirements. The coach, his objective firmly in view, has to think of the team unit and must often make a rapid assessment and decision. Hence the tendency to sweeping and contentious generalisations, such as Keith's: 'A loss of touch is always a loss of confidence'.

This generalisation in particular demands consideration. A player who is blaming everyone and everything but himself for his poor form would certainly benefit from such a challenge, for no one would argue long with the assertion that loss of confidence is accompanied by a loss of form. 'When my confidence is low, I can't pass accurately. When it's high, I can,' said Danny Thomas, at a time when he was still fighting his way out of Tottenham reserves and into the first team. However, loss of form

144

can result from physical disability, any number of distractions and the whole range of emotions. When the athlete is aware of such reasons for his loss of form, loss of confidence will only result much later, if and when he finds himself unable to eradicate the root cause.

Confidence grows with experience yet, whereas 'touch' or 'form' refers to total performance, it's quite possible for an otherwise mature and confident athlete to be deficient in a particular skill or technique and to be vulnerable and lacking in confidence in certain situations. Any athlete of whatever standing in whatever sport can respond to the question, 'What are you working on at present?' or 'What is it about your performance that you want to improve?' Often the response will be given in a positive way that shows excitement in the face of an identified challenge. Yet, just as often, the reply will be a wry laugh, followed by 'Well, there's always my backhand or my service', betraying the fact that in this aspect of performance the athlete is *im*mature, has never worked consistently or effectively towards improvement and has never become fully confident. It may be through inertia, a lack of attraction to this aspect of performance and a resultant skimping on practice or it may be that this particular technique is much more demanding. Diver Greg Lougarnis, even after his double Olympic win, said the tenth and last dive of a competition was as difficult for him as the first. 'You're up there thirty-three feet above the water, with not a whole lot on, and seven people judging you. It's a very vulnerable position. You've got to have a lot of confidence.' (*New York Times*, 13 August 1984.)

In *The C Zone: Peak Performance under Pressure* – a book for the business world that any athlete would benefit from reading – Bob and Marilyn Kriegel point out that it isn't mistakes or failures which block confidence, rather it is the fear of making such errors or of failing. Indeed, 'the main obstacle to confidence is fear'. Often this fear is not of physical danger, as encountered by Greg Lougarnis, but rather the fear of judgement by others. This can only be overcome when the athlete sets his own standards. As he matures and develops a strong self-image, he begins to realise that most limitations are self-imposed, that 'confidence is a constant positive experience' of himself 'that is not dependent on anything external'.

Golfer David Edwards commented on his change of self-image, when he won his first US tour event, the 1984 Los Angeles Open, after six years of trying. 'I've learned that to finish in the top ten, to beat 90% of the field, is not to lose and that's

improved my mental approach and made me more confident.'
(*Los Angeles Times*, 20 February 1984.) Contrast this to Ian Baker-
Finch's comment on leading after the third round in the British
Open, later that year. 'I'm not surprised to be leading but I *would*
be surprised to win.' Inevitably he compounded his self-image
by having a disastrous final round the next day. And then this,
from the golfer who was one behind the leader after the third
round of the Buick Open, Michigan, in August 84: 'I still think
I'm going to win. I don't think there's any question in my mind I
can win. When you're playing good, you can't wait to come back
the next day.' (*Los Angeles Times*, 12 August 1984.) Who else but
the forty-four-year-old Lee Trevino? As Peter Dobereiner says,
'In order to beat the world, a golfer must believe himself to be the
best in the world, a notion which players such as Ken Brown and
Sam Torrance have found impossible to accept.' (*Observer*, 5
January 1986.) Not, however, a notion that ever gave US down-
hill skier Bill Johnson any trouble. Ten days before winning the
gold medal at the 1984 Sarajevo Winter Olympics, he was pro-
claiming: 'They know I'm the guy to beat here. I don't know why
the rest of them ever bothered to come. It's going to be a helluva
race for second place. They might as well hand it to me now.' (*Los
Angeles Times*, 6 February 1984.)

'Misplaced' or 'over-' confidence is often not appreciated in a
team sport. Garth Crooks became unhappy at Tottenham, knowing that the manager and even some fellow players considered
him 'flash'. At times he may well have doubted his ability in private, for latterly he often found himself relegated to the reserve
team or substituted in the middle of the match. To those around
him, however, he never ceased to project a positive self-image
and when he was restored to the first team for a part of his last
season with Spurs, and scored goals in an unbroken run of
matches, he wore the mantle of his success with dignity.

Garth was a striker and it seems that a striker has to have a
stronger element of independence, indeed of selfishness (see
chapter three), if he is to be successful. Research seems to show
that people who are naturally independent 'have high ego
strength, favorable self-esteem and realistic images of themselves.' (Critchfield.) They also have 'a greater tolerance for differences and ambiguities in their world views'. I believe that
independents in a team will always run the risk of being outsiders, of being termed 'flash' unless the coach is able to teach his
athletes to discover and respect both their own unique abilities
and those of their team-mates. Again, there is a time for unity

and a time for withdrawal and the team whose team spirit is greatest is a team that blends synergistically the strength of strong, confident, independent members.

Players who join a team in search of strength based on the support of others have still to acquire self-confidence and until they discover confidence within themselves they are unable to contribute fully to the team of which they are a part. The acquisition of such confidence is a gradual process. Young athletes who display exciting ability on the field of play are often still in the process of purposefully building their confidence. In fact, at the beginning of the 1984/85 season, sixty per cent of the Tottenham professionals, when asked what part of their game – physical, technical or psychological – they most wished to improve, replied 'confidence'. Yet most of these players *enjoyed* their work and were clear in what they wanted to achieve: they were committed.

Provided such commitment is harnessed to a realistic goal and realistic steps towards that goal can be agreed, it will itself breed confidence and difficulties will again be perceived as thought-provoking challenges. Confidence is an attitude and attitudes are a mixture of thoughts and emotional feelings and even of physical feelings too. Confidence is experienced physically as a sense of well-being. The Kriegels quote research done at Purdue University which showed that self-confidence and self-assurance increase as physical conditioning improves. 'Participants in the study also became more out-going, more involved with others and more emotionally stable.' Gestalt practice takes the client's attention back to his body: 'And how do you experience that physically?' or 'Where do you experience that?' or 'I notice you're tapping your right foot, if your foot was to speak right now, what would it say?' are common interjections.

Working with footballer Gary Stevens to improve his aggression and 'dominance' in the air, as he searched to win more challenges for the ball in 40 per cent–60 per cent situations, I asked him to go back to a time when he did win such a challenge. He closed his eyes, relaxed and played such an incident through to himself, telling me when he'd finished. 'Okay,' I said, 'go back to the beginning, play it through again and this time tell me what you are experiencing physically.' In the middle of his description, Gary said: 'I feel as if I'm towering above my opponents like . . . like a mountain.'

This was a key exercise for Gary because a month later he had a severe leg injury – a ruptured medial ligament – that kept him out of the game for the rest of the season and well into the next season too. Prior to the injury, he rehearsed the feeling of towering over his opponent, just before each match and found that he began to win more and more 40 per cent–60 per cent balls in the air. Yet once he was injured, he refused to give up and feel sorry for himself. Most athletes are so disappointed and depressed when they get a serious injury, that they shrink into the background, away from the public eye. Not Gary. He realised that he could continue to develop the confidence he needed on the pitch by moving into difficult situations *outside* the context of sport, 'as if he were a mountain', recreating the physical feeling he'd experienced in the original on-the-pitch incident and expressing it in the new situation. This might be anything from speaking at an important or large meeting to going into a shop to buy shampoo. The result was that, despite his injury and prolonged absence from the game, he was able to return when physically fit, not only with much of the confidence which he'd built prior to his injury, but with the additional confidence which he'd developed in non-sporting situations.

I regularly ask my clients to cross reference their sporting and non-sporting lives – not just when helping them to develop some *mental* skill in their sports performance, such as Gary's work on dominance – but also when they want to improve a physical or technical skill. Once again, it means listening to the phrases they use as they describe their performance of the skill concerned. A young tennis player wanting to improve his volley said 'I must get away from it more, in order to volley better' ('it' being the ball), so I asked him 'When else in your life could you do something better if you were to get away from it more?' This particular session ended with the player deciding he would benefit by getting away from other people for a short time each day and by getting away from tennis for an hour or two as well. The connection the athlete draws is sometimes an important discovery and always interests him but the point of the exercise is also a simple one. By carrying out his decision daily – 'to get away' or whatever it may be – he will keep his full attention on the skill he wants to improve. I suggest that he carries out his new task for a limited period of time only, perhaps a week or ten days, the period of time he is going to spend practicing the skill itself in training.

I also explore the athlete's associations with pictures and music (see page 9), again that they become additional oblique reminders of his daily training's present focus. The tennis player put a picture on his bedroom wall for ten days of Ivan Lendl volleying. Gary Stevens found a picture of a mountain. One of the British track cycling team wanting to improve his ability to deal with nerves, when asked what piece of music gave him a feeling of confidence, said the Phil Collins track 'No Jacket Required'. As one of his mental training exercises, he decided to listen to that track before races for a period of three weeks.

Steve Archibald used to identify a lack of confidence with having a dull mind and a tense body. 'When I'm not scoring goals, I'm tense,' he said. 'Ask my wife! And somehow that's when injuries seem to occur.' The 'dull mind' element of reduced confidence is well documented. 'The less self-esteem people have, the less likely they are to try anything new,' say the Craigs, and the Kriegels add: 'Lack of confidence in one situation spreads to a lack of confidence in self.'

Confidence or its lack is often based on what we imagine about a situation rather than on what our physical senses tell us, yet what we imagine is based on what we see and hear. In other words, inappropriate experience can falsify our judgement. Boxing manager Cus d'Amato once said 'The young fighter always perceives his first time opponent as being bigger, stronger and faster than he is.' (Cus d'Amato, *Observations from the Treadmill*.) As a volleyball player, I would sometimes tighten up when I saw a line of tall blockers in front of me and fail to jump high and attack to my full ability. At such times, our coach would either sub me off or call a time-out: 'What's going on? Why aren't you jumping?'. 'Well, look at the size of those guys,' I'd say. 'Well? Yes, they're tall but haven't you noticed how slow they are? You could spike between them almost every time.' My fault was to see that the blockers were tall and to lose confidence because I imagined that meant they could block me, whatever I tried to do. I needed help to realise my imagination was leading me astray, that I was failing to check it with other pieces of information available to me.

In this case, I was able to regain confidence by switching my attention from one objective signal to another. Sometimes though, my assessment of external circumstances would be correct. Whether or not I then lost confidence depended on whether I continued to keep my attention on some factor outside my control (such as my opponent's strength) or whether I shifted my attention back to my own performance, which I could control. 'I don't dwell on things I can't control. What's past is past. It's gone. It's yesterday,' says Don Schula, coach to the Miami Dolphins. (*Los Angeles Times*, 22 January 1983.) As the Kriegels point out: 'the more you focus on the *can't do*, the angrier and more out of control you feel' and 'whether you win a game is outside your control. You can control how well *you* play but not how well your opponent plays'. 'A hitter doesn't have any control over whether he gets any hits or drives in runs . . . What a player *can* control is making sure he sees the ball well every time he goes up, making sure every swing he takes is a good one, making sure he knows the pitcher he is facing', says Karl Kuehl of the Oakland A's base-ball team. (*Sport Magazine*, August 1983.) Mark Falco overcame *his* goal famine by focusing on getting into the penalty box more often, getting into the right position to score, rather than on scor-ing itself.

How to gain confidence

(i) *Helping the individual*

No athlete lacks confidence *all* the time, not even in the restricted sphere of his sports activity. When he sits down, tells me he 'has a problem with confidence' and starts to relate how that is for him, I might well wait until he has had his say and then ask: 'How many times have you felt confident in the last twenty-four hours? Talk to me about one of those occasions' and he might tell me about a practice session he had with his coach or the feeling he experienced as he held his baby child. In this situation again, I listen carefully for phrases he uses to describe this feeling and feed one or two back to him for use as affirmations (see page 155). I might then ask that he close his eyes, relax, visualise the incident and *transpose* the kinaesthetic feeling it evokes into a vis-ualisation of him performing the element of his sport on which he had originally fixed his 'problem of confidence'. I'll come back to this scenario and explore visualisation and affirmations in more detail in a moment.

After this opening, I would ask him to observe and analyse his own pattern of behaviour, to identify the barrier that stands be-tween him and a confident performance, and make a detailed plan of how he may reach his objective. The way for an athlete to regain lost confidence often lies in turning his attention from the actual, imagined and feared judgement of others towards setting his own standards. Inner confidence comes primarily from knowing where he's going. What then are the *specific* situations in which he lacks confidence?

Sometimes an athlete won't know and gets stuck in the statement 'I've lost my confidence'. In this case, he should be asked to make no effort to change anything at all but instead to observe his feelings and behaviour in the next competition, with a view to making a detailed record afterwards. I always suggest to my clients that they go and buy a good-looking exercise book and use it to plan and record their mental training. Robert Nideffer, helping Roger Jones, an American miler who was lacking confidence, made a similar suggestion. 'In your training log, record your negative thoughts: how frequent they are, when they occur, how long they persist. Make a list of things that build your confidence. Set goals independent of winning the race.' (*Psychology Today*, July 1984.) Occasionally, the instruction to observe his reactions non-judgementally and with scientific interest is enough to renew confidence; usually it at least relieves tension and gives the sense of beginning to regain control.

After the competition, I might ask the athlete to divide it into segments and to score the degree of confidence he experienced out of ten, within each segment. Then I'd take the segment or segments that have the lowest score and ask 'What was happening then? What were you most aware of? What were you *imagining* and how was it connected with the object of your attention?'. There are numerous other questions which might be appropriate, beginning with 'What else might you usefully have been aware of?' and the suggestion that his attention might be focused in this direction next time. Pursuing the 'I see/I imagine ... and that makes me feel' tack further (see *Sporting Body, Sporting Mind*), I could ask 'Okay, so that was what you were aware of this time and that's what you imagined and felt but how else might you have interpreted this factor or event? ... What *positive* interpretation might there be?'. Then, if he gives one segment of the performance a notably high score for confidence, I'll ask the first set of questions again: 'What was happening then?' 'What were you aware of?'

I usually maintain this process of observation, self-assessment and questioning over a few performances, even as confidence returns. At the same time, other steps can be taken. Once an obstacle to confidence has been identified, the question must be asked 'Is this something that you can remove or change? and, if so, how would you do that?'. If the answer is 'no', then the question that follows is 'How can you change your *attitude* towards this thing?'.

Usually, the athlete will have good suggestions of his own. However, brainstorming with someone else, whether a sports psychologist, his coach or team-mates can spur new creative ideas, from which he can make an eventual choice. Making the choice himself is important, in that it is a further step towards taking control of the situation, in itself a remedy for lost confidence.

In addition to scoring his level of confidence after the competition, one golfer I worked with kept a journal, recording the ebb and flow of both his confidence and concentration and how the two interlinked. He came to recognise two distinct versions of himself, one who knew his ability and was able to express it, the other immobilised by doubt. Later we explored this with the Gestalt acting game, putting one version of himself on a chair facing him, pretending to be the other version and improvising a dialogue between the two. Often this exercise gives some surprising insights. It works best when there is someone else present to intervene in the dialogue and ask each 'character' leading questions. A question such as 'What *advantage* is there in behaving in this unconfident way?' posed to the self that is lacking confidence can give an important lead. Our actions and attitudes always have good reason. Where they result in discord, inhibiting our ability to achieve our avowed objectives, the tendency is to blank them out or at least to judge them harshly. Invariably, the way forward is not just to recognise but also to accept this part of ourselves, appreciating the logic and ingenuity behind the frustration. This may take some time. Jack Nicklaus was obviously upset at four-putting one green in the 1984 Masters: 'I apologised to myself as I walked off the green,' he said afterwards. 'Trouble was I don't think I could bring myself to accept my apology.' (*Los Angeles Times*, 12 August 1984.) However once the underlying logic is exposed and the hidden needs expressed, the way to find a new method to meet these needs is opened and the conflict can be resolved.

Brainstorming with my client for possible 'action steps' he might use to achieve his objective (in this case to gain or regain confidence), I draw the distinction between left-brain, verbal, logical techniques and right-brain, visual or intuitive ones. Into the first category fall realistic assessment and segmented goals. Any teacher will lead his student or player forward towards mastery of a subject or technique through a series of carefully-graded exercises. When confidence fails, the athlete must reassess his short-term objectives. Are they realistic or should he step back a pace or two? The need to score a goal every game may become an overwhelming burden, better to have an objective of making ten aggressive runs into the penalty box, something which is a step *towards* scoring goals.

At the end of a session with my client, I summarise, writing down (for his reference and my own) his objective and what he has chosen to do towards reaching that objective. So, in the case of a football striker, it might be:

Objective: to regain confidence
Decisions:
  (i) to review the next three matches and give myself a score out of ten for confidence, for each allotted segment
  (ii) to ask my coach to give a score out of ten for my achievement, for each segment
  (iii) to practice shooting an additional twenty minutes each day, after training

To these left-brain tasks will be added others, including relaxation and visualisation exercises, out of which other left-brain exercises, such as writing out affirmations, may arise. 'The key to overcoming fear and increasing confidence,' say the Kriegels, 'is not to think positively but to think realistically . . . Focus and act on what you *can* do. "Can-dos" are clearcut constructive, current and in your control.' 'I never play a shot of which I'm not sure,' says Lee Trevino. 'Improve weak shots on the practice ground . . . Consider the art of the possible . . . the only way you can score is with *your* game.' (*Sportsworld*, December 1973.)

'Control' is a key word for the Kriegels: 'Focusing attention and acting on what you can control maximises performance and effectiveness.' At Tottenham, this was related to basic skills. 'We must get back to basics' was a Tottenham slogan. Paul Miller prescribed this for himself at one session when his confidence was low and Steve Perryman once said 'Individuals must learn how to overcome a bad personal start to a game and get back to basics, things at which they are good'.

The same slogan is used in other sports. Derek Wyatt remembers Bedford RUFC first fifteen once having a very unusual run of three lost matches in a row, despite their six internationals and six international trialists. 'We hadn't just lost them, we'd been thrashed out of sight. We'd never had compulsory training – we thought we were too good – but after the third lost game, Pat Briggs our coach put us in a circle in the main club house and pondered the phrase 'back to basics'. 'Norman', he said to

Norman Baker our erstwhile hooker and a teacher and rugby coach in his own right, "what do you see as *your* basics?" 'Throwing in straight at the line-out," replied Norman. "Covering from the line out. On their ball at the line-out, attacking the scrumhalf. Supporting broken play. Defending the blind side of rucks and maul. Encouraging other players..." He paused. "Yes, that's about it." By which time I was laughing hysterically: our second most senior player had overlooked his main task, hooking the ball in set scrums. Perhaps the reason we never lost three in a row again was to avoid being so embarrassed by Pat's questions.'

When I arrived at Tottenham in 1980, the Argentinian player Ossie Ardiles' first words to me were 'I know what you do. Positive thinking, isn't it?'. 'Well ... not exactly,' I said and did my best to explain. Saying 'Think positive!' to someone lacking confidence is not much help. Even giving them a positive sentence to repeat is unlikely to work if the sentence is yours rather than theirs. In fact, half of the last minute instructions to be heard exchanged in the dressing room prior to a match have little effect on anyone but the person giving the instruction. Information of this kind, however simple, has to be translated by the recipient into right-brain imagined feeling before it can be absorbed.

Sometimes this happens and sometimes it doesn't. When Peter Shreeve told one of his strikers, minutes before the match 'I'm *insisting* that you do a supporting run to take the pressure off the player who has just the goalie to beat', the urgency of tone and the forceful choice of words probably penetrated but, unless the player to whom he spoke actually translated this message into what it would *feel* like to be in such a situation, he probably forgot the instruction in the heat of the game ... and, if he did remember it, if he kept this verbal as opposed to visual message in his mind until an appropriate moment, he very likely (i) made other mistakes and (ii) battered himself with the message 'I *must* do a supporting run ...', with the result that it didn't happen naturally. Ideally, the athlete doesn't need telling anyway and the positive thought, *visual* and *kinaesthetic*, is one he has already chosen and is there because he has trained himself to focus on it well in advance of the competition. 'Joe di Maggio was a great base runner,' explains Don Zimmer, Chicago Cubs third base coach 'because every time he hit a ball he thought of only one thing, a double. No matter where it was hit, he was thinking second base. And a lot of times he made it.' (*Los Angeles Times*, 5 March 1984.)

Simon Callow describes hearing from his agent that John Dexter wanted him to play Orlando in *As You Like it*. Initially shocked at the variance between his image of the character and his image of himself, he first found a way to view the suggestion positively and then began forming a kinaesthetic image of his new role: '"This is folly," I said. "Kamikaze casting. On the other hand, if John Dexter thinks I can play Orlando, I can. Besides, it's obviously going to be the kind of production in which someone like me would play Orlando. He's on." . . . I went into training. I lost weight. I stopped smoking. I thought young, romantic and handsome."' It is a clear *picture* that is required, a non-verbal positive thought. In the words of the *South Pacific* song: 'Gotta have a dream . . . If you don't have a dream, how yer gonna have a dream come true?'

When John Madden asked Vince Lombardi what separates a good coach from a bad one, Lombardi replied 'Knowing what the end result looks like. The best coaches know what the end result looks like, whether it's an offensive play, a defensive coverage, or just some area of the organization. If you don't know what the end result is supposed to look like, you can't get there.' Madden writes 'After that, whenever I put something new into the Raider playbook, I always tried to picture what the end result should look like. And then I worked to create that end result.'

'Attitude determines performance,' say the Kriegels, 'and involves much more than common thoughts. Attitude is influenced by feelings, instincts, mental pictures and physical conditions. Conscious thoughts, the only ingredient in positive thinking, are just a small part of attitude. In fact they are more the result of your attitude than the cause. Trying to change a negative attitude with positive thinking is therefore usually futile and frustrating . . . Using positive self-talk in an attempt to change negative self-talk is fruitless.' As Hersey and Blanchard point out, 'the addition of emotion often makes attitudes more difficult to change than knowledge'.

Yet there *are* positive sentences which can improve confidence and which I will ask a client to write out on a card and stick on his bedroom wall. Such sentences as we've just seen (page 150) are called *affirmations*, a left-brain exercise to improve performance, which is a verbal equivalent of right-brain use of images. Brad Lewis and Paul Enquist, the US Olympic champion rowers, who adopted the affirmation 'No-one beats us' as a part of their concentration training (see page 37), combined a second affirmation with a physical image to improve their motivation. This was a three-foot inflatable shark, with the words 'Stay Hungry' written on it. They also described themselves as 'warriors', and used this one word affirmation (termed by Sporting Bodymind an 'evocative word') to evoke the powerful feeling described by Carlos Casteneda in his Don Juan books. They sought to be warriors in all that they did.

How is an affirmation different to 'positive thinking' or 'positive self-talk'? Put simply, the difference is that an affirmation is a sentence that comes from something the athlete said, that the words are essentially *his own*. The sentence is positive because it is part of a description of a positive situation. The simplest though not the most effective way to get an affirmation that will help an athlete to improve his confidence is to ask him to describe a person who to him *has* this quality. Usually the person described will be another athlete, if not of the same team, at least of the same sport but it is important to note that the description could well be of *any* person doing anything confidently. I asked one golfer 'If I ask you to imagine someone who is confident, who would it be?' and got the surprising but perfect answer 'A man in a pin-stripe suit going in to a restaurant'. At Tottenham, on the other hand, I asked Mike Hazard and he said 'Ossie Ardiles'. Either way, my response is 'Imagine you *are* this person and describe what you're doing and what you're feeling and thinking as you do it. You can get up and act out the part completely if you like'. Then all I need to do is to wait, with pen and paper in hand, for the striking sentence, the affirmation to be spoken.

The response is often startling. Top athletes have great sensitivity; sometimes their words are poetry. 'I remember Ed (Moses) on T.V. at the Olympics in Montreal, with the hood up and the glasses,' says Andre Phillips, the man who has often been second to the seemingly unbeatable world champion. 'The dud had come out of nowhere and there he was and you still couldn't *see* him. No face. Edwin was like the Lone Ranger. No. He was more like a ghost. The Ghost. He was there but he wasn't. He was – like, wow! – hands-off, alone, cool. I *really* got into hurdles after that.' (*Sports Illustrated*, 30 July 1984.) From poetry to acting is a short step. 'Right, go out and train *as if* you're a ghost,' I might have suggested, had Phillips been a client wanting to develop cool confidence. Snooker player Alex Higgins has, for his part, the simplest of vivid affirmations. 'I am the Hurricane,' he said, on winning a match with a break of 142. (BBC TV, 25 February 1985.)

The most *effective* way to get an affirmation is first to do one of the visualisation exercises of the *performance practice* mental rehearsal category. If the athlete says that he has *lost* confidence, I sidestep the question 'What for you is confidence?' by asking him, as suggested earlier, to remember the last time he did feel confident. Should he claim never to have felt confident whilst playing his sport, I either ask 'Which athlete for you is the epitome of confidence?' or the original question: 'Think of a time outside your sporting life, when you felt really confident'. Either way, I suggest the occasion should be the most recent of the memories that come to mind (in the case of visualising another athlete, to see him demonstrating confidence recently) but this is less important than that the image should be vivid.

Having chosen an occasion to rehearse, the athlete then sits back in his chair and closes his eyes. I ask him to spend a moment noticing the sounds he can hear outside the room before bringing his attention back into the relative stillness of the room where he won't be disturbed and then draw back further into an awareness of the position in which he is seated. Having invited him to make himself more comfortable, I then ask him to take a deeper breath, hold it for a moment and then slowly exhale . . . and, as he does so, I lead a short relaxation by directing his attention to each of his main muscle groups, from head down to feet, suggesting that he allows each group to rest and the feeling of letting go to spread downwards till he is able to feel that he allows the chair and the floor to hold his whole weight.

A moment later I ask him to play through mentally a short 'clip', one particular sequence of movements from his chosen occasion which typifies the experience of confidence which he seeks. I ask him first to set the scene, being aware of the nature, colour, light and movement of his surroundings, noticing who else is there and what he is feeling and then ask that, when he's played the sequence right through, he lets me know. I ask him to repeat the process once and then to return to the beginning and this time to talk me through, to tell me what is happening as he experiences it again, talking in the present tense, 'as if it's happening now'.

As he does this, his eyes still closed, I write down as much of what he says as I can, taking special notice of any words or phrases that strike me as vivid or unusual. If the account is too short, dry or technical, I'll break in on a second hearing with questions, also asked in the present tense. Usually I would then ask, 'How does it feel physically to perform like that?' and, if the answer is 'Good!' as it often is, I'll ask how or where it feels good.

I may then suggest that he plays the scene through once silently as if *watching* his performance from outside: as if he is his coach watching himself. When he says that he's finished, I'll ask what he noticed and write that down too. Then, to finish with, I'll ask him to play through the scene silently twice more, this time from within himself, from the original 'inner' viewpoint, being particularly aware of how it feels *kinaesthetically* to perform in this way.

When he opens his eyes and readjusts to the room, I'll go through my notes with him, finding one or two sentences which can be good affirmations. Some slight change of tense or length may be required but the words and the feeling those words convey are not only his but are tightly connected to his personal experience of the confidence he is seeking to bring back to his performance. It is now that I can add items (iv) and (v) to the list of decisions I began to make earlier (see page 153). Decision (iv) will be to write out the affirmation and stick it on his bedroom wall (or into his wallet, purse or pages of a book he's reading, – Gary Stevens put his affirmation on to the board on which he keeps a note of pints delivered by the milkman); and decision (v) will be to sit down quietly in a room on his own at a specific time each day (usually before the evening meal) for five or ten minutes and repeat the relaxation and mental rehearsal exercise a few times over. Even the athlete who can find no memory of being confident whilst performing his sport and, instead of choosing another athlete as his model, worked with a memory of himself in a non-sporting situation – teaching a class, flying a kite or talking to a customer confidently – will find regular practice of visualising this situation will improve his ability to perform his sport confidently, particularly if he begins to do the rehearsal just before his sports performance as well as at home. And, as suggested on page 150, he may even manage to transfer his feeling of teaching – or whatever – confidently into a newly-constructed imaginary scene of himself performing his sport and begin to practice this new rehearsal too.

Visualisation is sometimes difficult for the type of athlete who wants a reason for everything and finds it hard to relax but most athletes take to it easily. Glenn Hoddle and Steve Perryman both told me they have *always* visualised but not as a deliberate regular practice. John Madden believes coaches must visualise too. After ten years coaching the Raiders, 'I got to the point where I couldn't coach any more. All my life, I've pictured myself doing things. Playing ball as a kid. Coaching on the sidelines. Even now, in preparing for my T V games, I picture players I'm going to be talking about. But in 1978, suddenly I couldn't picture myself on the sidelines the next year. That's when I knew I'd had it.' With practice, visualisation can be used in an increasing number of appropriate situations.

Practising a mental rehearsal daily at home will improve the skill or the attitude being rehearsed. This type of mental rehearsal is called 'performance practice'. There are however *other* types of mental rehearsal which can be employed immediately before and also during competition. Whereas a football or basketball player might learn to rehearse his 'confidence' visualisation in the dressing room lavatory, a golf player or gymnast or high jumper can eventually rehearse his technique and the manner of its performance just a few seconds before making his shot, vault or jump. Of all the entire sequence of ritual preparation that Greg Lougarnis completes as he stands on the edge of the high-board, an 'instant pre-play' rehearsal of the dive he is about to perform is the key element.

Visualising a quality *during* performance is called an 'As if . . .' visualisation. It also requires practice but this time practice is usually done during a physical practice session. Essentially, this technique is another acting exercise. Martina Navratilova, after losing to Steffi Graf in the final of the 1986 German Open tournament, spoke of the training she had been doing with her coach Mike Estep, for improving confidence. 'I get upset because I should have done better. That's me not feeling confident. Mike is working on that with me. He is always telling me to act confident and sooner or later it'll come back.' (Georgina Howell, *Sunday Times*, 22 June 1986.) Good players *can* act. 'Act confident' may be an American cliché but taken literally it is good advice.

Working with a client during a normal mental training session in our consulting rooms – a client who wants to regain or improve his confidence – I might give him a sheet of paper and ask him to write in the centre the word 'CONFIDENCE' and to put a circle around it. Then I would tell him to draw lines outwards from the circle, like spokes from the hub of a bicycle wheel and, at the end of each line, to write down a noun which for him is associated with confidence. Very often these words will be proper names, names of athletes whom he admires for this quality but sometimes his associative thought process might produce less *logically* obvious connections, which nonetheless are in some important way meaningful for him. So, such words as 'steel', 'wind' and 'lion' might appear. (See examples page 161.) When

Antony Sher described how he prepared for his acclaimed performance as Richard II, he said 'All the time, in thinking about the part, I was inspired by various animals: bulls, bisons, tarantullas and the shark from *Jaws*.' (*Observer*, 4 November 1984.)

The next stage of the exercise is to ask the athlete to put a cross against the noun he has written which he likes best. To make sure that the chosen image is clear, I sometimes circle the word and ask more questions, putting the answers at the end of a new set of 'spokes'. So if the chosen image is 'ship', I'll ask 'What sort of ship?', 'What is the ship doing?' and 'What's its name?'. Afterwards, I explain that the rest of the exercise consists in acting as if he *is* this noun, thereby introducing the feel and show of confidence to his performance.

As an initial practice, I might ask him to stand up, cross the room, stretch, turn, sit down, fold his arms, talk to me or whatever, as if he is the thing, person or animal he has chosen. Thereafter, I'll suggest that for the next ten days of training he acts his chosen role for five minutes of normal practice, paying attention to the kinaesthetic and emotional feeling of confidence that the performance produces. He must agree on this with his coach in advance, for during that particular five minutes he should *only* be judged on his acting ability, not on his technical skill. This is his confidence practice, not his passing practice.

In fact, since confidence is a feeling that may be expressed by the individual and perceived by others in an infinite number of ways, judgement of acting ability has to be tentative, preceded by the questions 'How did that feel to you?' and 'How many marks out of ten do you award yourself for your performance?'. Even then observations should only be made in the form of tentative suggestions. For instance, to a tennis player pretending to be Boris Becker in the Wimbledon 85 Final, the coach might say 'The way you came into the net on that last rally really convinced me ... but I didn't feel so sure about the way you prepared to serve. Do you have a clear image of the way Becker prepared? It seems to me that he ...' and so on.

During the 1984/85 season, as part of his drive to increase his confidence, Mark Falco spent some weeks developing his ability to 'shield' the ball, to keep it until a team-mate got close enough, doing nothing more than frustrate the efforts of an opponent to take the ball away. To this end, he wrote the word 'shielding' on the middle of a sheet of paper and around it wrote associated adjectives (in fact) as well as nouns. After focusing for a while on the memory of a match against Queens Park Rangers, when he'd

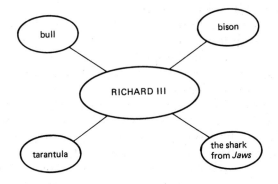

shielded particularly well, he settled on the image of a general in a green uniform. He then practised embodying this image on the football pitch for a few minutes each day and found that his 'shielding' improved.

A combination of visualisation and left-brain techniques can be used to increase confidence in physical ability after an injury has healed. In November 1984, Glenn Hoddle was recovering from a very bad leg injury. He told me he was fit but not match fit and that it was scary for him to make a sudden burst of speed. Also, because of the way he received his injury he had lost confidence in his ability to keep out of trouble when he had the ball and an opponent was approaching from behind. The objective of our sessions at that time was therefore to improve his confidence in his injured leg. 'I know in my mind that it's really okay,' Glenn said (and this was confirmed by club physiotherapist Mike Varney), 'but I can still suddenly lose confidence during a game.'

The first decision was to map out a progression of physical training exercises with Dougie Livermore, the reserve team coach. The second was to put himself in a position where he *had* to make a burst of speed, at least once each training game or match, after he'd caught himself hesitating and trying to avoid being in such a position. Two weeks later he increased this target to making such a burst, in such conditions, at least *twice* in each match. (Two weeks later still, it was no longer a problem.)

Glenn's third decision was to do a mental rehearsal twice a week in the evening, of an incident in a pre-injury match against the Dutch team Feynoord, where he'd felt total confidence. This exercise was reinforced by the decision to write out and pin up the affirmation 'I'm excited as I feel my opponent coming', which two weeks later changed to 'I'm in control of the situation'. Both affirmations came from reciting his mental rehearsal of the Feynoord match incident.

When Harold Ellis, a member of Haringey Cricket College, ducked to avoid what he thought was to be a bouncer and was hit hard on the elbow, he too lost confidence. In his case we used a different visualisation technique. Instead of going back to a time when he played such a ball confidently, I suggested that he replay the sequence as it actually happened. Having closed his eyes, relaxed and done the rehearsal a couple of times, I asked him how he *would* have played the ball, had he played it correctly. He told me. 'Okay, go back now, set the scene, see the bowler beginning his run, feel yourself there at the wicket and play through this new version of the event.' I asked him to do

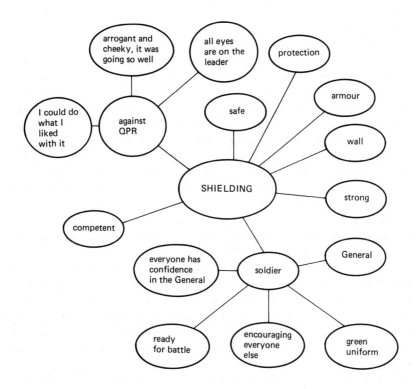

SHIELDING

arrogant and cheeky, it was going so well

all eyes are on the leader

protection

I could do what I liked with it

against QPR

safe

armour

wall

strong

competent

everyone has confidence in the General

soldier

General

ready for battle

encouraging everyone else

green uniform

Mark Falco
Tottenham Hotspur FC
6 April 1985

this three or four times and then to practice this new rehearsal each evening for five or ten minutes. A couple of weeks later, Harold had restored his confidence. Now, when faced with a bouncer, he responded as he did when practicing mentally, not as he did when he got injured. The original memory had faded and was no longer an issue. This type of visualisation is called 'visual re-editing'.

Having discovered at the start of the 1984/85 season that so many of the Tottenham players' prime objective was to improve their confidence, I began by asking *them* what steps they could take to this end. Answers such as Clive Allen's 'Strive for consistency', 'Believe in my ability' and 'Try to achieve what I feel I am personally capable of' are not complete because they invite the renewed question 'And how do you do that?'. Before returning the sheet of paper on which he'd written his replies, I added some suggestions: '(i) Decide where your ability is lacking; (ii) decide how to improve your ability in these skills; (iii) decide which skill needs improving first; and (iv) devise exercises with Peter Shreeve or John Pratt to practise these skills and ask them to assess your performance of them after each training and match, giving a score out of ten'.

Tony Galvin's answer 'Be more positive in front of goal' invited the query 'So how *do* you approach the goal when you are positive? When does that happen?', for on replies to these questions can be built a programme of physical and mental skill practices. Even his suggestion 'Practice goal-scoring attempts' needed further precision: 'Okay, so *when* will you do that and how often?'.

Other replies were more directly to the point. Carl Hoddle and Mike Hazard both showed a correct understanding of positive thinking: Carl wrote 'I think of the good things I've done after training or matches' and Mike: 'Spend five minutes each day thinking about the good things I done in a game'. Apprentice player Tim O'Shea also understood the importance of using visual right-brain thought. He wrote 'Watch senior players and imitate them'.

Carl's decision to think of the good things he had done could be achieved in either a left-brain or a right-brain way. He could keep a performance journal, noting the good things down, scoring his performance out of ten on the elements of his game in which he wanted to improve his confidence and recording objectives and strategies by which they may be obtained for the next match; or he could do a 'Performance Review' visualisation when he returned home after the match, singling out the good elements but also re-editing his mistakes, in the way cricketer Harold Ellis did his.

Keeping a mental training journal helps build confidence. Noting objectives and strategies and recording results always gives a sense of measured progress. By scoring possible new steps forward in terms of imagined difficulty or by scoring how able he feels to reach his goal, an athlete can change a daunting prospect into an intriguing challenge. Alternatively he might imagine the worst thing that could possibly happen and then rate the likelihood of it happening. If the difficulty he faces is really too high and he can see no first step towards overcoming it, he can begin to regain control by altering his attitude towards the difficulty. As a last resort he can always sit back, take a deep breath and let it out slowly . . . and then ask himself 'Okay, so what am I meant to learn from this?'

(ii) *Helping the team*
Many of the above techniques for increasing confidence may be reinforced by applying them at a team meeting. Part of the National Cricket Association's senior club coaching award examination involves giving a talk. This was a considerable test of confidence for several of the Haringey Cricket College players competing for the Award. Instead of sorting it out at a succession of individual sessions, we decided to address the problem at a team mental training meeting and for each player in turn to give a three-minute practice talk. Practice alone, with an audience of friends, might have improved confidence but it was much more effective to ask each player to think of someone who for them is supremely confident and to imagine themselves to be that person as they gave the talk – a practical 'As if . . .' visualisation exercise. This worked well and after each talk, the player was asked his assessment of his performance before feedback was given by his team-mates. To ensure that the feedback further improved his confidence, each team-mate who spoke was asked first to make a positive comment and only then a suggestion as to how the performance could become better still. Some of the players' confidence rose visibly whilst still in the middle of their rehearsal. The laughter they gained in response to their acting spurred them to act out their perception of a confident attitude even better.

When everyone had had their turn, each player agreed to rehearse the feeling of confidence at home and then to travel early to the hall on the day of the examination. Once there, they would do their rehearsal again in the actual surroundings (this time mentally) and even rehearse what it would be like to be an examiner listening to such a confident talk.

At Tottenham, I occasionally led a team session on individual review, which had several advantages. It allowed many more players to be involved than would have been, had I been conducting the exercise in individual sessions, yet it also gave a good basis *for* subsequent individual sessions. Just as importantly, since they were asked to write down part of their review, it gave players practice at withdrawing their attention inwards from the rest of the team, whilst the rest of the team was there. Withdrawal from team-mates whose span of attention is short and threatens to distract everyone else from the exercise is good practice for ignoring negativity in the match situation. When confidence begins to ebb during a match, it is felt by everyone and it is only with deliberate practice that a player can learn to insulate himself from the general trend. Once the players had completed the review exercise, there was the additional advantage of being able to learn about each other's challenges and to brainstorm on ways in which they could be met. Quite apart from producing results, the procedure itself strengthens team spirit, the ultimate source of confidence for all team players.

The format I used for these reviews came from a concern to increase self-confidence but the format could also be used to improve any other physical, technical or mental skill. Here it is.

1. ASSESS/SCORE your performance in Saturday's match. How far did you achieve what you set out to achieve? Score yourself out of ten. (Later on, get one of the coaching staff to score you as well, if you can.)
2. DECIDE what you want to RETAIN from your performance. What moment pleased you most?
3. MENTALLY REHEARSE what you want to RETAIN. Do a mental rehearsal of that moment, for five minutes each day. PRACTICE that skill in training.
4. DECIDE what you want to CHANGE OR IMPROVE.
5. Ask yourself 'HOW can I make this change?' SET yourself a first-step TARGET towards this change, that you will achieve in the next match.
6. MENTALLY REHEARSE how it would feel to play that way, for five minutes each day.
7. PRACTICE this way of playing in training.

Questionnaires can be a good way to start a team discussion. With a large group, half the individuals may say nothing unless provoked, either through choice (being embarrassed or uninterested) or through lack of time. As when dividing the group into smaller groups to start the discussion, questionnaires ensure that everyone puts his mind to topic of the meeting. Early in 1985, Tottenham were winning or drawing their away matches but frequently losing at home. Both management and players talked of an inexplicable lack of confidence in front of the home crowd. In order to introduce a discussion on this topic that would be led by Peter, I devised the following questionnaire:

1. What do you like about playing away?
     (i)
     (ii)
     (iii)
2. What do you like about playing at home?
     (i)
     (ii)
     (iii)
3. What do you dislike about playing at home, if anything.
4. Can you change this situation?
   If so, how?
5. If you can't change the situation, how might you change your attitude towards it?
6. Why do you think we lost so many home matches recently?
    (i) Reasons based on our performance.
    (ii) Reasons based on the performance of our opponents.

Since the discussion was to take place on a day when I was working elsewhere, I scribbled down a few thoughts of my own for Peter to read:

'... a non-supportive crowd becomes a "distraction" and there are two ways of dealing with any distraction: (i) getting rid of it, and (ii) changing one's attitude towards it. Perhaps it is possible to partially get rid of this problem by writing some message to the fans in the programme, as Mike Varney has suggested. More surely, the team can be helped to change its *attitude* to the problem. Perhaps the players would consider the following:

   (i) that in most criticism there is a germ of truth that can be used, when the husk of absurdity is cast away.
   (ii) that the hostility of a crowd can emphasis the bondedness

of the team, – as inter-family squabbles are forgotten in the face of an outside threat.

(iii) if someone is shouted at abusively, *he* should shout encouragement to another team member ... and that anyone else hearing the abuse should shout encouragement to him.

(iv) that they could actually welcome the abuse and criticism as a spur to them, supporting each other more closely and thereby enjoying the game more.

(v) that, in order to hold on to reality, they might openly discuss the critical element of the abuse to determine what part of it might be useful.

(vi) that they discuss the fact that 'words can't hurt' and that they either adopt Glenn's image of playing inside an invisible protective shell or find another such image, the name of which could become a key-word to defuse tension and restore confidence.'

Glenn Hoddle's image of a protective shell, behind which he could play, oblivious to the crowd – one which he had mentioned at a previous team meeting – reminded me of Tony Jacklin's 'cocoon of concentration' (see page 20), which he spoke of to Christopher and Sandy in 1979. I found it very evocative. Normally I stress that such images are personal and should not be foisted on another athlete whose associations with that image may be quite different but, if the team were to have a brainstorming session to find something appropriate, some image acceptable to everyone would probably be found. At very least, the discussion itself would serve as a focus of energy and become a positive touchstone for individual team members in a future match situation.

A further suggestion was to establish a practice whereby players always encourage a team-mate immediately after having made a mistake or having been dispossessed themselves. In such situations, the tendency is for the player to lose both confidence and concentration, his attention going inside to worries, negative thoughts, anger or simply to rehearsing the mistake. Switching his attention from the mistake to a team-mate who could use encouragement would be to keep his attention on the play around him. One way to build this patterned response would be to play a fifteen minute practice match, in which a 'goal' is given to the opposition every time a player, having made a mistake, forgets to encourage a team-mate. This practice is needed to make the response automatic but establishing the response as a norm is also the only way to combat fears the more retiring members of the team might have of being judged 'flash' if they speak positively after making a mistake. The point to emphasise is that cursing oneself makes one less effective, whereas encouraging a team-mate helps the team. In fact, *whenever* a player feels confident in the midst of a tough fight, he always does well to communicate that confidence both verbally and, if the game allows, physically, to other players in the team. Just as loss of confidence and withdrawal into silence is infectious, so too are shouts of excitement and well-being.

There are other ways to help a team with a loss of confidence. One is that the whole team should go 'back to basics', in terms of tactics and technique. Another, more drastic, is to play against weaker opposition. After the British men's tennis team came back into the First Division and beat Spain at the start of the 1986 Davis Cup season, John Lloyd told Nick Pitt: 'Going down to Division Two helped us a lot. Winning against anyone, is good for confidence and now every player in the team has confidence in himself.' (*Sunday Times*, 9 March 1986.)

A third exercise comes from my volleyball days. I knew that the Russian men's volleyball team used to train for playing in front of an antagonistic crowd by practicing in an empty hall at home, with loud speakers blaring the sound of whistles and cat-calls. Tottenham might have tried something similar: it would have been easy to set up mid-week at White Hart Lane. However, extreme pressure exercises, such as organising abuse from the touchline, in addition to the background noise, shouldn't be introduced until they will strengthen rather than overwhelm the players. If they are to learn new responses and behaviour they must be allowed to practise these changes without being punished for mistakes made along the way. New refinements of skill have to be presented in a way that inspires rather than threatens the developing athlete. Caring support from the coach and from each other is an important ingredient of success. In the words of Patricio Apey, coach to the young Argentinian tennis star, Gabriela Sabatini: 'You have to give them a lot of love, a lot of laughing and positive thinking.' (BBC 1 20 June 1986.)

An athlete should experience his own team-mates and coach as an affirmation of his own value. Footballer Garth Crooks' response to the question 'What steps can you take to improve your confidence?' was, in addition to other perceptive comments, 'I need to feel from my own players that I am a very good player. If that feeling is not there, I have to revert to my own strength which doesn't always give me necessary strength' and 'Lack of belief from the staff that I am their best striker, as opposed to just a good player distracts me. I'm always out to prove myself, which makes things somewhat tense'. And, in final defiance, 'I must insulate myself with me! No-one can chip away my confidence'. Most players will feel alone – often due to projected self-criticism – at some stage in the season and the humanistic coach consciously develops support systems between players so that, when in need, a player can reach out to contact someone else. No one can *give* me confidence but a solid support system will provide encouragement, relaxing smiles and, equally important, an objective reality check.

A good pre-match warm-up, the traditional team 'confidence builder', is an exciting mix of mental, emotional and physical preparation. When there is a need to calm things down, the coach should give a clear reminder of the task at hand and the agreed tactics to complete it. 'Okay, settle down lads', began Peter Shreeve on one occasion, 'If I can remind you of some of your comments, not mine, from yesterday's meeting . . .' and, more directly at half-time, in the same match 'Use your heads, not your hearts!'. (On the other hand, on a day when there was a hint of complacency at being ahead: 'The little practice we did yesterday, I want that to be the mood . . . Micky, Glenn, can we have a mean streak in you?')

In my view, the mental warm-up, whether initially or at half-time, should be a simple reiteration of agreed tactics, put across in an evocative visual way, such as Peter's reference to mood. This should apply when instructing individuals, as much as when talking to the team as a whole. So, better even than 'Can we have a mean streak?' would be: 'Glenn, Micky, when did you last show a mean streak on the pitch? Take a moment to play through that occasion in your mind. Have you got the feel of it? Okay, take it out with you on to the pitch and express yourself'. Confidence could be evoked directly in a similar way. The emotional warm-up for the team as a unit begins with the manager's final stirring words and continues with the all-important physical contact and verbal encouragement. The physical warm-up, massage, stretching, jogging or skills practice is part of the ritual.

However inspired the manager's pre-match talk, it won't achieve much unless team spirit and confidence in each other has been developed amongst the players long before. A lot can be done at team meetings, by encouraging each person to express his view, however contrary or ill-informed it might be. Understanding, respect and sometimes even caring can then take hold. Steve Perryman, as captain at Tottenham, wrote on one questionnaire 'I must improve my ability to help the team have confidence, help the players to believe in each other, so that if two or three people are not right, they can still give something to the team effort.'

To the same end, during the 1984/1985 season, I radically increased the amount of work I did with *pairs* of players. At first this was only with 'obvious' pairings – two strikers, two midfield players or two backs – but eventually I discovered that working with two players who *weren't* normally paired together was a stimulating and instructive experience for them both, as each expressed his awareness of the other's play. As an example of working with two strikers, here is a summary of a session I did before a European Cup match, with Mark Falco and Clive Allen. My objectives were to sort out any differences of perception, to allow criticism to be voiced in an acceptable way and to strengthen their confidence in themselves and each other.

First I asked 'What do you appreciate most about each other?' Mark said 'Clive is quicker than me and is good on the right.' Clive said 'Mark is strong and is better on the left.' Then 'What is your strength as a team?', which produced the answers 'We complement each other', and 'We support each other and don't shout at each other'. Then, 'How can the other make things easier for you?', getting the replies 'Clive can encourage me to hang loose and keep going' (this was at a time when Mark hadn't scored a goal for ten matches), and 'Mark can encourage me to get back'. Wondering if there might be any contradictions, I then asked 'What are you each aiming to do in this match?', and got the replies 'We must be more cagey than usual' and 'We must play closer together because we'll be two against three defenders'. Out of this also came the agreement that they should tell Gary Stevens and Mike Hazard that they would be welcome in the penalty box.

The sequence of questions so far had been designed (i) to evoke appreciation; (ii) to allow space for criticism, demands or requests; and (iii) to strengthen their unit. Finally, they chose and mentally rehearsed a moment from a past game (against Everton) when they felt they had played perfectly together. As they each recited their version of the rehearsal in turn, these two affirmations emerged: 'We're on our toes', and 'We're both

geared up', affirmations that they would be able to use for subsequent games as well. Throughout the session, I asked that they
face and speak to each other directly, formulating their answers
to my questions as statements made to each other, rather than to
me. So, in answer to the first question, Mark actually said to
Clive 'You're quicker than me and you're good on the right', and
so on. This is an important part of building full awareness each of
the other.

Such an exercise helps players to express support and confidence in each other, yet for it to be fully effective the manager
must demonstrate his own confidence in his players. In their
book on business management, Hersey and Blanchard say 'Managers must *clearly* specify what constitutes good performance in
each area... "Failures" are failures of the manager. He is responsible for making his personnel winners.' Peters and Waterman echo this sentiment, pointing out that, by thinking of
themselves as winners, people become winners and giving the
example of IBM who make sure that seventy to eighty per cent of
their salespeople make their quotas.

This policy is of course linked to realistic goal-setting and intro-
duces the whole question of good leadership which we'll look at
in more detail later on. Generally speaking though, it is not
enough to take players out of the first team 'to take the pressure
off', as Keith Burkinshaw would do, unless such a move is accompanied by *more* rather than less evident concern and supervision of their progress. Without this, the move will be
interpreted as a punishment and confidence will drop still further.

Confidence is indeed a quality which a good manager can
foster. Absolute statements such as Peter Shreeve's 'Some members of the team have no mental strength' only serve to express
the manager's own sense of frustration. In themselves, they lead
nowhere. Yet they do excite my curiosity. What is it that he *sees* in
a certain player that makes him *imagine* that the player has no
'mental strength' and (as *I* imagine!) causes him to *feel* so dis-
gusted? Obviously, some players are less confident than others
and an experienced coach does indeed pick up signals that suggest this lack of confidence. However, from then on, it is best to
be as precise as possible.

List the signals and check them out one by one with the player
concerned, for one's feelings – of disgust, dissatisfaction or whatever – are based on what one imagines, not on what one sees.
Checking with the player sorts out the true from the false and

clears the way for constructive goal-setting along a path that the player is able to follow. An important part of this confidence-building process will be strengthening the links between the player and the team unit.

8

STRESS

Excessive stress can drive an outgoing supportive athlete into reclusive isolation. This last chapter focuses therefore more on the individual team-member, with a view to suggesting ways in which he may cope with stress and retain or regain his ties with the rest of the team. After giving a definition of stress, I'll review the signs of stress, the causes of stress, the results of stress and some ways in which stress may be reduced.

Stress defined

Stress is a physical and mental reaction to any disturbance of one's normal state of well-being. The disturbance itself is called the *stressor*. Common stressors for sportspeople are fear of losing, fear of winning, of being dropped from the team, of injury and loss of control. A professional sportsperson may fear the loss of his livelihood. However, stress has also a positive form called excitement or arousal and some stress is necessary for optimal sports performance, just as a degree of stage fright is necessary for actors.

Perls defined anxiety, a form of stress, as 'the gap between the now and the then'. (*Ego, Hunger & Aggression.*) This definition holds good equally for negative stress as for positive pre-competition excitement. The narrow edge between excitement and anxiety can be related to the physical expression of these emotions. 'Anxiety', says Perls, 'equals excitement plus an inadequate supply of oxygen' and he explains that if an actor (or indeed a sportsperson) tries to suppress the excitement he feels prior to a performance, then, 'unable to stand the suspense of both waiting *and* being excited, his excitement will turn to an anxiety. Physically, the act of suppression causes tension across the chest, which in turn inhibits the intake of air.

Stress, then, is a negative phenomenon when we are unable to express our excitement and regain our equilibrium. Tennis players who are unable to let go of tension on the changeover, footballers who cannot relax between matches at the end of a full season, all maintain a high level of arousal across situations and suffer from what Nideffer calls 'trait anxiety'. Even if the tennis player, for instance, knows how and when to reduce his level of stress, he may not be able to reduce it sufficiently. This means that if he starts the match with a basic stress level of three out of ten and comes back to his chair, having lost the first set, with a level of six out of ten, he might only have relaxed back to a four out of ten level when the next set begins. As the match progresses, his base level could then slowly rise to eight out of ten, climbing higher at each crisis and only returning part way to the previous base level before the next crisis arrives. This process is described by Bob and Marilyn Kriegel in *The C Zone*.

There are of course many ways in which this trend can be reversed to the point where negative stress is once more experienced as excitement (and the stressor as a challenge), or to where a state of neutral relaxation is regained. In a team sport, one such method is to plug in to the synergistic experience of team spirit.

The signs of stress

After being unexpectedly beaten in the 1985 Wimbledon quarter-finals, John McEnroe said, 'Things speed up when you're losing. It's a difficult rut to get out of . . . It seemed like the changeovers were faster.' (BBC TV.) This was a perception of some poignancy from a man, on the lip of a downward curve, who was probably as familiar with the feeling of being 'in the zone' (where time seems to *slow down*) as any player past or present. He was identifying one common subjective symptom of stress. The tendency is to become locked into noticing any distracting factor outside oneself – in McEnroe's case, the scoreboard, the excited crowd sensing an upset, or Kevin Curren's power and accuracy – and reacting to it emotionally, unaware of one's own physical tension and unable to relax. Yet the slightest attention to the physical elements of the discomfort we feel would put us in touch with all the symptoms of readiness to flee or fight: 'increased muscle tension, perspiration, rapid and shallow breathing and increased heart-rate', even in the rest periods between physical exertion. (T Pasek and J Daniel, see bibliography.)

Other symptoms of stress are visible to the outsider. Fritz Perls points out that 'restlessness is commonly present in the state of excitement which doesn't find its natural outlet and that yawning and sighing are symptoms of "self-regulation" which don't occur when we are anxious'. Nideffer says that new behaviour is a sign of an unusually high level of stress. In business it can be a new carelessness in performing low priority jobs or the making of negative remarks and jokes about clients. In many occupations it can be failing to turn up on time, or working strictly to rule, rather than to the spirit of the rules. Billie Jean King tells of the players who reached match point against her and then, quite out of character, served two soft services. This betrayed that they were under stress and was all Billie Jean needed to take charge again. (Billie Jean King with Frank Deford, *Billie Jean King*.) One athlete may show stress in relationship to others in his team by detaching himself, refusing to accept responsibility for mistakes, and blocking out any new information he has been asked to deal with.

He's also likely to give up suddenly. Even just before Wimbledon 1985, John McEnroe said 'It's a scary thing to start understanding Borg. Before, I thought "Unbelievable! I'm No.2!" I was happy. . . Later I asked Borg "How come you quit?"' After his defeat, speaking to a different interviewer, he said 'I have a lot more understanding of Bjorn. Bjorn Borg is the best athlete that tennis has ever had. I feel the need to regroup a bit', and by the end of the year he had withdrawn from competition.

The causes of stress

There are just as many causes of stress as there are symptoms, although different members of a team will react differently to different stressors. The coach, manager or teacher will also be subject to stress and, although the stressors may be somewhat different to those that affect their charges, the performance of the team as a whole will be affected by the way that the leader chooses to cope.

Both positive and destructive levels of stress can be caused by stressors which are *external* to the individual or the team and by those that are generated from within.

Most literature limits itself to a consideration of those causes of stress which are *external* and experienced by the individual and John Adams identified *four* sub-types of this class. (John Adams, see bibliography.)

	Destructive stress		Positive stress	
	Occurring within Individual	Occurring within team	Occurring within individual	Occurring within team
Internal cause	Destructive stress created by individual 1	Destructive stress caused by team 3	Positive stress created by individual 5	Positive stress created by team 7
External cause	Destructive stress caused by factor outside individual 2	Destructive stress caused by factor outside team 4	Positive stress caused by factor outside individual 6	Positive stress caused by factor outside team 8

John Adam's sub-division of category 2 above
(ie negative stressors caused by factor outside individual)

	At work	Away from work
Recent events	Recent events at work (TYPE 1)	Recent events away from work (TYPE 2)
On-going events	On-going events at work (TYPE 3)	On-going events away from work (TYPE 4)

Type 1 are those which have occurred recently at work,

Type 2 are those which have occurred recently away from work,

Type 3 are those which are on-going at work, and

Type 4 are those which are on-going away from work.

If we broaden the context from business alone to all team situations, we can distinguish between those events that occur at work, school or sports club and those that occur away from these places. Type 2 factors (such as marriage, death of a family ıber and serious illness) and Type 4 factors (such as pollution, noise, financial concern, family problems and lack of fit with social milieu) all occur away from 'work' and affect the team only in so far as they distract the individual from full attention to his performance and relationships within the team. However, Adams' other two Types, 1 and 3, are actually generated within the team context and it is with these that Adams is most concerned.

Adams, describing a business situation, lists under 'recent events' at work: major changes in instructions, policies or procedure, requirement to work more hours per week than normal, a sudden significant increase in activity level or pace in work, any major reorganisation, a new supervisor, new co-workers, new subordinates, and any change in the nature of the job. Just *how* stressful these events are felt to be depends largely on how carefully the individual was prepared for them by his manager.

Demands on individuals can be very high. At Tottenham, the coaching staff had little respect for a striker who asked for a transfer when he heard that the management had signed on a well-known new striker who would obviously be in contention for his place. 'Am I meant to tell him all my plans?' asked the astonished manager. If competition for places was seen to be healthy, it was perhaps partly as a necessary conditioning for the analogous *physical* challenge players were expected to make on the pitch. The surprise element had also to be contended with each week by players on the verge of the first team. Very often they could only deduce who would be playing on Saturday, when the bibs were handed for the practice match at the end of the previous day's training, denoting a first team to play the rest. Even then there were often thirteen or fourteen players told to be there for the pre-match talk, unsure who would be playing and who would be substitute. The fact that this was often determined by last minute fitness tests didn't reduce the strain. That said, the players did indeed learn to display an outwardly calm stoicism, a 'professional attitude'. This inspired respect and probably increased team spirit amongst the squad.

That the appointment of a new supervisor or leader can be stressful for certain individuals is as apparent in schools and in sport as in business. It has long been recognised that children do better in some subjects than in others, simply because of their response to different teachers. Where a child's classes are almost all taught by the same teacher, the change of that teacher can produce significant results in the child's development, either for good or ill. Hidden somewhere under a sheet of lead on a roof of my prep school there may still be a defiant note that expressed my unhappiness at leaving the known for the unknown of the senior establishment. Years later, when I left the position of National Volleyball coach, I was aware of stress experienced by certain players in the team I'd been coaching as they responded to Nick Moody who took my place. Inevitably for one or two the experience was a difficult challenge, if for others the stress was experienced as positive excitement at the new possibilities that emerged. This was because Nick viewed the game differently and judged players accordingly. It was also because he was more rigorous in the demands of physical as opposed to technical training, so that in Adams' words there was a 'sudden significant increase in activity level or pace in work'.

Adams lists his 'Type 3' stressors (those that may be experienced continually 'at work') as: too much work and too little time to do it, feedback only when performance is unsatisfactory, conflict between one's own unit and the others with which one must work, unclear standards and responsibilities, role ambiguity and conflict, poor interpersonal relationships and unresolved interpersonal conflicts, lack of participation, territoriality, too many deadlines, lack of social support, lack of confidence in the manager and 'fire-fighting' rather than working from a plan. To these, still in a business context, can be added unnecessary meetings, interruptions, ambiguities, poor delegation and poor communication. Many of these stressors, being shared but unspoken ways of behaviour or expectations, are informal norms which cannot be legislated against from above. Any attempt to do so would simply drive interpersonal stress underground. As Adams says: 'Since everyone unwittingly participates in maintaining the norms of the organisation, everyone must participate in changing them.'

The best way to get rid of these stress-producing situations is to discuss them at a team meeting. Once the opposing parties can understand each other's position, the change to less stressful norms becomes possible. On-going stressful conditions other than the norms of interpersonal relationships are more directly the result of management. Neither the coach nor the teacher will draw the best from their charges if they only comment on a poor performance, indeed the stress this causes the individual is likely to perpetuate such performances. Similarly, the manager can avoid giving the individual too much work, too little time and too many deadlines. Demands must be reasonable, clear and even astute. Unreasonable expectations voiced by one's coach, friends or family are a prime source of stress and make one more vulnerable when an opponent increases the pressure during competition.

In fact, in sport, as opposed to business or education, the stress experienced by individual performers during competition can come from at least four external directions: the environment, the opposition, the coach or manager and other team members. Pressure created by speculative newspaper reports prior to the match, can also affect an athlete's performance. John Hopkins, in his book *Nick Faldo in Perspective*, refers to Faldo's 'old sore – his relationship with the press' and to how the press could distract him from his golf. (On the other hand, it's worth noting that the *response* to external pressure is in the hands of the individual. Steve Archibald's reaction to a contentious newspaper story was to play better than he had done all season.) Much of the stress experienced by Kevin Curren in the 1985 Wimbledon singles final came directly from the performance and antics of his opponent Boris Becker. A cricketer receiving a lethally aimed bouncer has no doubt at all as to the primary source of any stress he may experience. 'At Test level,' says New Zealander Richard Hadlee, 'the batsman is there to be tested.'

So far we've only looked at the category 2 of the Causes of Stress diagram on page 177. Let's take the other categories in turn, specifically in relation to sport, and consider each in terms of physical, emotional and mental stressors, starting with the negative or destructive ones. Destructive stress caused by the athlete himself (category 1) would include insufficient training or insufficient warm-up, possibly resulting in injury (physical), the need to impress or prove oneself or fear of injury (emotional), and unrealistic goals or unrealistic assessment of one's opponent (mental). George Brown suggested to me that unless there is a physical constraint, most stress comes out of making comparisons: comparisons with others, with one's idealised self, with how one should have done it. The idealised self is the perfect yardstick with which to beat ourselves. 'If you make comparisons', says George, 'you step out of the now and into a fantasy.' An athlete who is not fully in the now has little chance of success.

Other emotional stressors fitting in this category would be a fear of being dropped, a fear of failure, a fear of injury and even one's own contentious statements, such as McEnroe's claim midway through Wimbledon 1985 that champions should only play on the show courts (he hated playing anywhere else), when it in fact was always possible that he'd lose his title and find such a rule discriminating against himself the following year.

A fear of being different, the urge to conform, would also fit this category. 'Students feel insecure when their personal response is in opposition to a group norm,' write Richard and Patricia Schmuck. There is a fear of negative judgement, ostracism and worse. Steve Rowley writes of a group of highly anxious rugby players, 'who described themselves as not being self-seeking or autocratic but had that as an imposed ideal' and of 'constellations being held together by fear, anxiety and guilt in terms of what the other group members will do to the member who secedes or betrays'. (Steve Rowley, see bibliography.)

If we return for a moment to destructive stressors occurring within the individual but created by a factor outside the individual (category 2), we can add getting an injury mid-performance (physical); other players in the team succumbing to pressure, an unexpected change (for instance in the batting order), bad leadership or coaching, and opponents raising their game (emotional); and unrealistic goals being imposed by the coach (mental).

Destructive stressors occurring within the team and created by the team (category 3) would include too much or too little preparation and no opposition (physical); threats from coach or team-mate, internal power struggles, a team-mate determined to sabotage team effort (emotional); and unrealistic goals, poorly communicated goals and poor leadership (mental).

Finally, potentially destructive stressors occurring within the team but created by factors outside the team (category 4) would include overwhelming physical challenge from opponents and no time or place to practice (physical), being bottom of the league towards the end of the season and being threatened by relegation (emotional); and setting unrealistic goals (mental).

Many if not most stressors can prompt positive rather than negative results. In fact the better the team spirit, the more likely this is. Other positive stressors occurring within and created by the individual (category 5) include self-chosen punishing training (physical), self-psyching up (emotional); and demanding yet realistic self-chosen goals (mental). Positive stressors, occurring within the individual but created externally (category 6) include punishing training instituted by the coach (physical); psyche-up or in some cases even taunting or emotional winding-up by the coach, team mates, opponents or spectators (emotional); and following someone's example, or goal-setting and systematic analysis of performance by the coach (mental). Just before the 1986

Masters tournament, a friend of Jack Nicklaus went to the house that Nicklaus had rented and stuck a newspaper article on to the refrigerator. The writer claimed that Nicklaus was 'done, washed-up, through'. Nicklaus left the article in place. 'It had me sizzling,' he said, after winning the Green Jacket, 'but it egged me on. I kept reading it every day.' (Peter Finney Jr, *New York Post*, 14 April 1986.) Nicklaus, like Steve Archibald in the earlier example, chose to regard a negative article as a positive emotional stressor.

Positive stressors occurring within and created by the team (category 7) include pushing each other to train harder (physical); team-mates winding up those who are lethargic, a team talk by the coach and the offer of bonuses by directors (emotional); and appropriate goal-setting and systematic analysis arrived at through team discussion (mental). Finally, positive stressors occurring within the team but created by factors outside the team (category 8) include the physical challenge of opponents; the opponents taunting (emotional); and having an appropriate goal and analysis system imposed by the coach (mental).

Results of stress

Whereas a positive degree of stress results in positive arousal to meet the challenge at hand, too much stress or arousal maintained for too long a period results in chronic health conditions, a feeling of ineffectiveness at work and a lack of satisfaction and sense of growth. Physiologically, when one's equilibrium is disturbed, the cardiovascular system speeds up and digestion slows down, all in an effort to restore equilibrium. Over a period of time, this results in wear and tear, making illness more likely. In the *Sunday Times* of 9 February 1986, Rob Hughes began an article about Manchester United and England captain Bryan Robson with the words 'How much can one man, one body take?' and focused on the unreasonable damaging pressures which a stressed manager will sometimes impose on his key players. Players may willingly accept pain-killing injections to play in a vital Cup tie: but it can be shocking to see the week-to-week pressure sustained by key players recovering from injury, as the physiotherapist struggles to fend off a manager's intent. Hughes wrote: 'Atkinson himself put it most graphically in November 1984 when Robson, suffering from a debilitating bug, played his part in a United win over Arsenal. 'He wanted to come off at half-time,' said the manager, 'because he was dying out there, but we shoved him back out. We needed him even though he felt unwell.' Angela Patmore wrote an entire book called *Playing on their Nerves: Sport Experiment* to highlight the adverse stressfulness of sport. She claims that prolonged exposure to stress – for instance the batsman's experience of having to guess what a bowler is going to do – has 'made more than one athlete mentally ill'.

John Adams' Type 1 stress, resulting from recent events at work, can lead to more sick leave, more accidents and an increased inattention. Difficult situations seem more difficult and confidence in one's performance wanes. These patterns observed in a business context are equally apparent in sport. At Tottenham I noticed that players who had suddenly been dropped from the first team often became injured or *noticed* their injuries soon afterwards. In a team game excessive stress can result in negative confluence, in internal conflict or in inappropriate withdrawal. Team spirit can disintegrate as athletes lose individual inspiration and become increasingly dependent on the rigid structure of the team and on external encouragement.

Response to stress is however individual. In business, where physical release of stress is often impossible, those who are more driven, more competitive and more deadline oriented are more likely to have heart attacks than those who are more phlegmatic. Robert Nideffer observed that those swimmers who maintained a high level of arousal across situations ('trait anxiety') had difficulty in planning ahead, poor physical skill and poor performance, whereas those who became too anxious in particularly demanding situations ('state anxiety') suffered from choking, and an inability to adapt to change according to the demands of the competition. People who were high on either scale were poor leaders.

When we are anxious and stressed our attention narrows and we tend only to notice those things which increase our fear. Swimmers who let early mistakes disrupt performance no longer notice their environment and can't adapt 'to changes in strategy, plan ahead or listen to suggestions'. Whereas relaxation allows our attention to broaden, anxiety and arousal both tend first to narrow our attention and then to turn it inwards into ourselves. This can be appropriate when few cues are needed and a coach who gives a tough pre-match talk or even one who insults his players can be effective with some of them. However, if the athlete needs a broad external focus of attention, this type of talk will be counterproductive.

How to reduce stress

(i) What the coach can do

A good coach can do much to help his athlete avoid undue levels of stress, first, by monitoring his own behaviour; second, by introducing certain norms or exercises to the team as a whole; and third, by giving individual athletes the opportunity to learn how to monitor their own stress.

Somehow the coach must avoid causing debilitating stress whilst maintaining his role of ensuring the team is suitably aroused for competition. However, this requires him not only to empathise with his charges but also to *care* for them, beyond ensuring that they perform efficiently. This means, amongst other things, that he must give them positive feedback and encourage them in their drive towards perfection without burdening them with comparisons. Since a coach is himself often under pressure to produce results at all costs, it is not always easy for him to work exclusively towards the athlete's well-being and even if this is his sole intention, he may still feel so nervous himself that his nervousness affects his players. John Madden was a case in point. 'I stayed away from my players on game day. I was a basket case. I didn't want to add to a player's natural nervousness.'

Some of the advanced Sporting Bodymind courses I developed with Christopher Connolly are arranged so that participants divide equally into athletes and coaches. In one exercise we ask each coach to pair off with an athlete and then ask the athletes to sit in a circle and discuss 'How I experience my own coach deliberately or unintentionally increasing or reducing stress productively'. Meanwhile the coaches sit in an outer circle, each positioned so that he can watch his partner, listening to the discussion. After a while, the topic is changed to 'How I experience my coach deliberately or unintentionally increasing or reducing stress with *negative* results'. Eventually, the coaches sit in an inner circle and discuss the same topics from their point of view: how they personally increase or reduce stress deliberately or unintentionally, positively or negatively, when training their athletes at home. The point of the exercise is to help both coaches and athletes to become better aware and more sympathetic to the stressors that athletes experience, recognition being the first step towards change. At the end of the exercise coaches and athletes are all encouraged to take decisions about positive changes they will make within the next week and to write these decisions down.

One kind of decision that a coach might make is to improve communication between himself and the team and between team members. 'Excellent' business managers, as identified by Peters and Waterman, give each individual a clear job description and a statement of the standard of performance required. Graham Taylor introduced this practice with his First Division Watford football team, with startling results. At Tottenham, where the emphasis was on improvisation, players could be less than sure of their role within the team's performance, unless they made a point of asking. It wasn't always enough to *assume* that each player knew what he was required to do, just because the team's tactics as a whole had been made clear. Sometimes when I asked 'So what are you aiming to do in this match?', a player would reply 'We're going to play tight for the first twenty minutes and earn the right to "play"'. This was the *team*'s tactics. I had to ask again to find out what this individual player's role might be, given that the team's tactics were to be such as he'd just described.

Another principle of good communication which reduces stress is to ensure that any major change in job specification or in working conditions be announced as far in advance as possible. Where this is difficult, as in a selection of football team when several first team players require fitness tests just prior to the game, individuals need to be flexible and respond instantly to a rapidly changing situation. The stress involved remains high but an athlete can deal with it successfully, provided stress is reduced on other planes. If he has a three year contract for instance, he is less likely to be upset by the demands of the situation than if he has only two months of his contract to run. Less prosaically, if the importance of the squad rather than just of the playing team has been stressed and carefully developed into a strong 'squad spirit', the interchange of first team places is effected smoothly.

Once the performance is over or the week's work finished, you should find something positive to say to the team and to the individual, before pointing out all the faults. You may still criticise severely but put the faults in context. Such a discipline will also help you to keep your temper and put all your energy into creating the desired change. Even if losing your temper is the most effective way of communicating with your team, build a context for the occasion before letting fly. When I lose my temper too often, it is because one situation reminds me of numerous others and I fail to notice what might be different and positive about the present. Such outbursts tend to polarise relations and dig any rift between manager and 'problem athlete' deeper still.

Any number of norm changes or exercises could be appropriate to help your team avoid stressful situations or prepare them to cope. Which ones you choose will depend on the team's character and existing norms. One such change of norm would be to have fruit and fruit juices provided at breaks in training as options to or instead of tea and biscuits. Correct diet in an important element of stress management. Individuals, whether coaches or athletes, who eat a great deal of junk food containing large quantities of sugar and additives will be more likely to react angrily and ineffectively when challenged. Another adjustment, where you have the choice, would be to ensure that the rhythm of competition is not too demanding. The young Bulgarian tennis player Manuela Maleeva avoided the Austin-Jaeger burn-out syndrome by travelling with both her parents and having her schedule arranged by her mother, who insisted that the then seventeen-year-old player took one rest week in three. (*New York Times*, 3 August 1984.) Even in teaching a testing skill, such as a dive in volleyball, scaling demands to an acceptable level will help the athlete to avoid negative stress. If a volleyball player is intimidated by the request to imitate a dive, a good coach will break the skill down so that the player first practices a simple somersault and builds from there.

Scaling demands to an acceptable level also includes taking back some responsibility from the athlete who temporarily is overstressed. So the manager with a striker who becomes increasingly stressed as each game goes by without him scoring a goal backs off from telling him he *must* score goals, analyses what the striker needs to do *in order* to score goals (perhaps make more runs into the penalty box) and make clear that it is on this that he will be judged.

A different coaching technique is to prepare for stressful situations in competition by creating stressful situations in practice. A common pressure drill to *improve* diving in volleyball has been described in chapter five. Two players some eight paces apart feed balls in front of them alternately and the player under pressure dives first to one side and then to the other to save them. As has also been pointed out in chapter five, this drill can be used to improve team spirit, if other players gather round and shout encouragement to the player who is working.

When teaching the skill of dealing with stress, it is not much use calling 'Relax! Relax! Godammit, relax!' Instead, the athlete should be taught to notice where his body is tense, what is happening to his breathing and where his attention is focused. Listening to his body, he will soon learn kinaesthetically what adjustments to make in order to achieve the desired skill. In the process he becomes aware of his own physiological equilibrium and his sense of psychological peace, which together constitute the exact opposite to the stress response. John Biglow's first coach Frank Cunningham was exasperated by the young rower's constant stream of questions and finally exploded: 'John, when you do it right you'll *feel* it.'

That Biglow *did* 'feel it', could in effect withdraw from stressful circumstances to a point where he 'listened' to his body and to the performance of the crew as a whole was demonstrated when, his boat having gone out very high and being down a length after a few hundred yards, he brought the stroke *down* four notches. 'It was an unusual move, something that almost no other seventeen-year-old would have been willing to risk. The response of almost every other stroke would have been to send the stroke higher or go for power tens.' (Halberstam.) The boat steadied, found the tempo and eventually won.

Barcelona Football Club, champions of Spain in 1984/85, have a chapel at the entrance to the tunnel leading out to their incredible 100,000 seat stadium and I imagine that those players who visit it do so to gain a similar sense of equilibrium prior to a match. This is achieved in part through the religious ritual involved but a contributing factor may also be silence. Pre-match silence does not suit everyone but Greg Lougarnis, the double Olympic diving champion and Lucinda Green, the British horsewoman, are two first-class athletes who have reported being reduced to retiring to a lavatory prior to competition, as the only place where they could be quiet and alone.

In interactive team sports like hockey (field and ice), lacrosse, rugby, soccer, basketball, handball, volleyball and so on, there is likely to be competition for the lavatory. Each athlete arriving in the dressing room should be allowed to settle into his own routine in the initial stages of the warm-up, tuning in to the stretching he needs to do and the visualisation exercises or conversation that can help him to put aside distracting thoughts or feelings. Many need a long emotional preparation and have already begun before they arrive but others tend naturally towards over-arousal so need to start the process, by being alone, much nearer the start of the competition. This demands careful orchestration of time and space. When John Madden was at Hancock Junior College, one of his players approached him and said 'Coach, there are all different kinds of personalities in the locker room before a game. Some guys take a nap, some go to the bathroom, some throw up, some listen to music. Some like me tell jokes. We're not all the same.' 'After that,' says Madden, 'I always had two locker rooms at Hancock – one for the quiet guys, one for the guys who liked to play music or tell jokes.'

Two rooms are not usually available (hence the demand for lavatories) but this won't matter if you tune in to the needs of each athlete yourself and make sure that these are appreciated by his team-mates. Tony Parks, a loud cheerful Londoner, was normally the life and soul of the Tottenham reserve team yet, prior to a match, he liked to spend time on his own. This meant players who needed *company* as their way to monitor arousal, naturally wanted Tony's jokes and were upset by his refusal to be 'himself'. Coach Robbie Stepney sorted this out at a team discussion, the type of discussion from which all teams could benefit, especially at the start of a new season. As each person in turn explains his own warm-up rhythm, the level of respect and team spirit will rise perceptibly and, from that point on, there will always be more 'psychic', if not physical, space in the dressing room.

I actually feel that many noisy places in the world, including offices, airports and locker-rooms could benefit from a space or a time for silence. Pasek and Daniel report that in 1970, the Polish government set up 'calming centres' where people can take special two week holidays for regeneration and 'silencing'. 'The Centres are composed of a "hall of silence" and a tearoom with suitable decorations and furnishing to facilitate the development of inner calm, harmony and beauty.' At Findhorn we had both – a place for silence (a room called 'the sanctuary') and a time (the minute before any business meeting). Ever since, I have been aware of the benefit of designating a place or a time for silence at home, even if this is only a small carpet on which I can do some yoga.

Sometimes at Findhorn there was even a silent table in the dining room and to sit there was to experience increased awareness not just of my food but of the people sitting there with me. An imaginative coach, training his team to deal with the unexpected, might well make one meal-time silent as an exercise. Half-stifled giggles would punctuate a growing mutual awareness, an essential component of team spirit as experienced and expressed in competition. John Bertrand equated silence in competition with tension and it is true that when a team sport demands verbal communication, silence *during* competition may well indicate tense restraint. Initially, however, Bertrand *imposed* silence in training on his crew, so that messages which were essential would become apparent by their absence.

Silence is normally an adjunct of complete rest and withdrawal and an important part of both preparation *and* review. Used this way, it can promote a hundred per cent alertness on returning to competition. When, after his memorable defeat of South African Gerrie Coetzee, Frank Bruno was asked 'Where are you off to, for celebrations?', he replied. 'I might go for a walk with my dog – or even have a midnight run in the park'. (Frank Keating, *The Guardian*, 5 March 1986.)

After a time for individual preparations, players should warm up in pairs, talking and stretching, and then it is time for your pre-match talk. The very best and most skilful of these succeed in raising the level of excitement in players who were previously relaxed, whilst simultaneously lowering it in those who were overtense. As you evoke each athlete's sense of participation in a synergetic whole, you ensure the team is better able to deal with any external threat, than it could be as a group of individuals. However, a team in which no team spirit has previously been developed will not respond and may be more vulnerable to stress than its individual members would be alone. In tense situations, such a group may suddenly panic.

(ii) *What the individual can do*
The humanistic coach will not only modify his own behaviour in order to avoid causing stress that inhibits performance of his athletes but will give each athlete an opportunity to learn appropriate stress reduction skills. Stress invariably affects body, mind and emotions and can be reduced by working on any one of these aspects of the individual's being.

(a) *The physical approach*

Recognition of stress must precede change and very often the most recognisable symptoms are physical. Indeed the simplest way to change is to ask '*Where* am I stressed?' and pay attention to one's body. Having found the physical tension, one is half way towards letting it go. Tom Petranoff claims it was 'listening' to his body before throwing the javelin that enabled him to make his 327' 2" world record throw: 'I focused on a spot on the run way for ten or twenty seconds, just feeling my heart beat and my shoulders lower, and then – boom – I took off.' (Edwin Kiester Jr, *Psychology Today*, July 1984.) Usually it is the athlete who needs to learn some form of physical relaxation whilst the pressured sales-man or clerk needs to build a programme of vigorous exercise. Somewhere between the two is the need for disciplines such as yoga, the Feldenkrais method, meditation, and deep-breathing exercises in all their various forms. Anyone wanting to plan a correct, personal and enjoyable programme of exercise would be greatly helped be reading *The Fitness Jungle* by Christopher Con-nolly and Hetty Einzig.

Fritz Perls' advice to the actor with stage fright is to relax the muscles of his chest and give vent to his excitement. Like the stressed office worker, his greatest need is an increased supply of oxygen. Even the prima donna's hysterical outbursts attain this end. Yet most forms of physical exercise will do and when I find myself stuck with a block to my writing, I will often stand up, pick up my three dog balls and do five minutes juggling, finding that I'm more invigorated physically *and* mentally, as well as less tense, when I sit back at my desk. Lee Trevino once went so far as to say 'Warm-up exercises are to stay loose and *incidentally* to reduce the risk of pulling a muscle.' (*Sportsworld*, December 1973.)

The opposite solution for me, if I am physically tired as well as tense, is to lie on the floor, totally relax and take a cat nap. Ath-letes who are overstressed may find it easier to slow down rather than stop entirely and to practice some other form of physical exercise of a much slower pace. In our Sporting Bodymind course we teach a slow movement meditation, akin to *t'ai chi*, which helps athletes to slow down whilst retaining full attention and alertness. Hatha yoga of the Iyengar school is physically demanding, so good for the sedentary worker, but it also loosens and stretches the often over-tight muscles of the athlete. It has other benefits too. When taught by an experienced teacher (and in East Europe it is not unusual for a team to have yoga, medi-tation and relaxation teachers) and, when practiced in harmoni-ous surroundings, yoga not only reduces the intensity and frequency of stress but enhances one's mood and improves one's concentration.

In fact, the way to practice yoga is to focus attention on a par-ticular part of the body whilst in one position or posture, so that all other thoughts and feelings dissolve. At first one is aware of tension in the part of the body that is working but gradually one is able to allow even this tension to 'melt away', whilst continuing to hold the position. Yoga differs from ordinary athletic exercise in that it continually demands consciousness of the kinaesthetic sense. Yoga is a way to regain one's physical and psychological equilibrium. It is particularly apt for cyclists and other athletes who vary their posture little over a long period of time: relaxation is combined with stretching.

Correct breathing is an important element of hatha yoga and is also a yogic discipline in itself. Deep breathing, counted to a rhythm, such as *in* to the count of four, *hold* to the count of four, and *out* to the count of four, gives instant relief from intense anxiety and is a method I use to combat a fear of flying.

Here in the West, a more common physical method of preventing and dealing with stress is massage. During the 1984/85 season at Tottenham, Mike Varney began to encourage all the players to have a massage after their post-match bath. (Most of the players have massages *before* the match.) Massage allows a player to let go of the match both physically and emotionally. It also ensures that he takes time to relax, rather than rush from the dressing room to meet friends and relations in the overcrowded players' lounge.

(b) The mental approach

Stress can usually be reduced but an athlete can do a great deal to prevent it ever occurring. The challenge from his opponents becomes stressful in relation to how well or poorly he has prepared. If he prepared sufficiently well physically and technically, he's done much of the ground work to ensure that our response to the challenge is one of excitement but then he must prepare mentally. This means first deciding upon a realistic objective in meeting the challenge, which may well be something less (or more) than winning, and he must have decided exactly how he's going to achieve that objective. If he's done this, his opponents' performance is unlikely to be a source of stress. Robert Nideffer finds that swimmers who focus internally on their goals or their tactical plan (or on a pre-chosen fixed point outside themselves which evokes a positive feeling) are better able to mentally rehearse their performance in preparation for the next race and usually perform better as well.

When an athlete comes to me for his first individual session, I usually begin with the setting priorities exercise. I ask him to list ten lifetime, ten one-year and ten one-month goals and then to go back and order each set of goals into three 'A', three 'B' and the rest 'C' priorities. After this we review the one-month goals and look for steps by which the A and B priorities may be reached. This exercise may be used in many other contexts. If a businessman is to reduce the level of stress in his business environment, he must manage his time efficiently. Nothing is more stressful than unnecessary meetings or constant interruptions.

To gain a long-term reduction of stress, individual members of the team should first be helped to identify the causes of their stress. Christopher and I begin one Sporting Bodymind advanced course by asking participants to become aware of how much stress they feel in the moment, on a score of one to ten, then to notice whether the stress is positive or negative, then to decide what is its cause and, finally, if it is negative, how they could relieve it. An athlete who is continually anxious and unable to relax, who feels he would be happier and perform better if he were more relaxed, would find that responding to a sequence of such questions would help him to become aware of the signs, the causes and the results of his stress and thence to start devising an appropriate programme of exercises to reduce it to an acceptable and positive level. This programme will be one that suits not only his own needs but also his own preferences and prejudices.

A cricket team I worked with last summer was introduced to aerobics as a way of stretching and warming-up. Some players enjoyed it, others didn't and in the end the attempt to get everyone involved was abandoned. One of my clients found that relaxation and visualisation exercises prompted him to go to meditation classes. The coach or sports psychologist's role is to know what is available and where it can be found, just as the physiotherapist of a professional club knows which specialist to contact to gain treatment for a specific injury but with the proviso that, having made the options known to the athlete, it is the athlete who makes the choice.

If planning and goal-setting are left-brain mental approaches to stress management, available to the team as a whole as well as to the individual, visualisation is an associative right-brain mental approach, available to team members only as individuals. Very often a form of visualisation can be used in an emergency, provided the athlete is trained in the technique. Prior to one vault in her Olympic gold medal-winning gymnastics performance, Mary Lou Retton stepped in a puddle of Coca Cola. Seeing that this incident was stressful to her, her coach Bela Karolyi said: 'Never mind. Think of it helping you to stick to the floor as you land' and Mary Lou went on to win.

To any athlete wishing to deal more competently with stress, I suggest that he learns some form of relaxation technique and then make use of one of the Sporting Bodymind visualisation exercises. This might be the 'Quiet Place' visualisation, in which the athlete sits with eyes closed and relaxes in his chair, as described on page 157. He then imagines himself alone and undisturbed in a place that for him is peaceful, somewhere real or imagined but specific. If it is out-of-doors, it could be in a field by a river, in a forest, in the hills or perhaps by the sea. Imagining himself resting in a comfortable position, he first looks straight ahead, seeing the line of the horizon, the colours and shapes ahead of him, then looks at the ground, touches the ground, looks to his left being aware of the season, the time of day and the weather, then looks to the right, being aware of the sounds that belong to this place. He may look behind him, above him, and then he settles back into his original position, aware of the *feeling* of being relaxed and undisturbed in a place that is peaceful.

After a while I might ask him to return to the room where we are, without opening his eyes, and to take the thumb of his left hand in the fingers of his right, press it very gently and then return to his 'quiet place', looking again, straight ahead ... at the ground ... to his left and right ... behind him ... above him and again straight ahead, aware once more of the feeling of restfulness. This action of taking thumb in fingers, with practice, can become associated with the feeling of being in his 'quiet place' and can act as a 'trigger' to enable him to return there at will.

If I ask the athlete to describe his experience of being in this place, I may light on a phrase which he'll later decide to turn into an *affirmation* (see page 155). In this case, the affirmation would be a sentence which, for him, evoked a feeling of calmness; and he would copy it out and place it somewhere where he would notice it several times each day.

An alternative exercise would be to follow the initial relaxation with a variation on the 'Wise Old Person' visualisation described in chapter two (page 47). In this case, the athlete might ask 'What is the real source of my stress?' and 'What should I do to relieve it?'. Afterwards, I'd ask him to open his eyes, write down his perceptions and write a further commentary on them.

(c) The emotional approach

Some techniques fall between the mental and emotional categories. One such is changing one's attitude towards those
stressors which can not in themselves be changed. When the
order for the last round of dives in the 1984 Olympic high-board
competition was announced, the two Chinese divers, closely
challenging, were both placed between the Americans Greg Lougarnis and Bruce Kimball. After the event, when the Americans
had won gold and silver, one of the USA coaches Dick Kimball
said: 'You take the set of circumstances and you use it to your
own advantage, whatever it is. When we saw the order we said
"We've got them right where we want them, sandwiched between the two of you". But if Bruce and Greg had been together
at the end of the order, we would have said "Great! We have the
upper hand and they have to catch us". Either way . . . it doesn't
really matter.' And similarly, after the New York Knicks basketball team overcame a twenty-five point deficit to beat the Boston
Celtics, rookie centre Patrick Ewing reminded reporters 'It
proved we have heart. I told you before – we're not losers, we
were just losing.' (*International Herald Tribune*, 27 December
1985.)

Another technique is to plan and practice moving from a
narrow focus of attention to a broad focus: in doing this, one
learns to switch one's attention away from a potential stressor to
a broader view of the situation. Alternatively, if the occasion
allows, switching from a negative external focus to an internal
positive one – or, indeed, from an internal negative one (such as
worries) to an external positive one (see page 35 etc). Meditation,
relaxation and hypnosis have also all been learnt and used by
sportspeople to relieve stress.

George Brown suggests that focusing on the eighty per cent
that is right with a situation, rather than the twenty per cent that
is wrong, brings one back into the present, 'leaving anxiety in
fantasy land'. Greg Lougarnis, after winning his second gold
medal, said: 'I was scared to go into the last dive. But I stood
there and told myself that no matter what I do here, my mother
will still love me. That gives you strength.' And he backed up
this ploy with singing to himself before each dive. ('It's usually
Believe in Yourself from *The Wiz* that I sing.') (*New York Times* 13
August 1984.)

In the Gestalt idiom, relief is experienced through expressing
what is 'impressed' or blocked. This may be expressing one's

feelings with ink and pen on to the pages of a private journal or taking the time to write a long emotion-filled letter to a distant friend. It can be creating a work of art or playing a piece of music. It could be thumping a punch bag in the gym or even a pillow in the privacy of one's bedroom. Expression can also be direct to a friend, a team mate or a teddy bear. Greg Lougarnis, one of several famous athletes with mascot bears, says that 'the great thing about talking to Gar the Bear is that he doesn't answer back when his master lets off steam'. (*New York Times*, 13 August 1984.) If the source of your stress *is* someone you can speak to, getting together and 'finishing the unfinished business' is the best release of all.

Learning how to reduce stress is invariably a process of self-discovery. In the end, a businessman or an athlete may come to accept the need to reduce the element of conflict and competition in his life. A situation that for some colleagues or team mates remains an exciting challenge could be dangerously stressful to himself. This may mean changing his job or competing at a lower level or it may just highlight the need to develop a balancing element in his life. A player who lives alone or in a stormy relationship, without other affiliations, is always going to be prone to stress when things within his work or sports team become challenging. Such individuals may also be inclined to compromise or give in for the sake of peace, rather than face up to an important challenge, whether from within the team or without. Living alone, as I did in Edinburgh, I found my ability to deal with frustration within my volleyball-filled life to be considerably improved when I joined a yoga and later a dream-analysis group. Not only were these activities directed towards reducing stress but becoming a member of a new group, building new relationships, exploring new ideas and being able to distance myself from the challenges of volleyball was in itself therapeutic.

No individual, however strong, can do without social support, other people to whom he can turn in times of stress. 'In addition to friends and family, individuals also need people to respect them, challenge them, provide access for them and to be mentors, evaluators, experts or energizers,' writes John Adams, pointing out that most of us have too few such relationships. The coach or manager should encourage team members to 'evaluate their present support network, match it with their needs and identify improvements that can be made, asking "Who are the most relevant people around?" and "How can their support be rallied when needed?"' John Cassell suggests that 'Of the two sets of factors, it would seem more immediately feasible to attempt to improve and strengthen social supports than reduce exposure to stressors. (John Cassell, see bibliography.) When the external support system is strong, the athlete is better able to contribute to the team.

However, as suggested in chapter one, one reason people join sports teams in the first place is to experience a sense of belonging, looking to membership of the team to provide a balance to other areas of life. Some may even join to escape from rules, roles and values which they do not enjoy or for which they feel inadequate – or for a sense of order and some measure of control in a life which is otherwise experienced as chaotic. Where the team is held together by fear or negative confluence, and the level of positive creative energy is *lower* than the sum of the creative energies possessed by each member, the worst manifestations of negative team spirit may then result. Something like this must have happened in the case of the police unit patrolling the Holloway Road in London in 1983, where the officers of one van pulled in four young men, beat them up and then were protected not just by their own lies but by the lies of their colleagues in the two other vans known to be in the area.

Yet, when the team is a balanced positive synergetic unit, the individual member can not only find within it relief from outside problems but also find the strength and energy to step outside again and deal with those problems. This relates to the healing property of synergy. In fact I tend to think that a certain wistfulness for the experience of synergy, for the moment of realisation that we are part of a greater whole, where our concerns and doubts are seen in a different less daunting light, can be stirred within the most weathered of individualists.

In an interview with Alain Prost, the Formula 1 driver, and jockey Yves St Martin, Keith Botsford of the *Sunday Times* observed that 'Alain seems to envy the jockeys their *esprit de corps*'. He quotes Prost as saying 'I like their combatitiveness, their fantastic energy, their will to win at whatever they are doing. We are competitive also in F1 but we lack something the jockeys seem to have – normal human relations among ourselves. The teams are the main barrier. If we were too friendly, the teams could think we were swopping information, losing an advantage.' (29 December 1985.)

The coach who is as concerned that the individual perform at his best as he is for that individual's well-being (often in professional sport the first is a much greater concern) may also want to encourage an athlete to share his non-sporting difficulties with another team member, so that these difficulties be eased. However, for this to happen, the coach must first create a sense of safety and foster synergy within the team, which he will not be able to do if his intentions are purely manipulative. The synergetic team is not only a comfort and an inspiration to each individual member, a power that helps the individual to be strong in the face of threats from other areas of his life, but the spirit of such a team inspires stern resistance to any challenge to the team as a whole. The visionary architect Buckminster Fuller, inventor of the geodesic dome, describes such strength well in another context. 'In design synergism, we discover that, while chromium has one set of behaviour characteristics and nickel and iron still others, the association of the three in unique mathematical proportions provides a combined behaviour of superior performance in resistance to tension and impact, in contrast to the behaviour of any of its constituent parts.'(James Mellor (ed.), *The Buckminster Fuller Reader*.)

It was Buckminster Fuller who pointed out that if a chain is linked in a complete circle, the saying 'A chain is only as strong as its weakest link' does not apply: the circle will break at its weakest link, under great stress, but when it breaks it still remains a strong chain. The ritual of standing in a circle, discussed previously in the context of 'protection' (see page 38), if adopted and learned in non-stressful times, will serve to re-evoke the resilience of team spirit in times of stress. As with all technical skills, team spirit has to be practiced if it is to be available under pressure. When a team has suffered a severe set-back, the tendency will be (and the opposition will push) for it to fall apart. Several members may not want to join the circle and others may do so physically but come mentally and emotionally withdrawn. Yet once the circle is closed, the channel through which team spirit can flow is reconstructed and the coach or captain is better able to break the dam of disappointment and distress. Such was the lesson that Tottenham learned from the 1982 Milk Cup Final and which is described in the opening pages of this book.

EPILOGUE

Whatever I may have intended when I set out, this book has been as much about *leadership* as it has about team spirit. This is because team spirit can only grow in a certain climate and it is you the coach who creates the climate in which your athletes interact.

Each chapter has suggested different opportunities and options available to you. Some will stifle team spirit but ensure your wish is law. Others will foster team spirit with positive but unpredictable results. You can allow conflict to divide your team or ensure that it leads to greater understanding and unity. You can oblige your team to confirm to your pre-determined plan or encourage it to discover the full range of its skills. You can stay apart from your team or be close to it, developing your athlete's ability to communicate clearly with each other and the world at large. You can 'motivate' your team or help your athletes to maturity. You can increase or diminish your athletes' confidence and can *cause* stress, ignore it or teach your team to respond to it positively.

I have implied that the first set of options reflect a behaviourist approach and the second that of the humanist. I should add that, in doing so, I have focused on the negative qualities of the former and the positive qualities of the latter. In truth, neither the extreme behaviourist nor the extreme humanist makes a very successful coach – at least, not if his objective is to profit fully from the challenge of competition. Curiously, perhaps, the most enthusiastic humanist can find his energy drained by an unresponsive team. Athletes are not always prepared to take responsibility for their own actions and development. Many prefer to act on orders alone and a humanist who wants to change the norms of a team used to conforming to the coach's orders must introduce changes with care and patience.

Yet the idea of extremes is useful for it suggests a scale in between. We should now consider the two opposing systems of leadership in more detail and look briefly at the role of the trainer in relation to these sytems. Appendixes A and B describe proven examples of behaviourist and humanistic leadership – examples not directly related to sport but which contain a wealth of thought-provoking concepts which could help you to clarify your own approach.

Behaviourist coaching

The *behaviourist* coach is concerned to achieve a specific objective, usually winning, and considers how best to manipulate the environment so that his athletes are motivated towards achieving that objective. The most usual form of manipulation is reward or punishment. The most heavy-handed of this type of coach regards the team as a group of individuals that have to be shaped into a form of his choosing. This attitude is typified by P Chelladurai, when he defines leadership as the process of influencing subordinates towards objectives that are chosen for them and suggests that the coach should 'mould' the team by 'dispensing' rewards. (P Chelladurai, see bibliography.)

Most professional team coaches are assumed to be behaviouristic. After all, they are paid to succeed and their jobs depend on winning. It's true too that the best players are paid the most and a player who loses his form is not only dropped but often discarded. The *Guardian* football correspondent once suggested that professional football players are motivated by financial reward and that, deprived of the power of offering such reward, a coach has a hard time cobbling a team together: 'The greater freedom of contract enjoyed by players has made team-building more difficult and long-term planning well-nigh impossible.' (David Lacey, *Guardian*, 25 August 1984.) The success of teams in lower divisions and the fact that many players can't be tempted away from their clubs by offers of larger rewards suggests that this isn't the whole story. Despite heavy behaviourist overtones, many mangers are able to evoke flashes of genuine team spirit.

The behaviourist coach as here defined is a somewhat impersonal figure of authority, who feels with Keith Burkinshaw that 'It's very important to keep a certain distance from the players'.

However, as we saw in chapter four, neither Burkinshaw, nor Arok nor Parker have the guise of out-and-out calculating behaviourists. In all three cases, their reticence could charitably be taken as a matter of temperament. Not so with Tony La Russa it would seem (see page 72), nor with Dick Williams, manager of the San Diego Padres baseball team, who boasted to *Sports Illustrated* (6 August 1984): 'I'm as obnoxious as ever. I purposely stay away from the players'. These are the coaches whose sole concern is to build a winning team and who respond in astonishment to any suggestion that *listening* to their players might be part of their job.

Of course most coaches operating with systems of punishment and reward and clearly concerned to maintain a discrete distance and complete authority over their players are nonetheless adept at communicating in an amicable way and often enjoy the process of working towards their objective with their team. The best of the breed will make sure that not only the team but each individual player has clear and attainable goals, which are adjusted frequently. He knows that the experience of success is the best of all motivators. If he then rewards the player by praising him and showing his own positive response, he is experienced as effective *and* caring which motivates the player to still greater efforts. He will act similarly with the team as a whole, ensuring that the team too has realistic goals which are continually adjusted upwards towards new achievements. He plans his way to victory, taking account of the talent he has available and ensuring that the players he needs are happy. He even plans for setbacks along the way, establishing a code of rules and punishments in discussion with the players at the beginning of the season.

Chris Gibson, manager of Haringey Cricket College, at heart a humanist yet with a healthy behaviourist sub-personality, was still working towards such a scheme at the end of the College's first season. The day after one of his bowlers was told halfway though his run-up that his run-up was too long, and reacted by angrily throwing the ball way beyond the boundary, Chris suggested there should be a disciplinary sub-committee set up at the start of the next season. He proposed to the team that the committee be made up of two members of staff and two players and that they have the right to impose fines of up to one whole week's wages and to ban the offending player from match play. I knew that by his own terms, this was a reasonable suggestion and, in fact, with some reservations it was accepted by most of the young players. Chris Gibson isn't attached to winning each and every match but he is attached to the College being a success and to players adopting a code of behaviour that will help them to be selected for the staff of a county cricket club, all other things being equal. Disciplinary measures are the behaviourist's stock method of dealing with the 'problem athlete'.

Despite my bias against the behaviourist way of coaching, I can see that it has its points. Effective manipulation requires dispassionate calculation; the ability to assess athletes and situations coolly, especially in time of stress is invaluable to any coach, whatever his orientation. Furthermore, the concept of realistic stage-by-stage goal-setting towards an inspiring achievement is essential if an athlete is not to become discouraged. It is in this way that he acquires a sense of confidence and pleasure in his own ability. This is especially true of young players who, left to set their own goals, would probably not aim high enough and would therefore never reach their full potential.

There are however a number of drawbacks to the behaviourist style of leadership, even within its own terms. It was the results of the research at Hawthorn (page 101) which showed that if people are treated as if they are insensitive machines, only concerned with what money they can make, the lack of satisfaction of their needs for esteem and self-actualisation leads 'to tension, anxiety and frustration ... to feeling unimportant, confused and unattached – victims of their own environment'. (Hersey and Blanchard.) This is not just a reaction to the manager being too distant but also to having no control over decisions affecting them. The authoritarian behaviourist coach is actually encouraging his athletes to be passive and dependent. The more control that is imposed on the bowler who threw the ball over the boundary in disgust, the more likely he is to react immaturely. Furthermore, where a manager or coach closely supervise and take complete control, opposition will soon begin to simmer.

Teachers can be repressive too. As Hersey and Blanchard point out, it is strange that high school students 'are subject to more rules and restrictions and generally treated less maturely than their younger counterparts in elementary school'. This may in part account for adolescents being more troublesome than younger children. Despite a generally enlightened approach and research that shows that for adolescents an emphasis on winning is negatively correlated with 'having a good time', some school sports teams are still run with an almost military emphasis on discipline. In America, the pressure put on adolescents is probably greater than in Britain. However, at the higher levels of performance, even in Britain the coach can have an influence, second only to the child's parents – not just in terms of sport but in forming the athlete's general goals and values.

In business, a leader can become a prisoner of his own high position, with so many levels of subordinates, through whom information has to filter upwards, that he knows less about what is really happening than do outsiders. Although a sports club, even a large professional one, doesn't have many grades of staff between head coach and players, there is some point in drawing the analogy. The coach may be effective within his behavioural role without getting close to the players but he does need to be close enough to observe them accurately and he is wise to check out his conclusions with someone who knows the players well. His most obvious potential ally in this respect is his captain. To hold himself aloof from his captain is to risk losing out badly.

More of a problem though for the behaviourist coach is the fact that people respond in different ways to different stimuli (see page 127), so that what will be a reward for some athletes may hold no attraction for others, whose needs are different. Even what is meant as a punishment may not always be perceived as such. The 'behaviourist coach' is almost bound to discover the 'problem athlete', the athlete who does not respond to the coach's stimuli as he is supposed to do. There is also the problem of the athlete or team who consistently fails to achieve its allotted goal and as a result is never given the promised reward. After a while the promise of reward carries no significance to the athlete and his efforts will slacken further and results become even worse.

In fact the most serious drawback of the behaviourist coaching style is that enthusiasm is stifled and creativity wanes (see page 67). Players are continually told what to do, never asked and, as a result, if they accept the situation, they begin to lose the habit, if not the ability, of thinking for themselves. Here there is no synergy at all, no creative team spirit, no excitement. Edward Greenfield, in his *Guardian* article about Finnish conductor Esa-Pekka Salonen, writes 'What he likes about Anglo-Saxon orchestras is that the players are more flexible than in France, Germany and Italy. In particular, "the prestige business is not essential. It's delightful with the Philharmonia; I don't have to pretend to be authoritarian. We work in two-way communication."' (7 February 1986.)

It is a sad waste, a sacrifice to one man's need for power or fear of losing control, when the manager *doesn't* share the creative process with his players. Simon Callow, the actor, was outraged by the way he was directed in *As You Like It*: ' . . . What it seems to put in question is the propriety of so much standing or falling on one man's personal vision. Never at any point were any of us consulted on the meaning of the play or the gesture of the production. Forty intelligent and gifted people were committed without choice to embodying John Dexter's view of the play.'

Humanistic coaching

When it comes to the crunch, a *humanistic* coach is more concerned with the quality of the athlete's experience than he is with winning, although the one doesn't exclude the other. He seeks to stimulate the athlete's excitement and curiosity about his own and his team's potential so that he motivates himself to do well. Rather than mould his team into a predetermined shape, to achieve his own objective, he encourages team members to learn what they can about each others' strengths, weaknesses and motivations and creates the most exciting and efficient unit possible.

The humanistic coach spends time getting to know each athlete. He 'places individual expression above group conformity, self-discipline above authority and independence above dependence'. (George Sage, see bibliography.) Instead of punishing the bowler who threw the ball over the boundary, he would ask him a number of questions and suggest exercises he might do, to explore inappropriate outbursts of anger. The questions would be designed to help the bowler recognise his pattern of behaviour, accept it and eventually to bring about change. 'What do you want to achieve?', 'What blocks you from its achievement?', often lead to the recognition of conflicting motives and thence to the Gestalt dialogue exercise, (see pages 133 and 152), in which both 'selves' make their needs known and come to some sort of agreement. However, this would only be part of the story for it was the behaviour of members of his own team, the opposition and the umpires which sparked off his own action and a discussion of the incident in a team meeting would uncover patterns of interaction within the team in which the bowler only plays his part.

For any group to operate efficiently, there needs to be a balance between time spent focusing on the *task* at hand and time spent on *maintenance*, the feelings of team members (see page 88). Ideally, there should also be time spent on *processing* – discussion of the way the task is being fulfilled and of how members feel about the team. The extreme behaviourist coach will over-emphasise task factors, with the result that members become preoccupied with unresolved feelings, cease to contribute ideas and fragment into dissatisfied sometimes rebellious cliques. The extreme humanistic coach will over-emphasise maintenance factors, with the result that little gets done and in the end that many members get frustrated and leave.

Mark Anshel defines five principles of the good humanist coach: (i) that he interacts positively with his athletes, gets to know their backgrounds and adapts his coaching to their needs and styles; (ii) that he treats his athletes as individuals as well as part of a team; (iii) that he interacts with his athletes during the off-season; (iv) that he takes part in practice sessions himself, at least early in the season; and (v) that he gives all his athletes a chance to participate or to serve a useful role. His emphasis is on participation rather than the outcome. He wants his athletes to become more complete, fulfilled, self-motivated people without wanting this only for his *own* sake (ie believing such development would make his team more successful). He wants them to do well because it is in striving to do well that they develop as people.

Throughout this book I have made it clear I believe in humanist as opposed to behaviourist coaching. However, if there is a scale on which extreme behaviourism rates 'one' and extreme humanism rates 'ten', I'd place myself on about 'eight' and, when I've referred to *you* as a 'humanist coach', I've also meant 'eight' rather than 'ten out of ten'. As a sports psychologist employed by a team coach, I usually spend a large part of my time working with individual team members and, as with clients who come to my practice individually, I am concerned to help these athletes to identify and reach their objectives. Usually these objectives are in line with those of his coach but I secure an agreement with the coach before I start work whereby, if they are not so in line, I should have no part in manipulating the player towards satisfying the coach's needs. I view conflict positively as an indication that something important is being ignored and as a sign that the parties involved – in this case the coach and the athlete – should look again. I continue to reflect to the individual what I notice and occasionally give my personal response ... and then leave him to take his decisions.

In this I am no doubt nearer 'nine' than 'seven' on the behaviourist humanist scale but, *as a coach*, I'd probably rate nearer 'seven' than 'nine'. That is because the extreme humanist is one hundred per cent for the individual at the expense of the team. I am not. I know that, in so far as personal feelings affect an athlete's performance, they are relevant to the team's effort as a whole. Even feelings that are aroused by factors outside the context of the team can sometimes be relevant, although the need to discuss such matters at team meetings doesn't often occur. The fact is that the humanistic coach is so concerned to pay attention to the individual that he is in danger of forgetting that team spirit itself is a 'growth experience' and that the individual misses out if he is unable to allow himself to merge with the team in its efforts towards fulfilment of a chosen goal. In my view he is also missing out if he doesn't do his damnedest (by fair means not foul) to win.

The trainer

The *roles* of coach and trainer are distinct, even though they may often be played by the same individual. The coach is primarily concerned with tactics, selection and mental training; the trainer is responsible for teaching and improving physical and technical skill. The trainer, a leader in his own right as he conducts his training session, may *also* take a behaviouristic or humanistic approach. As a behaviourist he will tell his athletes how they must perform a given skill, as a humanist he will help his athletes to discover how to perform the skill.

The humanistic way is to prompt learning by experience: 'Experiential learning is learning through emanation. The abilities are assumed to exist and teaching is simply a process of providing the human and physical conditions for their growth. Basically this involves the student learning by seeing, trying out and becoming involved. Correspondingly, the teacher is involved in showing or modelling, helping the student try out through coaching him; and by being a guide for the student to become more deeply involved.' (Christopher Wainwright, see bibliography.) Once the student has acquired the rudiments of the skill, the humanistic coach helps him to make necessary adjustments, either by saying 'See what happens if you do this', or by adapting an Inner Game technique, which is to direct the student's attention to some aspect of the movement, placement of part of the body or distribution of weight for instance, and ask that they assess out of ten how much it is one thing or another – how much weight is on the top ski, how square the body is to the net on hitting the ball, how extended the arms as they claw into the water. All this is contrary to the behaviourist's direct-voiced analysis and instruction to make the desired change.

The Inner Game technique allows the student to explore on his own: He may even find that the most effective action for him is a little different to the way a behaviouristic trainer would have imposed. 'After a certain point of guidance, leaving the student to . . . explore and discover by himself enhances his capacity to learn . . . [Advice is then] usually a distraction to the student, inhibiting his capacity to become self-absorbed in the learning activities . . . Learning a physical skill is a scientific enterprise . . . hypothesising, experimenting . . . Only [the student] can engage in this. It is an independent activity.' And again: 'Learning can't be given to a person. Rather, learning emerges from a person when certain conditions prevail.' (ibid.)

The humanistic trainer won't always agree to give a repeat demonstration of something the student wants to see again. The student already has all the information he needs, now he must let the skill happen: 'Skills emanate from within the learner, they can't be grafted on.' Yet the trainer does stand by. If the student 'gets excited by a goal that is far out of reach, help him to be excited by the intermediate steps needed to reach it'. Also: 'Attention is paid to the learner . . . The experience of learning will affect the student's ability to learn . . . The coach is available to the learner. He is an auxiliary to the student and, as such, will operate according to the person's learning pace.' (ibid.) The coach/trainer's objective is to teach the student to respond and, indeed, to be responsible.

A leader doesn't always lead, for leadership is a *role* not a position and may be assumed from moment to moment by any member of the team. Hersey and Blanchard state this in behaviourist terms when they say 'leadership occurs any time one attempts to influence the behaviour of an individual or a group, regardless of the reason'. Only the most authoritarian of coaches will stifle all attempts at leadership other than his own.

Humanists view the process differently. 'The group has a wisdom of its own, extending beyond the wisdom of the leader alone,' say Erving and Miriam Polster, bringing us right back to our original definition of synergy and team spirit. First one individual's needs then another's come into focus. '. . . This movement of the group into concern with a particular person is an organically sound group phenomenon.' (*Gestalt Therapy Integrated.*)

For me, this not only describes a creative team discussion but also a sports team in the easy flow of action, a team that has momentarily captured the elusive experience of team spirit.

Appendix A

SITUATIONAL LEADERSHIP:
A BEHAVIOURIST MODEL

This section is based on Paul Hersey and Ken Blanchard's *Management of Organisational Behavior*.

This model was devised by Paul Hersey and Ken Blanchard and is based on the premise that different styles of leadership identified on a four-point scale, are demanded by different situations. It is a premise that was adopted somewhat earlier by Malcolm and Hulda Knowles, who distinguished between 'authoritarian' and 'democratic' leadership, where 'democratic' suggests 'fairness' rather than the humanist's overriding concern for the individual's process. They also extended the scale to a point beyond 'democratic' which they call *'laissez-faire'*. They suggested that, although some situations require authoritarian and some *laissez-faire* leadership, democratic leadership normally works best. The authoritarian style should be used in an emergency, when a decision has to be taken quickly. At the other extreme, the *laissez-faire* style can be appropriate with international level athletes, who are fully motivated and know how to achieve their objectives.

The four points on the Situational Leadership Scale are: 'telling'; 'selling'; 'participating'; and 'delegating'. Like the Knowles' model, it is designed to guide group leaders (in this case specifically business executives) in the art of gaining maximum effectiveness from their subordinates, in terms of the leaders' goals, rather than in terms of the holistic development of the subordinates.

Hersey and Blanchard view 'maintenance' discussion as a way by which the manager may better manipulate his subordinates towards his own ends. With this understood, they say that a leader can behave in one of four different ways: (i) high task and low maintenance behaviour, which they call a *'telling'* style of leadership; (ii) high task and high maintenance behaviour, which they call a *selling* style of leadership: (iii) low task and high maintenance behaviour, which they call a *'partici-*

pating' style of leadership; and (iv) low task and low maintenance behaviour, which they call a *'delegating'* style.

The aptness of any of these styles is related to the degree of 'maturity'
of the followers. *Telling* ('S1') is for people with low maturity, who are
both *unable* and *unwilling* to take responsibility to do something and
who are neither confident nor competent. *Selling* ('S2') is for people
with low to moderate maturity, who are *unable* but *willing* to take responsibility and who are confident but still lack skill. *Participating* ('S3')
is for people with moderate to high maturity, who are *able* but *unwilling*
to take responsibility, the unwillingness often being a result of their
lack of confidence or insecurity. *Delegating* ('S4') is for people with high
maturity, who are *able* and *willing* and confident enough to take responsibility. This can all be shown diagrammatically:

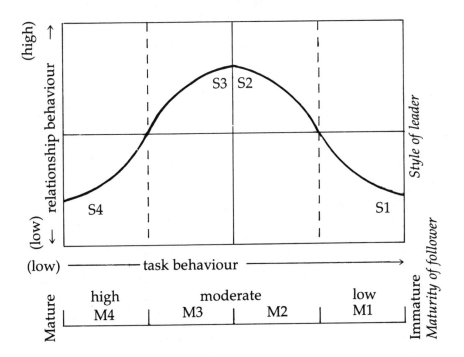

'Maturity' as used here by Hersey and Blanchard has little to do with
the humanistic concept of self-awareness and fulfilling inner potential.
Rather, it is 'a task-specific concept and depends on what the leader is
attempting to accomplish'. Since individual and team goals sometimes
conflict, it may be that one player will be considered inept and 'immature' at a certain skill, simply because he is not interested in developing
it: this definition of 'maturity' includes willingness. He would be
classed as M1 in respect of his skill. Similarly, a secretary may need

close supervision for paperwork but none for sales and be classed as M4 for sales but M1 for paperwork.

The behaviourist leader is only going to achieve his objective if his leadership style is right for the situation in which he finds himself and different styles of leadership will be needed for different members of a team if their needs and motives are different. Hersey and Blanchard give the example of a haulage firm where the drivers are loners and respond to supervisors who are task oriented, whereas the packagers work better with a relationship-oriented supervisor. In a sports team, some members' needs may coincide with the coach's and some not. In this case, some players may need a uniform 'S4' style of leadership, whereas those whose motives are quite at odds will require an 'S1' style, if the leader (at his most behaviouristic) is to use this player to reach his own objective. Furthermore the team as a whole will need to be led in a specific style, which may vary from the style required by many or even most of the individuals in the team. And different groups of people with whom the manager has to deal – the office staff, the directors, the press, the players and the coaching staff – may all need to be led in different styles.

The correct style with which to lead the team will depend on the task maturity of the team as a whole. In business, this means taking account of customs, level of education, standard of living and industrial experience. The choice of style must also take account of the followers' past experience of leadership. If this has been uniquely of a 'telling' S1 style, the introduction to anything more advanced would have to be done gradually.

There are many refinements that can be made to the table. For instance, Hersey and Blanchard make plain their behaviouristic bias when they add that the leader telling an 'immature' follower to do something (and showing him how to do it) can be friendly but must not reward the follower with a pat on the back until it has been earned. The delegating style is inappropriate for a follower 'lacking motivation and ability to direct his own work schedule' (this happened once to my own scholastic career) and the mistake can even 'encourage immaturity if the student perceives a lack of structure as permissiveness'. On the other hand, too much relationship behaviour with M4 maturity followers (treating them as if they were still at stage M3) 'is regarded as a sign of the leader's lack of confidence and trust'.

The leader's style – telling, selling, participating or delegating – is seen, in true behaviourist mode, to be an incentive to attain greater maturity. If the leader changes his style before the follower has completed his job and shown a new willingness or increase in ability, he will cut the follower's incentive and be thought 'a soft touch'. The young teacher, for instance, full of idealism and determined to do away with an established rule by punishment, is prone to make the mistake of changing the style of leadership too rapidly and finding that, instead of inspiring more initiative in his students as he'd expected, the change only stimulates irresponsibility. Other leaders make the mistake of making a sudden change from the telling (S1) to the delegating (S4) style and, in abruptly leaving their followers on their own, ensures that they are unable to achieve the goals that have been set for them. All too often the first mistake is followed by a second, as the leader angrily punishes his followers and reverts right back to the 'telling' style.

The reverse mistake is also made, in sport as much as in business. An athlete (and it could be an entire team) who had reached full 'maturity' and was coached in the S4 delegating style loses the edge of his performance, and is now 'able but not willing' due to loss of confidence. Instead of the coach going back to the participating style, which still involves low task but now involves high relationship behaviour, he does nothing for a long time. Then suddenly the coach loses his patience and jumps right back to either a 'selling' or even a 'telling' leadership style, involving high task behaviour – which in fact, by now, is necessary. The way back is now much more arduous and may well involve the athlete in a long spell of playing for the reserve team.

Hersey and Blanchard are concerned throughout with *task maturity* (being willing and able to perform an allotted task) rather than maturity in humanistic terms (development of the individual's ability to define and achieve his own goals). In the context of task maturity, they make very useful distinctions between ways of conducting discussions. For each level of maturity, there is an appropriate discussion leadership style. Level M1 athletes need to be given a talk, rather than participate in a discussion, so this requires S1 leadership style. Level M2 athletes need circle discussions in which the leader directs the conversation. Level M3 athletes conduct their own discussion with the coach acting as a supportive but non-directive member of the group. Finally, M4 athletes conduct their own discussion, with the coach only being involved when invited. As always, the match between style and maturity must be correct. Even S3 style, the coach intervening with supportive remarks, can be irritating to M4 athletes of international class; whilst an S4 style (the coach sitting back unless invited to speak) with M1 athletes would result not just in uproar but in uninformed uproar at that.

Hersey and Blanchard suggest that a manager should develop the 'maturity' of his subordinates to the point where one of them is able to take over his own job. For this the manager should be rewarded, usually by promotion. To develop maturity, 'a leader must first tell and show the follower(s) what to do; second delegate *some* responsibility (not too much or failure might result) and third, reward as soon as possible any behaviour in the desired direction'. The humanist's normal 'relationship' or 'maintenance' behaviour is seen by Hersey and Blanchard as a *reward*, to be proffered only after the follower has achieved the goal he was set. This then, they argue, makes it more likely that the action will be repeated. Task behaviour by the coach is the start which pushes the follower to take action to achieve his goal. A common mistake of managers is to give the initial push and then withdraw. They must follow the athlete's progress closely, if necessary through detailed reports of the coaching staff, 'so as to be in a position to reinforce the change appropriately' – that is, through reward.

Behaviourism relates closely to motivation, nowhere so obviously as in the question of *power*. However, what power is available and whether it is used, depends very much on the character and style of the leader. 'Power,' say Hersey and Blanchard, 'is a resource that may or may not be used.' There is power that is given to a leader by his superiors, called *'position power'* and power that can be earned on a day-to-day basis from his followers, called *'personal power'*. (Actually a manager needs to remember that he has to earn his position power as well – from his superiors. 'Most managers give considerable attention to supervising subordinates but some do not pay enough attention to being a subordinate themselves.') Position power is used to gain compliance from followers, personal power is used to influence followers. These are two different power bases. Generally speaking position power is best used with followers of below average 'maturity' and influence power with those of above-average 'maturity'. A dynamic leader – and a dynamic organisation – will gradually work his way from position power to personal power.

These two broad bases of power can be broken down further into seven categories in all, each category being more appropriate for a correspondingly higher level of 'maturity' of the follower. The first category is *coercive* power, based on fear of punishment, where the follower will obey in case he be penalised. The second is *legitimate* power, based on the leader's position, where a follower will obey almost unthinkingly because 'he's the boss'. The third is *expert* power, based on knowledge or expertise, where the follower obeys because he believes his leader knows best. This response is already one that involves an element of respect. The fourth category is *reward* power, based on the leader's ability to reward, where a follower responds as asked in the hope of recognition, closer relationship, a rise or a more responsible position. The fifth category is *referent* power, based on the leader's personality, where a follower responds because he likes and admires his leader. The sixth category is *information* power, based on a leader's access to information which the follower wants. The seventh and final category is *connection* power, based on the leader's relationship with people of influence, where the follower responds because he needs approval of some person of importance known well to the leader.

Research has shown that in a wide variety of business and academic settings, legitimate and expert power are the most effective ways to gain compliance; coercive and legitimate power provoke dissatisfaction but don't have an adverse effect on performance, expert and referent power tend to promote good performance and satisfaction. However, these generalisations are broad. The behaviourist coach will need to vary his use of the various power categories, according to the situation as the category that is the most effective at any given time depends primarily on the level of 'maturity' of the athlete(s) concerned. He should also realise that his own view of his power may not correspond to the view of his athletes and that, irrespective of the reality of the situation, it is the athletes' view that counts, since it is they who choose whether or not to respond. If he feels that his athletes are not responding as expected, it may be that he needs to demonstrate his power bases more clearly: the lack of response may arise merely because his power has not been perceived.

The following diagram shows how a behaviourist coach should relate his perceived categories of power to the lever of 'maturity' of his athletes.

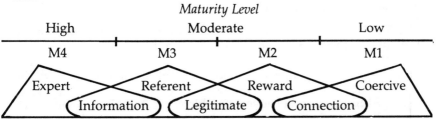

Maturity Level

High	Moderate	Low
M4	M3 M2	M1

Expert — Referent — Reward — Coercive
Information — Legitimate — Connection

With M1 he can use coercive and connection power, with M2 legitimate, reward and connection power, with M3 information, referent and legitimate power, and with M4 expert and information power. In terms of the two major power bases, positional and personal, positional power is the most effective base for dealing with 'low maturity' athletes, a mixture of the two for dealing with 'moderate maturity' athletes and personal power for dealing with 'high maturity' athletes.

Although not all coaches will have all seven categories of power at their disposal, it is clear that the majority of professional coaches at least are sufficiently of the behaviourist mode to use their power to gain their predetermined ends, a successful team. As a humanist, I would argue that this is not the only road to success. A coach who is able to lead his team to discovering its unique identity (that which is initially 'on the etheric' see pages 218–9) and its own team spirit, will find that even the 'low maturity' athletes in his team will respond. Of course, the humanist's *definition* of success is individual and concerned with the *process* of discovery and therefore different to the behaviourists but when a 'problem athlete' or a 'low maturity' athlete is inspired by a spirit that connects with higher and broader aspects of his experience than that of the task alone, remarkable changes occur which incidentally result in improved team performance.

As a final comment on this behaviourist's outline of power bases and categories, it should be pointed out that each base or category can be eroded and that leadership then becomes less effective as a means of achieving a set goal. Coercive power is lost through continual threats. Reward power is lost by lack of discrimination, as when a manager smiles and responds supportively to a player, irrespective of whether the player has accomplished his task or not. Connection power is lost if the influential person known to the coach doesn't become concerned with the team. Legitimate power is lost by making too many controversial and bad decisions. Referent power is lost by lack of discrimination as to who the leader compliments, and expert and information power are lost by giving away so much knowledge that the athlete doesn't need the leader any more – or when the leader is shown to possess little knowledge in the first place.

All managers are naturally better at one of the four leadership styles – telling (S1), selling (S2), participating (S3) or delegating (S4). Some have a secondary style and Hersey and Blanchard give a profile of each possible two-style combination:

The S1/S2 coach is good in a crisis and in getting things done under pressure. A person who is no longer a coach, having become an administrator, but still wanting to coach and who has to have the last word is an example. Such people are good with athletes of low 'maturity' but can't develop them to their full potential.

The S1/S3 coach will move M2 athletes up to M3 or down to M1, depending on whether or not he likes them. He keeps athletes locked into either the M1 or the M3 stages of development.

The S1/S4 coach can't develop athletes from a low to a high maturity, lacking empathy, but is good in a crisis. His M3 athletes tend to make it to M4 but his M2 athletes drop back to M1.

The S2/S3 coach plays it safe. He doesn't know how to delegate or discipline.

The S2/S4 coach insists on directing and has difficulty delegating. When he does his choice to delegate is often in trouble because he hasn't had the support needed to move through M3.

The S3/S4 coach can't direct or initiate structure. He can develop openness with youngsters but not basic skills. He is a good humanistic educator and very effective with top athletes.

Appendix B

LEADERSHIP AT FINDHORN
A HUMANIST MODEL

My time at the Findhorn Foundation gave me a very different experience of leadership to anything I had known before and became an important factor in my own understanding of group dynamics. That experience is therefore relevant and of interest, although it is unlikely that even the most humanistic of coaches would adopt some of the methods described below, on a day to day basis.

Findhorn was (and still is) one hundred per cent humanistic in its approach to leadership and, as such, is likely to spark creative reactions in any visiting leader. When I was there in the seventies, some two to three hundred members were grouped, by the location of their living quarters and by their work department, into smaller 'families'. Over a period of time, members might move living quarters from one part of the community to another and change work departments from housekeeping to maintenance, to gardening, to publishing, to cooking and so on but the principles by which these different groups were led were always the same. I personally always lived at Cluny Hill College in Forres and only worked for any length of time in two departments, the bookshop and the guest department, in both of which I had the experience of 'leading'.

Each work department had one part of an afternoon each week set aside for a discussion meeting. The meeting *itself* was called an 'attunement', as was the moment of silence which started this and 'all meetings in the community. The weekly meeting is divided into two parts, one 'task' – to discuss business matters of the department, both internal and those relating to the community as a whole – and one 'maintenance' – a space for each member of the department in turn to make a statement about his personal experience of the preceding week and of his current feelings, needs and ambitions. The departmental leader was called 'focaliser' to emphasise his role as a focus or point of contact for the department, within the community as a whole. He would begin the

215

business section of the meeting by announcing the agenda and then making a report to the department on community matters that had arisen at the focalisers' meeting he had attended earlier in the week. During the subsequent discussion, any member of the department who suggested a course of action agreeable to the rest of the group would be encouraged to explore the possibilities himself – to take responsibility for the matter that evoked his response.

We adopted much the same attitude in guest group meetings. Here people were together for just one week and, having come to Findhorn from very different backgrounds and, being of widely different ages and of many different nationalities, individual members had a great many different opinions to express about their daily experience. These groups would normally have a fifteen- or twenty-minute review or maintenance meeting each morning or afternoon before work. Because of the nature of the group, there were many opinions about what community members and the community as a whole should or should not do. As a guest group focaliser, I was inclined to give as much space as possible to someone expressing his feelings about his experience of the previous day (often feelings of moving intensity) and relatively little time to people expressing opinions as to what people in the community should or should not do. According to a distinction made earlier (page 98), the first kind of speaking I called 'talk', the second 'chat'.

In some cases it was possible to encourage the person with the opinion to go off and do something about it, to take responsibility for their response, but more often the need was more subtle and evoked from me the question. 'So that's what you *think* about what the community member is doing and should do. How do you feel as you give us this opinion? What is happening for *you* at this moment?' Sometimes this was sufficient to lead the speaker to an awareness of strong personal feelings that occurred regularly in certain situations for him and were perhaps a source of some distress, related to some other factor in his life entirely. That after all is the way our opinions are formed. Once the speaker was able to identify and express this feeling, he was back in touch with his 'response-ability' and taking responsibility for his experience. Usually, in the one-week-only guest-group situation, this tack was the most productive, but occasionally a guest would have such a strong positive sense of a specific change needed in the community, that he could and did initiate it to the benefit of all. (This would usually involve further visits and many more discussions with different groups within the community.)

Generally speaking, the community acted as a sounding board for the guest group as a whole, as did the experience recounted by each other individual in the group. Individuals had come to Findhorn attracted by the experience of community life, full of alert interest. The community did respond to their presence presence and sometimes changed because of it but the main experience of the week was a unique and personal one of the group members becoming aware of themselves and each other, awarenesses sparked off by the mix of their past experiences, their expectations and their surroundings. In the space of seven days a tight team spirit would develop as each member of the group took responsibility for his own experience and shared the process with everyone else.

Leadership at Findhorn in terms of government had gone through two distinct phases since the community was founded by Peter and Eileen Caddy and Dorothy Maclean in 1962. For the first nine years, during which time the community grew from one family and a friend to over a hundred people, leadership was outwardly directive and authoritarian. Peter, an ex-army officer and innate perfectionist, played the role of leader, whilst Eileen in particular, more retiring by nature, seemed content to dispense moral support. However, Eileen's times of reflection were not focused on Peter's actions as leader, rather Peter's actions were based on Eileen's quiet reflection. Peter was putting Eileen's inner vision into action.

Although there were no work department attunements (discussion meetings) at this time and people worked unremittingly from dawn to dusk, this style of leadership was not behaviouristic. Each morning and evening the entire community met for fifteen minutes of meditation and, right from the beginning, work was experienced as a form of close relationship, in which task and maintenance were consciously combined. At Findhorn there had always been an ethic of perfection, all work – especially the seemingly humdrum – was done with high awareness. Except in an emergency (Cluny Hill caught fire one night and was evacuated within minutes of the alarm), things did not get accomplished fast at Findhorn but they were done well. The process was considered more important than the objective.

Working one hundred per cent towards whatever objective one's team might have, with other members of the team who are similarly committed, brings its own satisfaction. Not every American coach is obsessed with winning, not even all the successful ones. Tom Landry, manager of the Dallas Cowboys football team says that 'the chase is more important than the winning. I don't think I'd enjoy it as much if I knew I would always be a winner.' (Bill Shirley, *Los Angeles Times*, 9 November 1983.) And Sebastian Coe makes the point that 'any reasonable coach knows that if the performance is measured solely in terms of winning or losing then little can be learned from it.' (David Miller, *The Times*, 7 February 1986.)

By 1971, word of the community had spread world-wide. Each week people would arrive from different countries. Eventually Peter Caddy accepted an invitation to undertake a tour of talks about Findhorn and, in preparing for this, twelve members of the community were appointed to a 'Core Group' who would run the community in his absence. The Core Group was never disbanded and, some eight years later, Peter and Eileen were no longer attending the meetings. Membership of the Core Group changed. People left and others were invited to replace them by the remaining members. Big decisions were only made after a full community meeting at which every member had the chance to make his view known. More recently – early in 1979, when membership was over 300 – a 'village council' was formed with representatives from each living, working and policy-making area of the community. This was not to replace community meetings but to provide a regular forum for creative discussion of Findhorn's vision and development and to ensure that the Core Group be in constant touch with the perceptions of the community as a whole.

The Faces of Findhorn quotes Stephen Clark's description of his leadership role in relation to the large publications department: 'Leadership at Findhorn is based on a hierarchical pattern not of power but of responsibility. If my responsibility as focaliser of the publications department is to ensure that deadlines are met, the way that's carried out is not to insist that someone meet a deadline but to share, in the most open and clear way possible, the reasons for it to happen. Being a focaliser, holding a broader awareness of the way a whole system operates, I try to share that awareness and allow each person to contribute his or her part.' (Findhorn Community, *Faces of Findhorn*.)

There were aspects of Findhorn which seemed strange and a little threatening to me. (The threat was of course my projection, see page 43.) I was never quite at home because I always held something in reserve, never allowed myself to join in completely. Yet I stayed (and was accepted) there for a long time, responding to some important aspects of the community with unremitting excitement. I arrived long after the first authoritarian stage of leadership was over and, knowing myself as I do, this was probably just as well. In fact, what kept me at Findhorn was a totally new and unexpected experience of team spirit. The message implicit in the change from government by one authoritarian (indeed ex-military) leader to government by a group of members was not only that anyone has the ability to tune in to a correct decision but that it could be done collectively by a group. The greater potential for disagreement and frustration in a group discussion is balanced by a potential for even deeper wisdom than can be attained by a leader on his own.

Despite all my initial doubts and caution, inspired by so much 'esoteric chatter', at least one concept that was totally new to me hit home with conviction the moment I heard it. This was that the correct decision, path of action or event exists before it is discovered. Indeed, I've used the word 'discover' in exactly this sense quite often in this book already, when referring to a coach's responsibility to lead his athletes to 'discover' their potential. The very word education comes from the Latin *'educare'* – to lead out, so that what is within may be known.

I still occasionally use my favourite Findhorn phrase. 'It's on the etheric', to denote a sense that something already exists before it becomes clearly manifest. This is at once an affirmation, a statement of faith, and an encouragement to push on. As I write this it is more than a year since I began mapping out the chapters of this book and, only last week as I thought ahead to all the revision that will have to be done, all the excisions and the additions to my untidy pages of writing, I was less than sure that I really *have* a book to produce. However, in the past few days, something has changed. Somehow I now know that a book called *Team Spirit* in a shiny jacket and with clear printed pages is out there 'on the etheric', ready to be pulled down into the material world.

So it is with group decisions or indeed any decision or answer to a given problem. Somewhere the correct decision or answer is out there *'on the etheric'* and all that needs to be discovered is the way to pull it down into our sphere of consciousness. Almost always, when a difficulty seems insuperable or a discussion hopelessly deadlocked, the obstacle is the tension of holding on to an incorrect answer – either because one *wants* it to be so for inappropriate narrowly personal reasons or because one is unable to 'trust the process' and hates uncertainty so much that any decision seems better than none. The fact that the correct group decision always gives overwhelming if totally unexpected advantages to the individual concerned is easily forgotten or ignored.

The whole field of lateral thinking and second order change is related closely to the concept of the etheric and to the difficulty one so often experiences in letting go of pet theories, trying endlessly to cram a square peg into a round hole. My favourite example of lateral thinking is a story quoted by Watzlawick at the beginning of *Change*. (See Bibliography: Watzlawick, Peter *et al.*) This tells of a siege laid by the Duchess of Tyrol on a castle in Carthinia in 1334. The siege had been going on for months and the beleaguered garrison within the castle were down to their last carcass of beef and last sack of grain. There seemed to be no answer to the cruel dilemma but to share these last remnants of food, hoping for the siege to be lifted by some mythical rescue force. Then, if no relief arrived they would either starve or capitulate. But the garrison's leader had an idea which cut right across such an habitual train of thought. To the astonishment and consternation of his followers, he ordered the carcass to be filled with the remaining grain and lowered over the ramparts. When the besieging party saw this happening and reported back to the Duchess, she called her troops together and rode away, convinced that if the garrison could afford to offer food to her troops she might as well give up the siege. This is an example of one man alone letting go of habitual thought patterns and turning his back on the predictable safe-in-the-short-term course of action, with startling results.

One of the advantages of problem-solving *in a group* and a source of much enjoyment, is the possibility of brainstorming, and finding an answer that no individual member would have found alone. This is an exercise in which every member throws out off-the-top-of-my-head solutions, with the proviso that there must be *no* judgement from anyone else, nor any from the originator of the idea. Nothing is 'rubbish'. Even the most outrageous of suggestions may contain a spark of the 'correct' solution, the solution that is up there, waiting on the etheric. Although this process strengthens team spirit and trust, there has to be a modicum of trust and good will before the exercise can be engaged in properly.

The insight I gained into team spirit at Findhorn came in part from the experience of trust. One of the most laudable aspects of Findhorn was tolerance. There was no dogma except that, whilst retaining the right to proclaim one's beliefs, one hadn't the right to inflict them forcibly on others. There was a constant war against negative thought-forms and an affirmation of 'the highest', the potential in every individual. It was a code which discouraged the put-down. This climate engendered trust and trust helped one to release fiercely held outmoded opinions and float again on a sea of discovery.

At the time *The Faces of Findhorn* was written, François Duquesne was focaliser of Core Group and he reflected that everyone at Findhorn 'is recognised as having the ability to tune in to the Universal Mind and offer his or her perspective and contribution to the government of the whole. This co-creative interaction leads to a government through synergy where individuals, knowing their own authority and power, are not threatened by each other but are working together to create a whole greater than the sum of its parts'

Although in the world at large, most people are still unclear as to what exactly meditation is, closing one's eyes, sitting still and 'emptying one's mind' is now a popular remedy for stress. The fact is however that the elements of physical, mental and emotional stress are inseparable and, if I take the trouble to relax for a moment physically, sooner or later I discover that I am momentarily less attached to my opinions. The healing effect of meditation is largely due to the action of letting go. The fact that letting go of fiercely held opinions allows a new perspective to present itself, quite possibly a perspective which has long been 'on the etheric' and is the answer to some deeply fraught problem, was used by Findhorn groups as an adjunct to brainstorming in the problem solving process.

The 'focaliser' or leader of the group was in effect the non-voting chairman of a business meeting, concerned above all to keep discussion on the rails but also to call a pause when it became repetitive. Long-term member Michael Linfield said: 'Another thing I like is that when we as a group get stuck, we usually realise that we are stuck and take positive action, such as getting on with some other business or meditating, or letting the problem rest and coming back to it later on. Basically, we accept that many of the polarisations or difficulties that come up in a group can't be solved at the level of the mind and need to be transcended in meditation.' And Leona Aroha simply said, 'When an issue is brought up it's important to examine it fully and then move into meditation holding that question in mind.'

Though this process of attunement could be usefully employed by a sports team at a moment of crisis – where a new approach has to be found or a difficult decision made – as I pointed out on page 110, it is not likely to be adopted by coaches as a preferred method, or to be used frequently. In fact, a coach can stay fairly within the bounds of humanism and still take a final decision on goals and tactics himself, provided the team feels it has had the chance to express its range of opinions and that they have been heard. Most often such decisions emerge clearly from a team meeting anyway and, if they don't, and the coach himself sees no over-riding reason for one tactic being preferred over another, he can always, for the sake of variety, wrap up the discussion by taking the decision by consensus. Even at Findhorn, it was only the rare item on the agenda of a business meeting that was decided by attunement. The meetings did all *begin* with an attunement, a moment of silence at which clarity and 'the highest' were invoked, and end with an attunement by way of warming-down but, for most meetings, that was it.

Appendix C

THE SPORTING BODYMIND

The Sporting Bodymind was founded in 1979 and is the first British consultancy to apply the principles of humanistic psychology to sport. It is a Scottish registered company based in London.

Christopher Connolly MA, co-founder of the consultancy with John Syer, is an American from Detroit who acquired his skill in water-skiing on a lake in north Michigan. His Masters thesis, on the use of visual rehearsal techniques to create change in the use and function of the body, was based on extensive consultancy work with individual sportspeople. Christopher is a staff member of the Psychosynthesis and Education Trust in London and is a qualified teacher and practitioner of the Feldenkrais Method. With John Syer he wrote *Sporting Body, Sporting Mind: An Athlete's Guide to Mental Training*, Cambridge University Press, 1984, and, with Hetty Einzig, *The Fitness Jungle*, Century Hutchison, 1986.

The consultancy's name was chosen to stress that body and mind are one. Your thoughts and feelings affect your physical performance, just as your physical state and activities influence the way you think and feel. Everyone experiences the changing relationship of body and mind in their daily lives. For sports men and women the relationship is critical.

The Sporting Bodymind exists to help sportspeople improve their performance through a systematic programme of mental training. We design this programme together with the individual or the team, ensuring that it reflects and complements their current physical and technical training. The programme includes a combination of exercises:

- to improve concentration and confidence;
- to improve relaxation and reduce anxiety;
- to improve technical skill through mental rehearsal and other exercises;
- to foster positive attitudes and set appropriate goals;

222

– to review performance realistically;
– to develop specific qualities in your performance.

These exercises may be applied to fields other than sport and, since 1985, we have made our services available to business organisations, particularly those where there is an interest in developing team spirit.

Courses.
(i) Individual.   Sports men or woman living in or near London can arrange to come to us for a course of 1 or 1½ hour sessions over several weeks. Working with you, we construct an individual programme of mental training exercises which you would practise between sessions and continue to employ at the end of the course.

(i) *Club or Squd.*   Athletes come to us from many different sports but we also act in an advisory capacity to a variety of clubs and national teams becoming part of their coaching team and travelling to them. We then design a course which is a combination of group presentations and individual instruction. In team sports we are able to suggest ways to improve team spirit and communication.

(ii) *Presentations.*   From time to time we are invited to discuss the principles on which our individual and team training is based, with colleges and departments of physical education, sport clubs and the governing bodies of various sports in the UK and abroad. In these cases we give precedence to invitations which allow for follow-up work with the athletes, either individually or as a team. Where the presentation is spread over a period of time, individual work can sometimes be incorporated.

We also administer introductory and advanced courses ourselves on occasion. These are open to athletes, coaches and teachers of any sport and are normally held on a weekend.

For further details of The Sporting Bodymind, please contact us at

The Sporting Bodymind,
18, Kemplay Road,
London, NW3 1SY
England.
Tel: 01 435 8145

or The Sporting Bodymind,
P.O. Box 224,
Birmingham,
Michigan,
48012
USA

BIBLIOGRAPHY

Adams, John, 'Improving Stress Management: An Action-Research Based on Intervention', W W Burke (ed), *The Cutting Edge* (University Associates, 1978)

Anshel, Mark, 'Behaviourism v. Humanism: An Approach to Effective Team Leadership in Sport', *Motor Skills: Theory into Practice*, Vol 2, 1978, 83–91

Assagioli, Roberto, 'What are the Laws and Principles of the New Age?' (MGNA Publications, PO Box 556, Ojai, CA 93023)

Bertrand, John, *Born to Win* (Sidgwick and Jackson, 1985)

Ken Blanchard & Spencer Johnson, *The One Minute Manager* (William Morrow, 1982)

Brown, Judith, *The Happily Ever-After Factor* (unpublished manuscript)

Callow, Simon, *Being An Actor* (Penguin Books, 1985)

Carron, A, 'Motivating the Athlete', *Motor Skills: Theory into Practice*, Vol 2, No. 2 (1978) 23–4

Carron, A & Chelladurai, P, 'Cohesiveness as a Factor in Sport Performance', *International Review of Sports Sociology*, 2 (1981) 69–77

Cassell, J, 'The Contribution of the Social Environment to Host Resistance', *American Journal of Epidemiology*, 4 (2) 1975, 107–23

Chelladurai, P, 'Group Cohesion, Leadership and Athletic Performance', *CAHPER Journal* (May/June 1981) 15–21

Connolly, Christopher & Einzig, Hetty, *The Fitness Jungle: Stage 2 Fitness: The Exercise Survival Guide* (Century Hutchinson, 1986)

Craig, James & Craig, Marguerite, *Synergic Power: Beyond Domination and Permissiveness* (Proactive Press 1979)

Critchfield, R S, 'Conformity and Character', *American Psychologist*, 10 (1955) 191–8

d'Amato, Cus, *Observations from the Treadmill* (OFT Union, 1976)

Dunphy, Eamon & Ball, Peter (ed.) *Only a Game: The Diary of a Professional Footballer* (Kestrel Books, 1976)

Festinger, L, Schachter, S & Back, K, *Social Pressures In Informal Groups: A Study of a Housing Project* (Harper, 1950)

Findhorn Community, *Faces of Findhorn* (Findhorn Publications, 1980)

Gains, Charles & Butler, George, *Pumping Iron: The Art and Sport of Bodybuilding* (Sphere Books Ltd, 1977)

Green, Geoffrey (ed), *The Encyclopedia of Association Football* (Caxton, 1960)

Halberstam, David, *The Amateurs* (William Morrow & Co, 1985)

Harris, Dorothy, 'Assessment of Motivation in Sport and Physical Education', W Straub (ed), *Sports Psychology: Analysis of Athletic Behaviour*, (Mouvement Publications, 1978)

Herbert, Frank, *Dune* (New English Library, 1969)

Hersey, Paul & Blanchard, Ken, *Management of Organisational Behavior* (Prentice Hall, 1969)

Hopkins, John, *Nick Faldo in Perspective* (Allen & Unwin, 1985)

Johnson, Wendell, *Living with Change: The Semantics of Coping* (Harper & Row, 1972)

Jones, M, 'Regressing Group on Individual Effectiveness', *Organisational Behaviour and Human Performances*, 11 (1974) 426–51

King, Billie Jean with Deford, Frank, *Billie Jean King: The Story of a Great Tennis Player* (Granada, 1982)

Knowles, Malcolm & Knowles, Hulda, *Introduction to Group Dynamics* (Follett Publishing Co, 1972)

Kriegel, Bob & Kriegel, Marilyn, *The C Zone: Peak Performance Under Pressure* (Anchor Press/Doubleday, 1984)

Lenk, Hans, 'Top Performance despite internal conflict: an antithesis to a functional proposition', J Loy & G Kenyon (eds), *Sport, Culture and Society* (The Macmillan Co, 1969)

Lewin, Kurt, 'Frontiers in Group Dynamics: Concept, Method and Reality in Social Science; Social Equilibria and Social Change', *Human Relations*, I, No 1 (June 1947), 5–41

Luft, Joseph & Ingham, Harry, 'The Johari Window, A Graphic Model of Interpersonal Awareness', *Proceedings of the Western Training Laboratory in Group Development*, Los Angeles: UCLA Extension Office, (1955)

McCluggage, Denise, *The Centred Skier* (Vermont Crossroads Press, 1977)

Madden, John, *Hey Wait a Minute (I wrote a book!)* (Ballantine Books, 1984)

Mellor, James (ed), *The Buckminster Fuller Reader* (Pelican Books, 1972)

Nideffer, Robert, 'The Relationship of Attention and Anxiety to Performance', W Straub (ed), *Sport Psychology: An Analysis of Athletic Behaviour* (Mouvement Publications, 1978)

Oh, Sadaharu & Faulkner, David, *Sadaharu Oh: A Zen Way of Baseball* (Times Books, 1984)

Oxendine, J, *Psychology of Motor Learning* (Appleton-Century-Crofts, New York, 1968)

Pasek, T & Daniel, J, 'Stress Management Through Relaxation Concentration Training', *CAHPER Journal* (May/June 1984), 17–36

Patmore, Angela, *Playing on their Nerves: Sport Experiment* (Stanley Paul, 1979)

Perls, Fritz, *Ego, Hunger and Aggression* (Vintage Books, 1947)

Perls, Fritz, *The Gestalt Approach* (Bantam, 1976)

Perls, Fritz, *Gestalt Therapy Verbatim* (Bantam, 1971)

Perryman, Steve with Ball, Peter, *A Man For All Seasons* (Arthur Baker Ltd, 1985)

Peters, Thomas & Waterman, Robert, *In Search of Excellence* (Harper & Row, 1982)

Polster, Erving & Miriam, *Gestalt Therapy Integrated: Contours of Theory and Practice* (Vintage Books, 1974)

Roebuck, Peter, *Slices of Cricket* (Allen & Unwin, 1982)

Rowley, Steve, 'The Myth of the Male Sports Type: Some Methodological and Theoretical Considerations' (unpublished MPhil thesis, University of Loughborough, 1985)

Sage, G, 'Humanistic Psychology and Coaching', W Straub (ed), *Sport Psychology: An Analysis of Athletic Behaviour* (Mouvement Publications, 1978)

Schmuck, Richard & Schmuck, Patricia, *Group Processes in the Classroom* (William Brown, 1971)

Singer, R, *Motor Learning and Human Performance* (The Macmillan Co, 1975)

Strawberry, Darryl with Castellano, Dan, *Darryl!* (Contemporary Books, 1985)

Syer, John & Connolly, Christopher, *Sporting Body, Sporting Mind: An Athlete's Guide to Mental Training* (Cambridge University Press, 1984)

Tucker, Robert, 'Maximum Man', *United Magazine* (February 1985)

Wainwright, Christopher, 'Learning from Experience . . . A Communications Approach to Coaching', *The Coaching Clinic* (December 1982), 14–17

Watzlawick, Peter, Weakland, John & Fish, Richard, *Change: The Principles of Problem Formation and Problem Resolution* (W W Norton & Co, 1974)

Zander, Alvin, 'Motivation and Performance of Sports Groups', W Straub (ed), *Sport Psychology: An Analysis of Athletic Behaviour* (Mouvement Publications, 1978)

INDEX

Abrahams, Harold, 60
Action steps, 164
Adams, John, 177–9, 183, 195
Adams, Katherine, 38
Adhesion, 19
Affiliation needs, 15–6, 17, 195–6
Affirmations, 37, 134, 150, 155–6, 162, 171–2, 193
Aggression, 30, 39–46
Ali, Mohammed, 36, 96
Allen, Clive, 43, 90, 164, 171
Allen, George, 41
Anshel, Mark, 204
Apey, Patricio, 169
Appreciation, 88
   see also Resentments
Archibald, Steve, 1, 4, 15, 46, 57, 58, 79, 83, 149, 180, 182
Ardiles, Ossie, 87, 135, 154, 156
Arok, Frank, 86, 200
As If visualisation, see Visualisation
Aspiration, 52
   see also Invocation
Assagioli, Roberto, 53
Assistant, 68, 74, 82
Atkinson, Ron, 182
Attitudes, 145–6, 151, 155, 194
Attunement, 52, 53, 110, 142, 215, 221
   see also Silence
Australia II, 55
   see also Bertrand, John
Authoritarian coach, 48, 62, 108, 128
   see also Behaviourist coach

Baker-Finch, Ian, 146
Ball, Alan, 136
Ballesteros, Seve, 86
Bamford, Maurice, 55
Barcelona FC, 15, 46, 80, 187
Barnes, Peter, 62
Baruah, Sandy, 131–2, 138
Becker, Boris, 160, 180
Beechams, 124
Beerbohm, Max, 18

Behaviourist coaching, 10, 50, 66, 71, 100, 102, 108, 121–2, 123–32, 198, 199–203
Bell, Martin, 135
Benedict, Ruth, 24, 26
Biglow, John, 17, 21, 94, 187
Bingham, Billy, 24
Black Orpheus, 39
Blanchard, Ken & Johnson, Spencer, 102
Blanchflower, Danny, 5, 45
Body awareness, 26, 116, 131, 138, 147, 150, 154–5, 158, 160, 175–6, 187, 189–90
Borg, Bjorn, 21, 31, 176
Boyle, Jimmy, 23
Brady, Liam, 127
Brain-storming, 51, 151–2, 166, 219–20
Breathing, 174–5, 190, 191
Breland, Mark, 79
Bremner, Billy, 96
Bromides and Sulphites, 58
Brooking, Trevor, 62
Brown, George, 4, 60, 78, 89, 180, 194
Brown, Judith, 4, 78, 98, 112
Bruno, Frank, 189
'Buddy system', 89–91, 140, 189
   see also Pairs work
Burgess, John, 45
Burkinshaw, Keith, 5, 6, 43, 62, 63, 69, 72, 79, 80, 86, 102, 114, 135, 139, 144, 172, 200

Caddy, Peter & Eileen, 38, 217
Callow, Simon, 73, 84, 87, 91, 155, 203
Campbell, Neil, 131, 140
Captain, 69, 74–5, 84, 85, 111, 141, 202
Carron, Albert, 126, 134
Carron, A & Chelladurai, P, 17
Cash, Pat, 119
Cassell, John, 197
Castelijn, Boudewijn, 91
Casteneda, Carlos, 156
Catastrophic expectations, 165
Chattering mind, 116, 154, 170
   see also Body awareness

227

Chelladurai, P, 119
Chilcott, Gareth, 61
Christensen, Todd, 15
Circles, 38, 107, 141, 197
Circle quality exercise, 159–162
Clark, Michael, 26
Clemence, Ray, 1, 21, 51, 90
Cliques, 16, 17, 18, 23, 27, 32, 48, 67, 93
Close, Brian, 117
Co-acting, interacting & reactive/proactive
    sports, 18, 87
Coe, Sebastian, 47, 217
Cohesion, 15–9, 24–5, 29
Collins, Phil, 149
Commitment, 28–9
Concentration, 26, 34–8, 118–9, 149, 167–8, 183,
    187, 191, 194
Confluence, 19–22, 25–6, 29, 196
Connolly, Christopher, 4, 106, 131, 168, 184, 192
Connolly, Christopher & Einzig, Hetty, 190
Control, 81, 153
Counselling, 6, 46
Cowans, Gordon, 92
Cox, Bobby, 63
Craig, James & Marguerite, 23, 24, 27, 100, 149
Crawford, George, 94
Critchfield, R S, 62
Criticism, 115, 117
Crooks, Garth, 146, 169–70
Cruising, see Peak experience
Curren, Kevin, 96, 119, 175, 180

Dalgliesh, Kenny, 68, 72
    see also Liverpool FC
D'Amato, Cus, 149
Dawes, John, 75
Dean, Christopher, 38
Defence, 39, 64
Di Maggio, Joe, 154
Disidentification, 78
Dixon, Rod, 37
Dunlop, Sandy, 4, 168
Dunphy, Eamon, 114

Edwards, David, 145
Eisenstaedt, Alfred, 136
Ellis, Harold, 162, 165
Ellison, Andrew, 18
Encouragement, 118–20, 168–9, 186–7
Enjoyment, 128, 135, 137–8, 201
Enquist, Paul, 37, 155–6
Esalen Institute, 4
Etheric, on the, 86, 213, 218–20
Everton, FC, 24
Evocative word, 112, 156
Ewing, Patrick, 194

Facilitating, 6
Falco, Mark, 42, 43, 60, 90, 96, 150, 160–3, 171
Faldo, Nick, 180
Family therapy, 72, 78, 81, 110, 203
Farr, Tommy, 42
Feedback, 105, 106
Feldenkrais Method, 190
Festinger et al, 15

Fields, Randolph, 23
Findhorn Foundation, 3–4, 52, 130, 142, 188,
    215–21
Flow, see Peak experience
Focaliser, 215, 218
Fonda, Henry, 66
Ford 1, Henry, 68
Friendship/respect, 16, 72–3, 86–8, 199–200, 201
Fuller, Buckminster, 197

Gains, Charles & Butler, George, 63
Galvin, Tony, 20, 33, 39, 40, 60, 87, 114, 164
Gamesmanship, 35, 41, 96–7
    see also Concentration
Gestalt, 12, 20, 30, 39, 137, 147, 194–5
Gestalt dialogue, 46, 82, 133, 134, 152, 203
Gibson, Chris, 82, 200
Goal-setting, 33, 126, 129–30, 138–9, 147, 150,
    153, 166, 172, 191–2, 200–1, 206
Gove, Andrew, 101
Gower, David, 57
Gray, Andy, 64
Green, Geoffrey, 45
Green, Lucinda, 187
Group Being, 83, 110, 140

Hadlee, Richard, 180
Halberstam, David, 17, 27, 72, 94, 141, 187
Half-time, 132
Hardison, Barb, 42
Hare, David, 84
Haringey Cricket College, 82, 96, 132, 162, 165,
    200
Harris Dorothy, 135–6
Hawthorne project, 101, 201
Haydon, Laurie, 22, 102
Hazard, Mike, 60, 135, 156, 164
Herbert, Frank, 25
Herisher IV, Oriel, 36
Hersey, Paul & Blanchard, Ken, 48, 67, 69, 103,
    105, 108, 125, 127, 135, 139, 155, 172, 201,
    206, 208–214
Heseltine, Michael, 25, 67
Heysell Stadium, 32, 39
Higgins, Alex, 136, 156
Hoddle, Glenn, 21, 33, 54, 57, 58, 87, 158, 162, 168
Hopkins, John, 21, 180
Houllier, Gerard, 101
Howe, Don, 43
Hughton, Chris, 13, 91, 114
Humanistic coaching, 11, 50, 71, 108, 123, 139,
    184–5, 189, 198, 203–7
Hypnosis, 194

IBM, 172
Images, 168
Immaturity, 62
Individual in the team, 7, 100
Injury, 16, 26, 147–8, 162
Inner Game, 205–6
Inspiration, 2–3, 22, 55, 63, 73
    see also Team talk
Instructions, 116–8
Intermediate goals, 113, 134, 152–3, 186, 191, 201
Invocation, 38, 52, 140, 221
    see also Team talk

Jacklin, Tony, 20, 143, 168
Jackson, Reggie, 47
James, Carwyn, 75, 134
James, Dave, 3
Jianhua, Zhu, 36
Johari Window, 103–6
John, Barry, 75, 134
Johnson, Bill, 146
Johnson, Wendell, 61, 98
Jones, Alan, 73, 80, 122, 131
Jones, MB, 24
Juggling, 190

Keegan, Kevin, 135
Keen, Sam, 44
Kimball, Bruce, 194
Kimball, Dick, 194
Kinaesthetic sense, see Body awareness
King, Billy Jean, 20, 176
Knott, Alan & Underwood, Derek, 90
Knowles, Malcolm & Hulda, 57, 58, 70, 89, 208
Kriegel, Bob & Marilyn, 145, 149, 150, 153, 155, 175
Kuehl, Karl, 150

Landry, Tom, 217
La Russa, Rony, 72, 200
Lateral thinking, 51, 219
Lauder, Nikki, 29
Lawrence, T E, 55
Lefebvre, Jim, 59
Left brain/right brain, 7, 9, 33, 131, 152, 164, 192
Leighton, Gus, 60
Lenk, Hans, 15
Lever, John, 119
Lewin, Kurt, 47, 66
Lewis, Brad, 37, 155–6
Liverpool FC, 1, 40, 51, 68
    see also Kenny Dalgliesh
Lloyd, Chris, 31, 53
Lloyd, Clive, 19
Lloyd, John, 53, 169
Lombardi, Vince, 41, 155
Lopes, Carlos, 137
Lougarnis, Greg, 21, 145, 159, 187, 194, 195
Louis, Joe, 42

McCluggage, Denise, 93
MacDonald, Malcolm, 43
McDonald's, 124
McEnroe, John, 31, 36, 41, 58–9, 96, 133, 136, 175, 176, 180
McKinney, Tamara, 41
Madden, John, 12, 32, 55, 62, 69, 73, 74, 95, 99, 100, 101, 109, 155, 158, 184, 188
Mahre, Phil, 41
Maleeva, Manuella, 186
Marshall, Malcolm, 40
Massage, 191
Meditation, 53, 190, 192, 194, 220–1
    see also Attunement
Mental rehearsal, see Visualisation
Mental skills, 7
Mental Training Exercises, 7–10
Mental Training Journal, 85, 151, 152, 164–5

Middle zone, 26, 27
Miller, Paul, 36, 40, 42, 96, 153
Mob, 25, 66
Moody, Nick, 179
Morale, 14, 29
Moses, Ed, 28, 31, 156
Music, 9, 55, 142, 148–9

Nakamura, K, 59
Navratilova, Martina, 31, 97, 159
Negative thought forms, 77, 220
Nicklaus, Jack, 21, 152, 182
Nideffer, Robert, 34, 151, 175, 176, 183, 191
Non-sporting situations, 148–9, 150, 158
Non-verbal communication, 114
Norms, 56–7

O'Connor, Carol, 98
Oh, Sadaharu, 19, 23, 52, 59, 64, 71, 86, 93, 97, 119
Open discussion, 50, 51, 57, 65, 84–6, 88, 89–90, 93, 98, 107–8, 110, 139, 167–8, 218
    see also Task/Maintenance
Oxendine, J B, 125

Pairs work, 112–3, 171–2
Park, Daphne, 23
Parker, Harry, 27, 72, 141, 200
Parks, Tony, 1, 90, 188
Pasek, T & Daniel, J, 176, 188
Patmore, Angela, 183
Peak experience, 21, 135–7, 175
Performance practice, see Visualisation
Perls, Fritz, 12, 20, 21, 22, 31, 32, 33, 43, 45, 46, 61, 84, 93, 108, 174, 176, 190
Perry, Fred, 95
Perryman, Steve, 26, 39, 42, 58, 68–9, 74–5, 83, 87, 90, 96, 101, 135, 153, 158, 171
Peters, Thomas & Waterman, Robert, 49, 88, 101, 172, 185
Petranoff, 189
Phillips, André, 156
Pictures, 9, 148–9
Pimm, Gerry, 69
Pinero, Manuel, 28, 86
Polster, Erving & Miriam, 206
Positive thinking, 65, 154, 155, 156
Power bases, 212–4
Pratt, John, 114
Preservation Hall Jazz Band, 142
Pressure exercises, 169, 186
Primary needs, 122, 127–8
Problem athletes, 50, 57, 58, 69, 77–82, 84, 111, 124, 186, 201–2
Problem solving, 46–7
    see also Visualisation
Projection, 43, 45, 170
Prost, Alain, 196
Protection, 38–9
Psyching-up, see Team talk

Questionnaires, 166–7
Questions, 99, 100, 109, 115–6, 141
    see also Pairs work
Quiet Place, see Visualisation

Rah-rah-rah, 13, 45, 50, 52–3
Relaxation, 157, 187, 190, 192–3, 194, 220
Resentments, demands & appreciations, 81,
    112–3, 171
Respect, 87–8
Retton, Mary-Lou, 192
Review questionnaire, 166–7
Rhodes, Steve, 37
Richmond Rugby Club, 47
Richardson, Dougie, 76
Riggs, Bobby, 96
Ripley, Andy, 53
Ritual and Superstition, 20, 21–2, 55–6, 142, 187
Roberts, Graham, 33
Robson, Bobby, 58, 63, 122
Robson, Bryan, 92, 182
Roche, Stephen, 88
Roebuck, Peter, 19, 32, 48, 95, 96, 141
Rose, Brian, 49
Rowley, Steve, 181
Ryder Cup team, 142–3

St. Martin, Yves, 196
Sage, George, 203
Salonen, Esa-Pekker, 22, 202
Sanderson, Tessa, 28
Sanders, Red, 41
Scandinavian Airlines System, 6
Schmuck, Richard & Patricia, 27, 89, 181
Schula, Don, 149
Schumacher, Fritz, 51, 70
Schwarzenegger, Arnold, 63
Scoring performance, 164–5
See/imagine/feel, 149, 151, 172
Selfishness, 43, 146
Session summary, 153, 158
Setting priorities exercise, 134, 191–2
Shapiro, Stuart, 46
Sher, Antony, 160
Sherwen, Paul, 88
Shilton, Paul, 117
Shreeve, Peter, 5, 6, 32, 42, 49, 68, 76, 80, 91, 95,
    110, 119, 132, 141, 144, 154, 167, 170, 172
Shriver, Pam, 97
Silence, 48, 110, 141, 187, 188–9
    see also Attunement
Singer, R N, 126
Small groups, 90, 93, 139–40
Social support, 195–6
    see also Affiliation needs
Somerset Cricket Club, 32, 48, 95
    see also Peter Roebuck
Sportsmanship, 40
South Pacific, 155
Sporting Bodymind, The, 4–5, 10, 51, 106, 122,
    134, 137, 184, 190, 192, 193, 222–3
Sporting Body, Sporting Mind: An Athletes Guide to
    Mental Training, 5, 6, 8, 9, 51, 72, 111, 115,
    151, 156
Spurs, see Tottenham Hotspur FC
Star players, 63
Stein, Jock, 73
Stevens, Gary, 46, 60, 62, 147–9, 158
Strawberry, Darryl, 64

Substitutes and injured players, 91–2, 93
Sundström, Hendrik, 140
Synergy, 22, 26, 29, 196, 197, 220

T'ai chi, 190
Talk and chat, 98, 111, 216
Task/maintenance, 16, 18, 68–9, 88–9, 106, 203–
    4, 217
Taylor, Graham, 185
Taylor, Ian, 50
Teaching, counselling and facilitating, 6, 10
Team discussion, see Open Discussion
Team talk, 21, 123, 130–2, 140–2, 170, 189
Thatcher, Margaret, 23, 25, 67
Thomas, Danny, 144
Thompson, Daley, 28, 137
Torrance, Sam, 146
Tottenham Hotspur FC, 1, 5–7, 14, 16, 21, 46, 49,
    54, 56, 57, 60, 68, 77, 90, 92, 93, 95, 106, 107,
    110, 116, 139, 147, 153, 164, 166, 177, 185
Touch, 102
Trainer, 205–7
Trammell, Alan & Whitaker, Lou, 90
Trevino, Lee, 146, 153, 190
Trust, 21, 88, 220

Varney, Mike, 5, 40, 162, 167, 191
Venables, Terry, 80
Violence, 40, 43–5, 94
Virgin Atlantic Airways, 23
Visualisation, 9, 10, 158, 192
    Mental rehearsal:
    Performance practice, 46, 134, 147, 150, 157,
        159, 162
    As if visualisation, 79, 156, 159–62, 165, 192–3
    Instant Pre-play, 159
    Performance review, 164
    Problem Solving:
    Quiet place, 193
    Visual re-editing, 9, 10, 115, 162–4
    Wise old person, 47, 193
Visual re-editing, see Visualisation

Waddle, Chris, 135
Wainwright, Christopher, 205–6
Walker, Rob, 73
War, 26, 43–4, 65, 96
Watching, 74, 76, 95, 100, 131, 144, 158, 202
Watzlawick, Peter et al, 219
West, Jeremy, 87
Williams, Dick, 200
Winning, 41, 63, 201, 203, 205, 217
Wise old person, see Visualisation
Withdrawal, 7, 25, 27, 139, 147, 166, 189
    see also Silence
Wooden, John, 130
Wyatt, Derek, 45, 153

Yoga, 190–1

Zander, Alvin, 88, 129, 142
Zoeller, Fuzzy, 28
Zone, in the, see Peak experience